THE GOD WHO ACTS IN HISTORY

THE GOD WHO ACTS IN HISTORY

The Significance of Sinai

Craig G. Bartholomew

WILLIAM B. EERDMANS PUBLISHING COMPANY

GRAND RAPIDS, MICHIGAN

Wm. B. Eerdmans Publishing Co.
4035 Park East Court SE, Grand Rapids, Michigan 49546
www.eerdmans.com

26 25 24 23 22 21 20   1 2 3 4 5 6 7

ISBN 978-0-8028-7467-2

Library of Congress Cataloging-in-Publication Data

Names: Bartholomew, Craig G., 1961– author.
Title: The God who acts in history : the significance of Sinai / Craig G.
    Bartholomew.
Description: Grand Rapids : Wm. B. Eerdmans Publishing Co., 2020. | Includes
    bibliographical references and index. |
Summary: "Bartholomew merges his interests in philosophy and Old Testament
    studies by exploring what it means to recognize God's voice in the Biblical
    text and recognize that God actually acts within history and how one can
    come to terms with this idea in a way that makes strong philosophical sense"—
    Provided by publisher.
Identifiers: LCCN 2019031041 | ISBN 9780802874672 (paperback)
Subjects: LCSH: Providence and government of God—History of doctrines. |
    Philosophy and religion. | Revelation. | Revelation on Sinai.
Classification: LCC BT135 .B337 2020 | DDC 231/.5—dc23
LC record available at https://lccn.loc.gov/2019031041

Dedicated to Gordon J. Wenham, mentor, colleague, friend—
a giant in the field of Old Testament scholarship

CONTENTS

FOREWORD

In the mid-twentieth century, debates about divine action suddenly broke like troublesome waves on the shores of biblical studies and systematic theology. On the philosophical side, Ian Crombie of Oxford took up the challenge that had emerged from logical positivism. Henceforth, the debate became focused on how to delineate the necessary and sufficient conditions of divine action, taking human action as the obvious analogue. More importantly, Langdon Gilkey, working from within the Barthian tradition, found himself puzzled by claims of Old Testament scholars who talked a lot about divine action but ended up reading the relevant texts like the Liberal Protestants they despised. Divine actions turned out to be entirely natural and historical events interpreted in the minds of the biblical writers as specific and sometimes spectacular divine actions. Gilkey proposed that, by getting hold of a doctrine of general divine action in history (effectively a doctrine of providence), we could then proceed to deal with the kind of special divine actions that showed up again and again in the biblical materials.

Taken together, these challenges became the mainstay of a host of efforts to solve "the problem of divine action." There was, of course, not just one problem but a nest of metaphysical, epistemological, and theological problems buried in talk of "the problem of divine action." There was only one problem with the projects that showed up: all the efforts assumed that the concept of action was a closed concept that could be defined in terms of relevant necessary and sufficient conditions, say, the condition of intentionality. However, this assumption simply does not hold. And even if it did, it would not help us distinguish one divine action from another. The concept of action, like the concept of event or happening, is a radically open concept. Hence the effort to transfer any concept of action derived from cases of human action to divine action was doomed to failure. In the end we have to return to the rough ground of particular divine action, and once we do that, we are knee-deep in theology. Moreover, any effort to veto this or that divine action, or range of actions (most notably miraculous action), will simply beg the crucial question at issue. Over half a century of assiduous research has taken us right back to where we started. What did God do at Sinai?

In these circumstances it is a pleasure to welcome this splendid volume by Craig Bartholomew. Rather than take flight into abstractions about divine action, he launches his investigation straightway into a quest to find out how to tackle questions about the specific divine actions related to Sinai in the history of Israel. Unlike earlier treatments of the debate, this allows him to draw on the Jewish tradition of discussion, for it is Sinai that is at the heart of the Jewish heritage. Also unlike earlier discussion, he realizes implicitly that it is crucial to get behind the modern rejection of a whole range of divine actions in the Jewish and Christian tradition. Hence he travels back intellectually behind the modern debate in order to enrich his eventual treatment of what God did at Sinai.

However, the full force of the critical inquiries of Spinoza and Kant cannot be ignored; it is they and their offspring who have been handing out the contraceptive pills that prevent the very birth of crucial affirmations about divine action in the modern period. Their assumptions have again and again found their way into the presuppositions of historical investigation and thus made it virtually impossible to explore the relevant theological claims head-on. The upshot is that Bartholomew has provided crucial philosophical and theological resources that need to be brought to bear on adjudicating what really happened at Sinai. Hence, he not only takes us back to the beginning of the twentieth-century debate; he provides a new angle of vision for looking afresh at absolutely crucial claims about what God did at Sinai, claims that Jews and Christians cannot cast aside without shedding theological tears.

The last two chapters bring the whole project to a pleasing conclusion. Bartholomew tries his hand at developing models of divine action that would better serve in making sense of what God really did at Sinai. No doubt, there is room for critical assessment of this move as a way to tackle the relevant challenges of discourse about divine action. Then, to round it all off, he comes clean on what we should say happened at Sinai. It was a strenuous journey to get there. However, it is a delight to see the philosophical and theological issues tackled with such sophistication and clarity. And we now have a substantial and specific set of claims that keep to the rough ground of the critical acts of God that are at the heart of our Jewish heritage and that deserve to be revisited and reappropriated with gusto by Christian theologians and preachers.

I realize that in this foreword I have run the risk of butchering the full range of issues taken up in this work. My goal has been to set this volume in the stream of discussion that I know best; on this score, as already noted, I find it wonderfully refreshing. However, it would be remiss not to mention that I have barely touched the hem of Bartholomew's garment. This is a book to be read and pondered by historians of Israel, biblical scholars, theologians, and philosophers. It should be taken up by seasoned scholars and by beginners. It is, moreover, a fitting prolegomenon to a fresh reading of the Old Testament that the author promises at the very end. I can only wish our author Godspeed in this endeavor.

WILLIAM J. ABRAHAM
Southern Methodist University

PREFACE

In the Bible, and in our liturgies, we encounter not only a God who is the creator, sustainer, and ruler of the universe, but also a God who acts decisively in history at key points to reveal himself to us, and to draw us into relationship with him and into the *missio Dei*. The exodus-Sinai event in the HB/OT and the Christ event in the NT stand out as two mountain peaks of Scripture in terms of such special divine action. The focus of this book is the Sinai event.

This book emerged from my time as a Senior Research Fellow of the Herzl Institute in Jerusalem, as part of a Templeton-funded project on philosophical theology. The theme of this book is divine action in history, and it emerges from a puzzle. Jewish authors in particular, but also Christians, assert the fundamental importance of the Sinai event as foundational and generative for Israel and the HB/OT. At the same time many are reluctant to affirm the historicity of this "event" or at least retain what one of my readers of this manuscript refers to as a "prudential agnosticism." This is the puzzle: how can an event that is so formative, so foundational and so generative have no basis in divine action in history, and perhaps turn out to be an imaginary projection onto the past by later Israelites? The aim of this book is to explore closely the reasons for such reluctance, to see if they withstand careful evaluation, and, if not, to propose an alternative approach to the Sinai event.

My hope is that this book will be read by biblical scholars, theologians, and philosophers. However, it is aimed in particular at biblical exegetes. Part of what I hope to achieve in this work is to bring into focus elements in such reluctance that are far too often glossed over by biblical scholars, and yet that are formative upon such reluctance. There are reasons for such reluctance that biblical scholars may well be aware of; for example, the alleged incoherence of the Sinai story in Exodus. However, the narrative of how so many scholars come to deny or be agnostic about the historicity of Sinai is complex and composed of multiple strands. Part of what I am doing in this work is teasing out the different strands so that we can have a close look at them and see how the position we take on such issues influences our reading of the Sinai event, for better or for worse.

Readers may, for example, be surprised by the amount of philosophy and theology in this book, but that is no accident. It is still by no means uncommon to find scholars asserting that biblical studies is largely—and should remain—unaffected by philosophy and theology. In terms of philosophy, as late as 2000 James Barr could write:

> The typical biblical scholarship of modern times has been rather little touched by philosophy—certainly much less than it has by theology. Going back to the last century, one remembers Vatke and his Hegelianism and it has long been customary to accuse Wellhausen of the same thing though the accusation has long been proved to be an empty one. And after that we do have an influence of philosophy, but mostly on the theological use of the Bible rather than on biblical scholarship in the narrower sense.[1]

Writing in 2007, John Barton argues that the bracketing out of "questions of theological truth" is "methodologically essential" for biblical criticism.[2] What I hope to show in this volume is that philosophy and theology are already at work in modern biblical criticism, albeit far too often unconsciously, and that what we should be focused on is not whether or not they are present but *how* they should be present.

I am not proposing that biblical scholars need to become professional philosophers and theologians, but rather that we need to be conscious and honest about the philosophical and theological presuppositions at work in our biblical interpretation. There is much more to exegesis than philosophy and theology and one is aware of the many years of specialized study required for an exegete. Nevertheless, as I seek to show in this book through close attention to the Sinai event, philosophy and theology exert far more influence on biblical interpretation than Barr and Barton allow, and work-

1. James Barr, *History and Ideology in the Old Testament: Biblical Studies at the End of a Millennium* (Oxford: Oxford University Press, 2000), 26–27.
2. John Barton, *The Nature of Biblical Criticism* (Louisville: Westminster John Knox, 2007), 164.

ing consciously with such knowledge can make a major difference. As my readers have alerted me, biblical scholars are not generally trained in philosophy and theology, and thus I have sought to make the philosophical and theological parts of my argument as clear and accessible as possible, with regular signposts along the way.

Outline of the Argument

In Chapter 1 I elaborate on the puzzle from which this research emerges. In Chapter 2 I focus on Benjamin Sommer's recent and lauded book on Sinai. It is greatly to Sommer's credit that he openly sets out the many different components that constitute his reading of the Sinai event. The result is that Sommer's work provides an effective foil for an excavation of the different dimensions shaping one's reading of Sinai. As will become apparent in this book, I disagree with Sommer on many issues, but I respect his work and would, for example, hope that his work read alongside mine could make for a very interesting seminary or university course. I provide an overview of the key elements in Sommer's book but would encourage serious readers to read it for themselves.

Philosophically, Sommer leans on Maimonides for his view that God cannot speak, and in Chapter 3 I explore Maimonides's approach to the Hebrew Bible and the very different approach of his close predecessor, Judah Halevi. Here, and below, readers should note what I am doing methodologically. By focusing on Halevi I am showing that if one leans on Halevi's work philosophically, with its very different doctrine of God, rather than that of Maimonides, one ends up with a significantly different approach to the Sinai event.

In the Christian tradition the great representative of the classical theism or perfect-being theology of Maimonides is Thomas Aquinas, and we explore Aquinas as a Christian parallel to Maimonides in Chapter 4. We will have much more to say about this, but for now it may help readers to know that perfect-being theology works with two major assumptions: God is the most perfect being, and human reason is able to and should use philosophy to explain God as the most perfect being.[3] Aquinas is a giant in theology and philosophy and some of the contours of his thought relevant to our project

3. Katherin A. Rogers, *Perfect Being Theology*, Reason and Religion (Edinburgh: Edinburgh University Press, 2000), vii.

are contested. Aquinas is central to the revival of analytic theology[4] and much contemporary Christian philosophy and so we do well to investigate whether or not he rectifies the deficiencies in Maimonides's doctrine of God or whether his thought remains vulnerable to them. I will argue that Thomas's approach does not provide us with an adequate theology and philosophy of divine action in history.

In Chapters 5 and 6 we turn to two modern philosophers, Spinoza and Kant, both of whom are influential on modern biblical criticism. Sommer is a proponent of the neo-Documentary Hypothesis of the Pentateuch, a type of historical source criticism that can be traced back to Spinoza, and Sommer draws on Kant for his understanding of law. Both Kant and Spinoza develop philosophies that exclude the very possibility of the sort of special divine action we appear to find at Sinai. Biblical scholars are often unaware of just how influential Kant has been on modern HB/OT studies and so we need to look closely at how and why he and Spinoza came to discredit the historicity of the HB/OT, and of Sinai in particular.

In Chapter 7, as an alternative to the perfect-being theology of classical theism, I turn to Colin Gunton's work, a theologian who is strongly critical of classical theism, and examine his doctrine of God, of the divine attributes, and of divine action. In Chapter 8 we focus on the philosophy and theology of divine action. This leads in to Chapter 9, where the journey comes home in an examination of divine action in the Sinai event (Exod 19–24).

Methodologically it may help to note key elements at work in my argument. One is to identify the reasons why so many doubt the historicity of Sinai, ranging from the state of the text in Exod 19–40 to philosophical and theological assumptions. A second is to show that such reasons are not *defeaters* for affirming the historicity of Sinai. This could be thought of as a ground-clearing exercise. So many elements in modern approaches to Sinai go unnoticed that this is an essential part of the argument. A third, however, is to show that there are rigorous and rich alternatives to the threads that constitute the cord of those who deny the historicity of Sinai or are agnostic about it. A fourth is to bring these constructive alternatives together in a reading of the Sinai event that affirms its historicity with appropriate nuance and is theologically fecund.

---

4. William J. Abraham, *Analytic Theology: A Bibliography* (Dallas: Highland Loch Press, 2012), 6, proposes that "analytic theology can usefully be defined as follows: it is systematic theology attuned to the deployment of the skills, resources, and virtues of analytical philosophy."

A moot issue is what I achieve with such an approach. As I explain in the final chapter, I do not think that one can "prove" that Sinai took place. This, of course, opens up the discussion of the nature of historical proof, and we will have more to say about that in the final chapter. What I do aim to show is that the reasons for doubting the historicity of Sinai are not persuasive and that there are very good reasons for affirming it, so that scholars like myself and many others are rationally justified in affirming that Sinai happened. Having taught philosophy of history for several years I am aware of the complexities involved in "history," and I endeavor to take these complexities into account. However, when all is said and done, it surely remains a fair question as to whether or not the Sinai event took place.

I am very grateful to the anonymous readers to whom Eerdmans sent my earlier manuscript. Their comments were all helpful and have made this a much better book. One reviewer thought that while I was pointing out the assumptions of others, I seemed to be assuming my own neutrality. I should clarify such confusion at the outset. Hermeneutically, I think that any such neutral position is a myth and I am glad to alert the reader that I operate in the evangelical tradition and draw deeply from the well of Reformed theology and philosophy, as readers of my other works will be aware. I agree with Gadamer that it is only on the basis of our "prejudices" (pre-judgments) that we make progress in our quest for knowledge. Your prejudices may be very different from mine. While, of course, I hope to persuade readers of my approach to Sinai, this book will have gone a long way towards achieving its aim if exegetes become more conscious of the different threads that constitute their biblical hermeneutic and subject those threads to critical scrutiny. If, for example, one follows Kant in his approach to the historicity of the Bible and Sinai, it would be good to hear the arguments for this. If not, then what are the alternatives?

I gladly dedicate this work to Gordon J. Wenham, supervisor, colleague, and friend, a true giant in the field of HB/OT studies.

CRAIG G. BARTHOLOMEW
Advent 2018

ACKNOWLEDGMENTS

This book has its origin in my time as a Senior Fellow of the Herzl Institute in Jerusalem from 2015 to 2017. I am grateful to that institution for my appointment there. In particular I thank Yoram Hazony and Joshua Weinstein for their leadership and friendship. Jeremiah Unterman has become a good friend and has pointed me to many good resources during countless cups of coffee in Jerusalem. Excavating and diving into Jewish scholarship has been wonderfully stimulating and I hope this book encourages other scholars to do likewise. The Pontifical Biblical Institute in Jerusalem kindly granted me, an Anglican, residence for a month. I am also grateful to my research assistants Keegan Lodder and Mark Standish for their good work. During the writing of this book I moved from Canada to Tyndale House in Cambridge, UK, a good context in which to complete this manuscript. I remain grateful to my former employer, Redeemer University College, for the freedom the H. Evan Runner Chair provided for my research. The chair also provided me with the opportunity to teach a course on the philosophy of history several times, indispensable help in writing this book. It is a joy to work with Eerdmans, and I am grateful to my editors there, Michael Thomson and Andrew Knapp, as well as the anonymous readers who commented on my manuscript.

ABBREVIATIONS

ANE	ancient Near East
BA	*Biblical Archaeologist*
CD	Karl Barth, *Church Dogmatics*. Edited by G. W. Bromiley and T. F. Torrance, translated by G. W. Bromiley et al. 4 vols. Edinburgh, 2004
CWS 1	Spinoza, *The Collected Works of Spinoza*. Volume 1. Edited and translated by Edwin Curley. Princeton, 1985
CWS 2	Spinoza, *The Collected Works of Spinoza*. Volume 2. Edited and translated by Edwin Curley. Princeton, 2016
EJT	*European Journal of Theology*
EncJud	*Encyclopaedia Judaica*. 16 vols. Jerusalem, 1972
HB	Hebrew Bible
HTR	*Harvard Theological Review*
JQR	*Jewish Quarterly Review*
JSOTSup	Journal for the Study of the Old Testament: Supplement Series
NJPS	Tanakh: The Holy Scriptures: The New JPS Translation according to the Traditional Hebrew Text
NRSV	New Revised Standard Version
NT	New Testament
OT	Old Testament
RWBMR	Immanuel Kant, *Religion within the Boundaries of Mere Reason and Other Writings*. Edited by Allen Wood and George di Giovanni. Cambridge, 1998
RRT	Immanuel Kant, *Religion and Rational Theology*. Edited and translated by Allen W. Wood. Cambridge, 1996
SDA	special divine action

ST	Thomas Aquinas, *Summa Theologiae*
TCTF	Immanuel Kant, *The Conflict of the Faculties*. Edited and translated by Allen W. Wood. In Kant, *Religion and Rational Theology*. Cambridge, 1996, 233–327
TTP	Spinoza, *Tractatus Theologico-Politicus*. In *CWS* II, 65–354

CHAPTER 1

The Puzzle

The decisive event in the spiritual history of our people was the act that
occurred at Sinai. . . . It was an event that happened at a particular time
and also one that happened for all time.

—Abraham Joshua Heschel[1]

It seems safe to say that the structure of Exodus 19–24 presents more
unanswerable questions than any other part of the Old Testament. . . .
Sinai may have been from the beginning, then, less a part of history
and more a part of worship than the other traditional materials used
in the Pentateuch.

—Donald E. Gowen[2]

In the Hebrew Bible God is known through his engagement with his people *in history*.[3] We only know about his nature and how he relates to the
world through such engagement. As Heschel notes, "The God of the philosopher is a concept derived from abstract ideas; the God of the prophets[4]

1. Abraham Joshua Heschel, *Moral Grandeur and Spiritual Audacity*, ed. Susan-
nah Heschel (New York: Farrar, Straus and Giroux, 1996), 15.
2. Donald E. Gowen, *Theology in Exodus: Biblical Theology in the Form of a
Commentary* (Louisville: Westminster John Knox, 1994), 173–74.
3. Note that in my view a theology of God acting *in history* is inseparably related
to a theology *of history*. Underlying both is a theology of God as creator (cf. Craig
G. Bartholomew and Bruce R. Ashford, *The Doctrine of Creation* [Downers Grove,
IL: IVP Academic, 2020). The specific focus of this project is a theology and philosophy of God acting in history.
4. Note that for Jews throughout history and in the HB/OT, Moses is the first
great prophet.

is derived from acts and events. The root of Jewish faith is, therefore, not a comprehension of abstract principles but an inner *attachment to those events*; to believe is to remember, not merely to accept the truth of a set of dogmas."[5] According to Miskotte, "It is precisely the act-character of God's being that distinguishes himself *in* the world *from* the world. . . . From God's deeds there grows the knowledge of his 'virtues' and in the knowledge of his virtues his nature."[6]

It would appear, then, that God acting in history is fundamental to Jewish and Christian faith, and that one would expect such an emphasis to be expounded and defended among their representatives. Somewhat surprisingly, this is often not the case.

The Puzzle in Jewish Scholarship

Jewish scholarship has attracted my attention because of its overt public dimensions, an emphasis not nearly so common in Christian scholarship as it ought to be. Its public dimension involves taking all aspects of life seriously as worthy of attention and effort, an emphasis related back to Sinai and the Torah of the HB/OT. It is puzzling, however, that this Jewish emphasis on *human* action, on our action in history and in the world, often goes hand in hand with a pronounced skepticism about God's action in his world.

An example of this quandary is found in Michael Walzer's *Exodus and Revolution*.[7] He acknowledges that through the centuries religious men and women have found both a record of God's actions in the world and a guide for themselves in the narrative of the exodus. However, he is adamant: "my subject is not what God has done but what men and women have done, first with the biblical text itself and then in the world, with the text in their hands" (x). Walzer wants to retell the story of the exodus in political history "even though it is also, in the text, an act of God" (7). Walzer resists making any claims about the authorial intention of the text or to any view of the history of the exodus and Sinai. "What really happened? We don't know. We have

5. Abraham Joshua Heschel, "The Moment at Sinai," in *Moral Grandeur and Spiritual Audacity*, 12–13.

6. Kornelis H. Miskotte, *When the Gods Are Silent* (New York: Harper and Row, 1967), 193.

7. Michael Walzer, *Exodus and Revolution* (New York: Basic Books, 1985). Hereafter, page references to this work are given in parentheses in the text.

only this story, written down centuries after the events it describes. But the story is more important than the event" (7).[8]

Walzer reads the exodus as a paradigm of revolutionary politics. He notes that "the Exodus is an account of deliverance or liberation expressed in religious terms, but it is also a secular, that is a this-worldly and historical account. Most important, it is a realistic account" (9). Exodus is the story of a people, "hence not a story simply but a history" (12). For Walzer, the exodus shapes the Jewish conception(s) of time and breaks with the cosmological kind of storytelling.[9] "Exodus is a literal movement, an advance through space and time, the original form (or formula for) progressive history" (15).

Walzer's reading of the exodus is what we today would call a literary—and perhaps theological, certainly political—reading, but one that brackets out the question of whether or not God acted in the exodus and at Sinai. In the text, according to Walzer, the exodus is indeed an act of God, but the story is more important than the event. At the same time the exodus is a this-worldly and history-like account that gave permanent shape to the Jewish view of time and history. Walzer's reading of the exodus is thus riddled with major tensions between God who acts and the extraordinary influence and paradigmatic significance of the exodus while leaving open the possibility that it is entirely imaginary.

Jewish scholar Jon Levenson is rightly well known for his creative work on the Hebrew Bible. In his rich and fecund *Sinai and Zion* he observes that "the experience of Sinai, whatever its historical basis, was perceived as so overwhelming, so charged with meaning, that Israel could not imagine that any truth or commandment from God could have been absent from Sinai."[10] As with Walzer, we find an emphasis on the epochal nature of exodus-Sinai, which, "whatever its historical basis," betrays the same quandary. Indeed, Levenson uses much stronger language: "What really happened on Mount

8. Cf. Walzer, *In God's Shadow: Politics in the Hebrew Bible* (New Haven: Yale University Press, 2012), x.

9. He refers to Herbert N. Schneidau, *Sacred Discontent: The Bible and the Western Tradition* (Baton Rouge: University of Louisiana Press, 1976); but he also notes the qualifications urged by Robert Alter in *The Art of Biblical Narrative* (London: George Allen and Unwin, 1981), 24–28. For a more positive reading of the historicity of Sinai see Nahum M. Sarna, *Exploring Exodus: The Origins of Biblical Israel* (New York: Schocken, 1986, 1996).

10. Jon D. Levenson, *Sinai and Zion: An Entry into the Jewish Bible* (New York: Harper and Row, 1985), 18–19.

Sinai? The honest historian must answer that we can say almost nothing in reply to this question."[11]

Michael Fishbane is another major Jewish scholar from whose work many have benefited. In 2008 he published *Sacred Attunement: A Jewish Theology*.[12] Fishbane is adamant that Jewish theology finds its inception at Sinai. Sinai is *the* formative event for Israel. It is the time when the Israelites are called upon to embrace God's rule personally and over history and the entire world. According to Fishbane, "For Jewish theology, there is no passage to spiritual responsibility that does not in some way cross the wilderness of Sinai and stand before this mountain of instruction" (47). At Sinai the Israelites received from God the basic theological principles that were to govern their life and thought, including the Decalogue, "which forms the matrix of covenant values" (46). The Sinai covenant contains apodictic and casuistic laws signaling the comprehensive nature of God's reign over Israel. "Sinai set the standard. It is a metaphor for cultural *nomos*. It is an axial moment of consciousness" (47). In the HB and Jewish tradition ongoing development connects laws and other materials to the foundational event of Sinai. So powerful is Sinai that it becomes for Jews an ever-contemporary reality. "Focused on God's teachings, and their meaning, the adept was ever bound to the foundational moment of Sinai and its theological core" (49). For Fishbane, "One might even say that there is no authentic Jewish theology outside this covenant core, however diversely it might be conceived or elaborated. For it is the Sinai covenant that has shaped Jewish life and thought over the ages" (49).

For Fishbane, Sinai is not a one-off event but one for all times; it "stands *at the mythic core of religious memory*" (49; emphasis added). Having placed such strong emphasis on the Sinai event, it is somewhat surprising to encounter this expression: "the mythic core of religious memory." That Fishbane here moves away from any kind of strong affirmation of the historicity of Sinai is confirmed when he moves on to articulate the center or core of the Sinai event, stating that "this last query is less a historical question than a hermeneutical one" (49). It is fine and good to assert that "Jewish theology thus begins at Sinai—but it is hermeneutically so much more" (62). We might further enquire as to whether it indeed began at Sinai, and if this matters.

11. Levenson, *Sinai and Zion*, 16.
12. Michael Fishbane, *Sacred Attunement: A Jewish Theology* (Chicago: University of Chicago Press, 2008). Hereafter, page references to this work are given in parentheses in the text.

Yair Zakovitch is rightly well known for his creative, close readings of the HB as a Jewish scholar. His book on the concept of the exodus in the HB is extremely useful and he demonstrates the centrality of the exodus throughout the HB. Indeed, he asserts that "the Exodus, the central event in the historiography of the Bible and in the collective memory of the biblical period, represents an historical watershed. It shapes the recounting of events both before and after it: at the dawn of history and the time of the patriarchs, as well as events and periods long after the Exodus itself."[13]

Zakovitch begins his book on the concept of the exodus in the Bible with a quote from the Passover Haggadah: "Therefore, even if we were all sages, all men of understanding, and all experts in the Torah, it would yet be our duty to tell of the departure from Egypt, and the more a man tells about the departure from Egypt, the more praiseworthy he is."[14] Zakovitch asserts that no other *event* is given as much attention as the exodus in the Hebrew Bible. In his "Preface" he expresses his gratitude for being able, with this book, to observe Exod 13:8: "And you shall explain to your son on that day, 'It is because of *what the Lord did* for me when I went free from Egypt.'"[15]

Once again, we are led to expect an affirmation of the historicity of exodus-Sinai. Astonishingly, then, some two pages later, Zakovitch says that "historical issues find no place in such a study as this one. We need not consider whether the Exodus actually took place, who left Egypt, or in what numbers. It is a different history altogether that engages us: the history of ideas."[16]

The impetus of Walzer's, Levenson's, Fishbane's, and Zakovitch's work appears to push strongly in the direction of the exodus-Sinai event as *historical* revelation of the living God. However, they resist this direction and appear content or compelled to live with a view of Sinai as remarkably generative and yet something about which we can say nothing or little historically. This constitutes a genuine puzzle: Why do they feel that they cannot affirm the historicity of an event that they regard as so epochal for Israel and the entire world?

---

13. Yair Zakovitch, *"And You Shall Tell Your Son . . .": The Concept of the Exodus in the Bible* (Jerusalem: Magnes, 1991), 46.
14. Zakovitch, *Concept of the Exodus*, 9.
15. NJPS. Emphasis added.
16. Zakovitch, *Concept of the Exodus*, 11–12.

The Puzzle in Christian Scholarship

There is a sense in which we would expect Sinai, and YHWH as "the One of Sinai" (Judg 5:5), to be of more consequence for Jews than Christians. However, historical revelation is central to Christian theology with the Jesus event regarded as the fulfillment of the Old Testament and thus Christian understanding of Sinai remains of major importance. Surprisingly there is a lack of serious theological engagement with Sinai by Christians, and in what engagement there is, we find a similar reticence about its historicity among Christian scholars.

In his commentary on Exodus, Durham has a section on the exodus in history and the exodus as history.[17] He helpfully alerts the reader to scholarship that has established what he refers to as the contextual plausibility of the story of the exodus[18] but asserts that we lack proof of any one part of the narrative. Durham never elaborates on what he understands by "proof" but says that we should be content to speak about the narrative of Exodus *in* history rather than speaking of it *as* history. Either way, for Durham, historicity is the province of historians and other disciplinary specialists and not that of the commentator. Certainly, in his view, the question of historicity should not be a primary concern of the commentator, who has so many other tasks to attend to. Durham assumes a late date for the exodus in the nineteenth dynasty of Egypt, "but the chronology of the events described in Exodus is of little importance to the theological message of the book in its present from, a form vastly removed from the connection of any of these events with an historical time-frame."[19] As with the Jewish scholars discussed above, here again we find exegesis and theology separated from historicity.

The distinguished twentieth-century German theologian Emil Brunner is clear that historical revelation is utterly central to the Bible. He argues that everything the Bible teaches us is based on revelation in history.[20] Indeed, Brunner argues that we find in Scripture a unique conception of world his-

17. John I. Durham, *Exodus*, WBC 3 (Waco, TX: Word, 1987), xxiv–xxvi.

18. Durham, *Exodus*, xxv.

19. Durham, *Exodus*, xxvi.

20. Emil Brunner, *Dogmatics*, vol. 2: *The Christian Doctrine of Creation and Redemption*, trans. Olive Wyon (Philadelphia: Westminster Press, 1952), 193. Hereafter, page references to this work are given in parentheses in the text.

tory that has no parallel in the ANE or among the Greeks. He is adamant that outside of the particular history we find in Scripture "we do not know the living God" (198).

The HB/OT is clearly central to such historical revelation, and yet Brunner asserts that "the picture of 'revelation-history' which is given to us in the Old Testament can no longer be ours. Historical research has shown it to be a later Priestly theological construction, which probably contains historical elements, but at the same time conceals as much as it reveals of the real course of events" (199). However, in subsequent pages Brunner goes on to assert that unique to the HB/OT is the view that God acts in history, in events like the exodus, the deliverance at the Red Sea, and the formation of a covenant people at Sinai. Indeed "there is something in the Old Testament which does not exist outside it . . . the revelation of the Living God of History, of the Holy and Merciful God, of the God who marches towards a goal with his people" (201). The book of Scripture is of less importance to Brunner than the fact that God has intervened in history.

Of Israel, he notes that it "is the only nation in world history whose existence and distinctiveness is based upon historical divine revelation. Israel is what it is in virtue of the Covenant. Its historical existence is not a natural one, nor is it a simple political fact, but it is the product of the Mosaic revelation, of the divine Election as this particular people" (205). Brunner immediately qualifies this statement by arguing that Israel's origins are somewhat obscured and should not be equated with the picture we find in the HB/OT; nevertheless "this one point cannot be refuted, that at the outset of the history of Israel there is the Event of Moses and the Exodus from Egypt, in the remembrance of which Israel continually renews its unity and its distinctive character" (205).

Walzer wants to use the exodus as a paradigm for political action but will not go near the historicity of the event. Brunner sees the exodus and the Sinai covenant as a leading example of historical revelation but leaves the door open as to whether we can know anything about what happened at Sinai. Living amidst the homeland of modern historical criticism, Brunner ought to have known better than to think that the rhetorical flourish—"yet this one point cannot be refuted"—would for a moment prevent contemporaries or subsequent scholars from rejecting or questioning any historicity to Sinai.

Questions Emerging from This Puzzle

We have seen that it is by no means uncommon to find Jewish and Christian scholars affirming the unique generativity of Sinai while denying or remaining agnostic about its historicity.

A question that immediately comes to the fore is, Why are scholars so cagey about Sinai? To answer that question in some detail and to do justice to its complexities we will focus in detail on Benjamin Sommer's 2015, award-winning *Revelation and Authority: Sinai in Jewish Scripture and Tradition* in the next chapter. This book was published as I was embarking on my research, and, while I disagree with it in many ways, to Sommer's credit he sets out the different elements that constitute his approach to Sinai. For now, we highlight the following questions:

- Does it matter whether or not the Sinai event happened? The twentieth-century Jewish philosopher and theologian Eliezer Berkovits thinks it does: "For if the biblical encounter did not take place, religion as we understand it becomes a worthless mirage, and it would be so much foolishness to pursue it any further. On the other hand, if the encounter did occur, it was undeniably the most important event in the history of man."[21] However, clearly many Jewish and Christian scholars regard its historicity as of marginal or secondary importance.
- Can we appropriate exodus-Sinai as a literary and/or theological paradigm while bracketing off its historicity, without subverting the very theology or political theory we draw from the narrative?
- How should we go about assessing the historicity of the Sinai narrative? Is Levenson right, for example, that if we are "honest historians" we can say almost nothing about what happened at Sinai? Or, with Durham, must we remain agnostic in the face of a lack of "proof"?

Alternative Approaches to Sinai

We have focused on approaches that are agnostic about the historicity of Sinai, regard it as impossible to know, and/or regard it as unimportant. In this section we attend to alternative Jewish and Christian voices that regard the historicity of Sinai as central to the truth of the Sinai event.

21. Eliezer Berkovits, *God, Man and History*, ed. David Hazony (Jerusalem: Shalem Press, 2004), 19.

Jewish Alternatives

Rabbi Joseph Herman Hertz (1872–1946) was born in Hungary and appointed Chief Rabbi of the United Kingdom in 1913. Hertz produced a rich and influential commentary on the Torah (Genesis to Deuteronomy) and the corresponding Haftorahs (1929–36, and a one-volume edition in 1937). Throughout much of the twentieth century this classic was used in synagogues and classrooms throughout the English-speaking world. It remains a rich and useful commentary, not least because of the short essays at the end of each of the five books of the Torah.

Hertz is adamant that "Judaism stands or falls with its belief in the historic actuality of the Revelation at Sinai."[22] Revelation is the unveiling of the nature and will of God to humans. Theism and a view of God as the personal creator and source of life make revelation "a logical and ethical necessity" (402). Believers and scholars will, according to Hertz, differ on the exact *means* of this communication between God and humankind, but "no interpretation . . . is valid or in consonance with the Jewish Theistic position, which makes human reason or the human personality the *source* of such revelation" (402). The prophets experienced revelation from God to differing degrees, but when it comes to Moses,

> Not in dreams or visions or occasional flashes of Divine intuition was the manner of revelation in his case, but "face to face"; i.e. in the form of self-luminous thought and complete self-consciousness. In his mind, the Rabbis say, the Divine Message was reflected as in a clear mirror. . . . The supreme revelation in the life of the Lawgiver, however, that of the Covenant at Mount Sinai, he shared with the whole of Israel. To all of them was then vouchsafed the psychic experience of a direct communion with God. (403)

As does Zakovitch, Hertz notes how deeply the motif of the exodus and Sinai is woven into the HB and Jewish tradition, but for Hertz this is inextricably related to its historicity. In terms of the story of Israel's origin as slaves in Egypt, Hertz finds it unthinkable that a nation would invent such a

---

22. J. H. Hertz, ed., *The Soncino Edition of the Pentateuch and Haftorahs with Hebrew Text, English Translation, and Commentary*, 2nd ed. (London: Soncino, 1960), 402. Hereafter, page references to this work are given in parentheses in the text.

narrative for itself unless compelled to do so because this is what in fact took place: "No people has ever yet invented a *disgraceful* past for itself" (396).

Eliezer Berkovits (1908–92) was a theologian, philosopher, and Talmudic scholar. For many years he taught philosophy at the Hebrew Theological College in Chicago. Berkovits specifically addresses issues that are central to our project in his *God, Man and History*, but equally important is his *Major Themes in Modern Philosophies of Judaism*. In his preface to the latter work, Berkovits provocatively says that at present (1974) we possess neither a Jewish theology nor philosophy that relates integrally to Jewish teaching about God, humankind, and the world as articulated in the classic sources of Judaism. "Judaism is awaiting a reformulation of its theology and philosophy."[23] In his *Major Themes*, Berkovits reviews several major Jewish philosophies of the twentieth century and regularly focuses on their views of historical revelation and of Sinai. We will have good reason to refer to his review of these philosophies in subsequent chapters. For now, it should be noted that his other works move toward the reformulation he calls for, and, in this respect, *God, Man and History* is of particular relevance for our work.

Berkovits urges us to return to the sources: *Ad Fontes*. He reviews the epochal work of Saadia and Maimonides in the medieval era but notes that they subject faith to intellect. Building on Arabic Aristotelianism, Maimonides developed a view in which Judaism and metaphysics become ultimately identical so that "religion becomes absorbed by metaphysics. . . . If religion is so eminently reasonable, what need is there for revelation?"[24]

In the modern era, Berkovits notes how the philosophies of G. E. Lessing, Immanuel Kant, and G. W. F. Hegel are reflected in Jewish thought. In Hermann Cohen's work, for example, reason becomes the conduit for the contents of revelation and "the fact of revelation at Sinai is explained away as a mere political act, serving as it were, the practical purpose of committing the national consciousness of the Jews to the cause of monotheism in history" (6). The danger here is that metaphysics or anti-metaphysics becomes the religion of the scholars. For Berkovits, "the entire structure that was built around the identification of religion and reason must now be seen as lying in ruins" (12). He thus elects rather to follow the path of Judah Halevi (ca. 1075–1141), who came to assert the independence of the religious realm while retaining a deep

23. Eliezer Berkovits, *Major Themes in Modern Philosophies of Judaism* (New York: Ktav, 1974), vii.

24. Berkovits, *God, Man and History*, 5. Hereafter, page references to this work are given in parentheses in the text.

respect for reason. Halevi sought to liberate Judaism from bondage to various philosophical systems, exemplified in his book *Sefer ha-Kuzari.*

Berkovits develops his concept of God from the HB and Jewish tradition, rather than starting with philosophy. He asserts that "the foundation of religion is not the affirmation that God is, but that God is concerned with man and the world; that, having created this world, he has not abandoned it, leaving it to its own devices; that he cares about his creation" (15). At the heart of biblical religion is the view that God encounters and addresses humankind, and we can know this only by participating in it. "Everything in the Bible is communication between God and man; everything is relationship. God spoke; God commanded; God called; God appeared—all reflect events that take place between God and man. In all these situations man experiences the presence of God, which seeks him out and addresses him" (16).

Berkovits draws attention to the continual reference to sense perception in relation to what happened at Sinai. The biblical text insists on the incorporeality of God but also insists on the sensory impressions at Sinai. For Berkovits, the full story is that of a paradox; the invisible God revealed himself to the senses of human beings. "Moses was saying to Israel: At Sinai, you knew God—his presence, his word, and his command—by actual experience, in which all of your senses were involved. . . . The event itself brought the awareness of its own certitude" (17). This, for Berkovits, is the huge discovery of the living God; indeed, *that* God addresses humankind is the central religious concept, and is more significant even than *what* God communicates.

As already noted, for Berkovits it really matters if the encounter at Sinai took place or not. Certainly, such an encounter is not logically impossible. Historical encounter is different from science and the appropriate reference to an encounter is testimony.[25] There can be no science of the particular. "Biblical religion is history; and history is not taught by means of treatises on logics or mathematics, but through the records of eyewitnesses, or such as are based on them. Therefore, biblical religion, based as it is on man's encounter with God, could be established only by the testimony of the witness" (27). Who, asks Berkovits, are the witnesses? He answers: the prophets and Israel. The patriarchal narratives, the exodus and Sinai, the witness of the prophets, and so on, are not legends but events in the history of the Jews. Jewish children are not taught "these are the things we believe in," but

25. Cf. C. A. J. Coady, *Testimony: A Philosophical Study* (Oxford: Clarendon, 1992).

"these are the things that happened." Judaism is constituted historically by a number of encounters with God: "Eliminate Abraham, Isaac, and Jacob and their intercourse with God, deny the revelation at Sinai and the worlds of the prophets, and you have destroyed the foundations of Judaism" (43).

Encounter is inherently personal, and, like Fishbane, Berkovits stresses the ongoing encounter with God at Sinai: "The revelation at Sinai never belongs to the past; it never ceases to be. It is as if the divine Presence, never departing from the mountain, were waiting for each new generation to come to Sinai to encounter it and to receive the word" (44).

Whereas Hertz focuses on exegesis and the theology of the text, Berkovits is important for his attention to the philosophical—and theological—issues related to historical revelation and Sinai. He provides us with some important clues as to why some scholars are so cagey about affirming historical revelation at Sinai, including possible limits of the perfect-being theology so dominant in the medieval era. Berkovits also provides us with an indication of how a move from the text to theology and philosophy, rather than the other way around, might reshape our perspective.

Christian Alternatives

Walther Eichrodt (1890–1978) is well known for his discerning covenant as central to OT theology. Unlike Rabbi Hertz, Eichrodt follows the main lines of source criticism of the Pentateuch but, nevertheless, he, like Hertz and Berkovits, finds the historical revelation in the Sinai covenant to be foundational to Israelite religion. Like Zakovitch, Eichrodt notes the ways in which exodus-Sinai is built into the warp and woof of the OT. Unlike Zakovitch he finds in this strong confirmation for the historicity of Sinai: "If one observes the completely unique importance which these events have gained in the total religious praxis and tradition . . . then no doubt can exist that this first experience of a Divine encounter was decisive for the fundamental conception of the Divine revelation in Israel. Here one learned to understand the being of God from history and to exhibit his works in the forms of history."[26]

Like Walzer, Eichrodt recognizes in the HB/OT a unique view of history. Unlike Walzer, Eichrodt relates this to Israel's unique historical expe-

---

26. Walther Eichrodt, "Offenbarung und Geschichte im Alten Testament," *Theologische Zeitschrift* 4.5 (1948): 232. Quoted in G. Ernest Wright, *God Who Acts: Biblical Theology as Recital*, SBT 8 (London: SCM, 1952), 43–44.

rience at Sinai so that the two are inseparable: "In this way history acquires a value which it does not possess in the religions of the ancient civilizations."[27] The external event of Sinai leads to an interior view of history and the historical process that is unique in the ANE. Intriguingly, and here he moves in a somewhat different direction to Berkovits and Fishbane, Eichrodt acknowledges that there may be similarities with pagan rites to those at Sinai but, utterly different to such pagan rites is the fact that the Sinai covenant sacrifice cannot be repeated; it is a once-for-all event that creates the legal relationship at its first performance. Like Berkovits, Eichrodt emphasizes the relational aspect of the Sinai event and notes that "it is the manifestation of power with which Yahweh preludes the actual covenant-making which gives the Yahweh worship of the Mosaic period this character of trembling prostration before the jealous God, who will admit no derogation from his majesty."[28]

Wright points out that Israel's understanding of God did not originate in theoretical and speculative thought but from attempts to explain the events that founded Israel as a nation.[29] Eichrodt concurs, and notes that the nature of Sinai led first to a strong emphasis on living according to the covenant, and then to reflection on the God of the covenant. However, pressure in this direction is already present in the circumstances of the Sinai event.

The great twentieth-century theologian Karl Barth held a similar approach to historical criticism to that of Emil Bruner. However, in his *Doctrine of God*, amidst a discussion of God's constancy and omnipotence, Barth asserts that "His [God's] action is a conscious and planned activity; His operation is history."[30] Immediately following this statement is a smaller-font discussion, which begins, "Who and what is God in the Old Testament?" Barth replies:

> He is definitely the One who leads Israel out of Egypt, and saves it at the Red Sea from the power of Pharaoh, and leads it forward into the wilderness to Sinai and through the wilderness to the land of Canaan. This history and this recollection of this history as the primal history of the covenant between God and man are for all time the revelation

27. Walther Eichrodt, *Theology of the Old Testament*, vol. 1, trans. J. A. Baker (Philadelphia: Westminster, 1961), 41.

28. Eichrodt, *Theology of the Old Testament*, 1:44.

29. Wright, *God Who Acts*, 44.

30. Karl Barth, *CD* 2/1, 200.

of the God of the Old Testament, and therefore the revelation of His being as power. . . . It is a unique action in which He knows Israel for the sake of its elected fathers, and therefore calls Moses and sets him face to face with Pharaoh, strikes Egypt with all the plagues, lets the waves of the sea pile so that the people may pass through, lets them close again over Pharaoh and his host, and finally confirms and seals His election and will publicly concluding His covenant: I am thy God and thou art my people.[31]

Barth points out that that the Bible's interest in God's omnipotence is not primarily a general interest in a universal doctrine; rather the *particular* action of God in power, as at Sinai, precedes the general reflection, even if they are inseparably connected.[32] A great strength of Barth's dogmatics is his immense sense of the reality of God. Barth affirms in so many ways, and not least at Sinai, the centrality of God and his action to the life and existence of Israel.

Brevard Childs was deeply influenced by Barth. Childs studied under Barth, and once he grasped what Barth was doing, he spent the rest of his career seeking to redirect biblical studies so as to focus its work on the canonical witness to the God who has come to us in Christ. In his canonical hermeneutic Childs seeks to do justice to both historical criticism and the final form of the text as we receive it. Childs's work is rich and refreshing but, in my view, a tension remains in it between historical criticism and his final-form reading of the text. In his discussion of God's revelation through history in the HB/OT, for example, Childs finds this theme most completely affirmed by the prophets rather than drawing attention to the exodus-Sinai events.[33] In his discussion of the canonical shape of the witness at Sinai, Childs acknowledges the canonical centrality of Sinai to the Pentateuch. However, in the light of the texts' complex history of development over a long period of time, he thinks that it is a mistake to make HB/OT theology dependent on any historical reconstruction of the Sinai event.[34]

---

31. Barth, *CD* 2/1, 600–601.

32. For Barth on Exod 3 see *CD* 2/1, 60–61. He says of Moses's encounter with YHWH at the burning bush that "this incomprehensible event is the revelation of Yahweh" (60).

33. Brevard S. Childs, *Old Testament Theology in a Canonical Context* (London: SCM, 1985), 36–38.

34. Childs, *Old Testament Theology in a Canonical Context*, 53.

In his commentary on Exodus, as we will see later in this volume, Childs reviews historical critical reflection at each stage. Nevertheless, he says that "Exodus 19 remains as a witness that God did enter a covenant with a historical people at a particular time and place."[35]

Conclusion: "History Matters"

The puzzle in which this book originates will now be clear to the reader. What we call "the Sinai event" is clearly central to the HB/OT, and Jewish scholars in particular continue to mine it for its rich theological and public resources. One goal of this volume is to affirm such mining and to encourage and promote similar work by Christian scholars. We live in a day that cries out for a recovery of the public dimension of the HB/OT and its application to our many religious, social, political, and economic challenges.

However, another goal is to attend to the deep tension between taking exodus-Sinai as somehow paradigmatic and yet denying that we can know anything about the historical revelation of God involved in the Sinai event. As Abraham Joshua Heschel in his "The Moment at Sinai" puts it, "To ignore these events and to pay attention only to what Israel was taught in these events is like tearing out a piece of flesh from a living body."[36] The Bible presents us with the living God who speaks and acts, and whose speaking and acting is fundamental to his revelation of himself.

A way of focusing the question is to think in terms of speech-act theory, which distinguishes in a performative speech-act between the locution (saying something that is meaningful), the illocution (the act performed in saying something; the force conveyed in saying something), and the perlocution (the achieving of certain affects by saying something). Austin sums up these distinctions as follows: "Thus we distinguished the locutionary act . . . which has a meaning; the illocutionary act which has a certain force in saying something; the perlocutionary act which is the achieving of certain effects by saying something."[37] To provide a simple example, the statement "There is a snake in the garden!" makes sense. But what is its force? It could,

35. Brevard S. Childs, *The Book of Exodus: A Commentary* (Louisville: Westminster John Knox, 1974), 384.

36. Heschel, "The Moment at Sinai," 13.

37. J. L. Austin, *How to Do Things with Words*, 2nd ed. (Oxford: Oxford University Press, 1962, 1975), 121.

for example, be a warning to get out of the garden quickly, and its effect could be to make us evacuate the garden ASAP.

A speech-act like the Sinai narrative can have multiple illocutions: it can tell the story of what happened at Sinai, it can evoke the character of YHWH, it can call for obedience to his law, and so on. A crucial aspect in speech-act theory is that a speech-act can misfire or be rendered infelicitous if certain conditions are not met. For example, the act of marrying a couple is not achieved if the person conducting the service is a fake minister. Or, in our example above, there does indeed need to be an actual snake in the garden if the warning is to function fully and effectively.

We can therefore ask, Is the illocutionary force of the Sinai narrative rendered *infelicitous* if the events did not in fact happen? Another way of expressing this is to ask, Does the speech act *misfire* if the events and the description of Sinai as an act of God are imaginary? It would seem that this is indeed the case, especially when we take the witness to God in the text seriously. Heschel would seem to be right that to attend to the teaching while ignoring the events is like tearing out a piece of flesh from a living body.

However, we need to explore far more closely what it is that drives so many Jewish and Christian scholars to feel that we simply cannot have any idea what happened—if anything—at Sinai. Some of our best scholars hold this view and the basis for it requires close attention and critical scrutiny. In order to focus our investigation, we will use Benjamin Sommer's treatment of the topic as our basis in the following chapter.

CHAPTER 2

The Problem Explored

> If the Pentateuch was not revealed in the stenographic sense but results from a dialogue between God and Israel, then its words, as human formulations, are tentative and searching rather than definitive. It follows that the distinction between. . . . Written Torah and Oral Torah falls away entirely. Scripture is simply another form of tradition.
>
> —Benjamin Sommer[1]

In the previous chapter we explained the puzzle that is at the heart of this book. It revolves around what we make of YHWH as "the One of Sinai." On the one hand, Jewish and Christian scholars see the Sinai event as central to the Bible. It is of particular importance for Jews, but hardly less so for Christians, since the NT is built upon, and professes to be a fulfilment of, God's actions in the OT. At the same time, there is a surprising reluctance among Jewish and Christian scholars to affirm the historicity of Sinai.

In this chapter we will look closely at the reasons for this by attending to Benjamin Sommer's award-winning *Revelation and Authority: Sinai in Jewish Scripture and Tradition.* This is not to suggest that Sommer is necessarily representative of Jewish approaches to Sinai, but he is a believing Jew and certainly representative of the puzzle discussed in Chapter 1, and the great advantage and strength of his work is that he lays out all the components that shape his view of Sinai, something that is far too rare among HB/OT scholars.[2]

---

1. Sommer, *Revelation and Authority*, 147. Hereafter, page references to this work are given in parentheses in the text.

2. For three responses to Sommer's book, including one by Jon Levenson, and a reply by Sommer, see https://marginalia.lareviewofbooks.org/revelation-authority -forum/.

As with many of the Jewish scholars we discussed in the previous chapter, Sommer asserts that "the event that transpired at Mount Sinai some three months after the Exodus belongs to the threefold cord that is fundamental to all Jewish existence. Along with the redemption from slavery and the gift of the Land of Israel, the experience at Sinai created the amalgam of religion and ethnicity that we now call Judaism" (30). This would appear to make belief in divine action and revelation at Sinai fundamental, but Sommer's view turns out to be different from what this quote suggests.

Sommer points out that many biblical texts that narrate the giving of the Torah move in two directions: they anchor it in the revelation at Sinai and simultaneously destabilize that authority by teaching that we cannot be sure how the rules in the Torah relate to God's self-disclosure. "These texts deliberately ground the law's authority in the divine will, which God deliberately made known to a group of human beings" (1). However, they also problematize this view of revelation, pointing toward the human role in the production of the texts and thus suggesting that they arise through contributions by both God and Israel. In order to account for this, Sommer develops a *participatory* understanding of revelation.

Sommer's Participatory View of Revelation: A God Who (Perhaps?) Cannot Speak

Sommer distinguishes between *participatory* and *stenographic*—or dictation—understandings of revelation. The latter relates particularly to the view held by Orthodox Jews that the whole of the Torah was dictated to Moses by God at Sinai. Examples of the former are, according to Sommer, Franz Rosenzweig (1886–1929), Abraham Joshua Heschel (1907–72), and Louis Jacobs (1920–2006), and Sommer argues that they have medieval and rabbinic predecessors. Sommer develops his *participatory* understanding of revelation in a variety of ways but at its heart is the view of revelation as *dialogue*, which greatly enhances the human dimension in revelation.

According to Sommer, scholars have not noticed the ways in which the Bible itself anticipates a participatory approach to revelation. He is concerned to discern how the biblical texts themselves conceive of revelation and of their own status. Jewish and Christian theologians tend not to engage in close readings of the biblical text in their work, but Sommer argues that the religious relevance of the biblical texts emerge when we do the sort of close readings done by historical critics. Indeed, a central motif in Sommer's work is to defend *biblical criticism* as a legitimate way of reading Scripture and important for Jewish and Christian appropriation of the Bible today. He explains that a core idea in the book is that an Assyriologist can help a Jewish or Christian reader understand a verse in a way that is theologically relevant. "The major methodological goal of this book is to reconceive the Bible—and in particular, the Bible as understood by modern biblical critics—as a work of Jewish thought that should be placed in dialogue with medieval and modern works" (5).[3] The literary, philological, and historical challenges of biblical criticism to a view of the Bible as sacred are well known, and Sommer affirms a neo-Documentary Hypothesis approach to the Pentateuch. Sommer's emphasis on the Bible as *a work of Jewish thought* flows from this and relates to his strong view of human/Jewish involvement in its production.

However, for Sommer, biblical criticism is not the strongest argument in favor of a participatory approach to revelation. The strongest argument for him is the problematic, ideological nature of some biblical texts. He refers to texts that embody genocide, pervasive sexism, and so on, and notes that it is such texts rather than the contradictions identified by source critics that prevent him from embracing the traditional Jewish and Christian views of the Bible. "Moral issues rather than historical-philological ones pose the most disturbing challenge to the Bible's status as scripture" (28).

There is something of a paradox in Sommer's view; the very biblical texts that problematize revelation nevertheless assert the authority of the laws that emerge from it (6).[4] Sommer is aware of the dual temptations of

3. By comparison, Jon Levenson, "Do Bible Scholars Need Theology?," https://marginalia.lareviewofbooks.org/bible-scholars-need-theology/, concludes his review of Sommer's book by noting that, "And that brings me, finally, to what I think is the largest and most fundamental difference between how Sommer and I see things. In his thinking, the classical biblical and rabbinic tradition can be brought into harmony with modern historical critical thinking. In my thinking, the relationship is one of tension and mutual judgment." John C. Cavadini, "Can We Separate Scripture and Tradition?," https://marginalia.lareviewofbooks.org/can-separate-scripture-tra dition/, wonders if Sommer's rejection of an authoritative canon of Scripture "is not finally analogous either to a Catholic view or a Protestant view but is actually a rejection of religious authority in favor of a secular magisterium."

4. For a similar, clear articulation of this view see Bernard M. Levinson, *"The Right Chorale": Studies in Biblical Law and Interpretation* (Winona Lake, IN: Eisenbrauns, 2011), 30–39. Levinson asserts that "literary history—human authorship and revision of law, the obvious need for new laws to develop in response to ongoing

reading the Bible critically and ignoring its relevance to Judaism, or ignoring historical critical readings and engaging with the Bible simply through the Jewish tradition. Neither is acceptable to him, and his participatory model is an attempt to articulate the role of a historical critical approach within Jewish thought, thereby bringing together what seems, to many, irreconcilable.

Sommer follows John Barton in his explication of the nature of historical criticism:[5]

- It attends to the genre of texts.
- As part of the humanities it shares an emphasis on reason and evidence.
- It seeks to be objective by attending to what the text actually says.
- Diachronic analysis is not nearly as central as is often thought.

Sommer adds that historical criticism must situate the text in its ANE context.

Sommer notes the difference between approaching the Bible as an artifact (biblical criticism) or as Scripture (religious). "The very core of modern biblical criticism consists of an attempt to understand biblical texts as their first audiences understood them in ancient Israel" (19). He acknowledges that approaching the Bible as Scripture is more difficult for those who accept the methods and conclusions of modern biblical scholarship. However, "An intellectually honest person addressed by the Hebrew Bible today must read the Bible at once as artifact and as scripture" (13). But is this possible? Only in relation to a particular, local, religious tradition and only if we revise our view of revelation. Throughout his work, Sommer engages in dialogue with the Jewish tradition, but in particular with Rosenzweig and Heschel. He finds support for much of his participatory view of revelation and what he calls his dialogical biblical theology in these two thinkers.

To his credit, Sommer affirms the centrality of Sinai as an event to and for Judaism: "The event that transpired at Mount Sinai some three months after the Exodus belongs to the threefold cord that is fundamental to all Jewish existence" (30). Sinai is clearly generative for Sommer, but what he grants with one hand he seems to withdraw with the other. Chapter 2 of his book is

---

social and economic change—is everywhere ostensibly denied by means of the attribution of law to God or Moses. Yet precisely the thoroughness of such attribution undermines the veil of redactional illusion. The very repeated denial of literary history succeeds in affirming it" (34).

5. John Barton, *The Nature of Biblical Criticism* (Louisville: Westminster John Knox, 2007).

entitled "What Happened at Sinai?" He begins chapter 2 with a discussion of difficult biblical texts and thus the human origins of the Bible. He asks, "How can a contemporary Jewish theology come to terms with obedience to the tradition based on this text along with the need to construct correctives to it? How can a theology express both love of Torah and readiness to study it critically and with an open mind?" (28–29).

One response from Sommer is to stress that the results of historical criticism are not as radical as they are often taken to be. The sources posited by the Documentary Hypothesis, JEDP, for example, all agree that the events at Sinai were bound up with lawgiving. For Sommer there are no archaeological or historical reasons to doubt the core elements of the biblical presentation of Israel's history. However, he also argues that the question of historical reliability is far more pressing for Christians than Jews and that such concern is a modern development: "Concern with Scripture's historicity is a recent development; it is shared by fundamentalist Protestants and anti-religious skeptics, who are equally influenced, in their thoroughly modern view of scripture, by historical critics" (258).

A further response is to argue that the category of "Scripture" is a chimera, and Sommer resituates the Bible as a work of *tradition*. "This approach implies that for Judaism there really is no such thing as scripture; there is only tradition" (8). As a work of Jewish thought and part of a much broader tradition, readings oriented toward the final form of the text need not be privileged; for Sommer atomistic, fragmented readings are as legitimate as focusing on the final form, and sometimes more interesting. We must face the fact that the canon of Scripture is imperfect, and Scripture is flawed. Resituating Scripture within tradition makes it a partner for dialogue and debate, as well as alerting us to the fact that Scripture is itself already a book of dialogue and debate, an anthology of divergent views. Biblical traditions and voices can be *correlated* with voices in the tradition and with the modern knowledge yielded by biblical criticism. Sommer refers to Uriel Simon's view that the apparent clash between biblical criticism and Jewish faith is a psychological problem and not a problem of principle. Sommer's means to overcome this clash or tension is his participant view of revelation.

To help him accomplish this, Sommer finds resources in Rosenzweig's and Heschel's views of the Bible as a *response* to revelation, and particularly in Rosenzweig's view of the Bible as akin to *midrash*. For Sommer, along with Jewish tradition the Bible is a *response* to God's revelation. The Bible thus mixes human and divine elements, but Sommer is open to going much further than this: "Alternatively, God's act of revelation may not have con-veyed specific content, so that all the words and laws we find in the Bible are human interpretations of revelation" (29).

Sommer acknowledges the centrality of Sinai in Jewish liturgy, which repeatedly states that God gave Torah to his people with Moses as the inter-mediary. But what, asks Sommer, do "gave" and "received" mean? Sommer, as we have noted, is deeply committed to modern biblical criticism and indeed to the neo-JEDP Documentary Hypothesis. Sommer asserts that "I primarily follow the rigorous, massively detailed, yet elegant revision of the classical theory known as the neo-Documentary Hypothesis, available and defended in the works of Menahem Haran, Joel Baden, and above all Baruch Schwarz" (270). He maintains that "the story of revelation in Exodus 19–24 defies a coherent sequential reading" (31). In light of this he observes that Exod 19–20 and 24 contain gaps, discontinuities, and contradictions. For example, Sommer finds in Exod 20:18–22 and 24 a bewildering aggregate of verses describing Moses's ascents and descents. Moses, according to Som-mer, seems not to be located at the right place when the Decalogue is given. All these strange aspects of the Sinai narrative make us feel as though we are witnessing it through a fog, or that so overwhelming was the experience that it could not be articulated in human words. Sommer notes that the theoph-anic imagery here and elsewhere in the Bible is also found in ANE literature, as, for example, in the Baal stories.

Sommer makes no attempt to attend to literary readings of Exod 19–24, readings that understand that narratives are often not coherently sequential in nature. There are not many of these but the major ones we attend to in Chapter 9 are not referred to by Sommer or included in his bibliography. Instead he privileges JEDP and likens these sources to rabbinic voices try-ing to tell the story of Sinai. Sommer relates this philosophically to the fact that "human language cannot encompass an event in which heaven comes to earth and the transcendent becomes immanent" (45). The JEDP narra-tives of Sinai were written centuries after Sinai, but, according to Sommer, each preserves memories going back to it. "Because the revelation was so overwhelming, the way people perceived it as it was happening must have varied; different Israelites noticed, and missed, different aspects of what took place" (45). Over time, Sommer acknowledges, the differences be-tween the accounts grew. Remarkably, he relates this divergence among the JEDP versions to God's intention to provide an account that alerts us to Sinai as overcoming the limits of human perception. The divergence also yields interpretive freedom.

A central concern of ours is divine action and especially divine speech. Sommer discerns five ambiguities in Exod 19–24 concerning sounds as he seeks to discern precisely what the Israelites heard at Sinai:

1. The word *qol* occurs seven times in 19–20. But does it refer to God's voice or to thunder? "Did God communicate with Moses using a human voice or a very loud noise? Our understanding of revelation's nature and its very content changes drastically depending on which understanding we adopt" (36).
2. The extent to which the nation heard God speak is unclear.
3. In 20:1 Sommer maintains that the recipient of "God spoke all these words, saying . . ." is unclear. The unprecedented phrasing lacking an addressee calls us to wrestle with the question, according to Sommer, from whom did Israel receive the Decalogue? Were one to concede the point, which I do not, that the addressee is unclear, one might expect Sommer to explore different options, but instead, he turns the question around, seeking to make the addresser unclear!
4. Exod 19:25–20:2 can be read with either God or Moses as the speaker.
5. The mode of the nation's perception at Sinai is unclear. For example, in Exod 20:18 we read that all Israel saw *haqol*. Sommer discusses Cassuto's view that this is a case of zeugma, in which a word applies to others in different senses, but remains with the view that the text is unclear. This is important for Sommer. In Exod 24 revelation is visual and for Sommer this suggests a completely different understanding of revelation, one in which God's revelation is *nonverbal*.

For Sommer, these ambiguities support a participatory view of revelation: "If human intermediaries wrote the laws found in the Torah, even those in the Decalogue, as an attempt to translate God's nonverbal *qol* into human language, then the authority behind the law in general remains fully divine, but the specifics of any given law are human" (43). For Sommer the motif of Mosaic mediation represents the attempt by authors of the sources to raise precisely these sorts of questions. All the laws may be Moses's personal formulations and thus "the book forces us to hover between two models for understanding revelation" (44). For Sommer we cannot, however, invoke the refrain "God spoke" to solve this issue. "The Pentateuch encourages us to conclude from *the web of ambiguities* in Exodus 19–20 that we are unsure whether God talks, even to Moses, in human language" (44; emphasis added). This is vital for Sommer because "if human intermediaries wrote the laws found in the Torah, even those in the Decalogue, as an attempt to translate God's nonverbal *qol* into human language, then the authority behind the law in general remains fully divine, but the specifics of any given law are human" (43).

Sommer connects this with his view of JEDP and Exod 19–24. "An intellectually honest modern reader of scripture will regard some redacted texts less as the product of synthesis than as a record of debate and polemic" (72). JED and P differ substantially in their account of "Sinai." For example, the unity of place of the revelation each source championed is gone. Indeed, "the redacted Torah relativizes the sources, replacing their clarity with cacophony" (74). This forces us to wonder about revelation; only the person who attends to a single source can achieve that most dangerous thing: certainty. For Sommer, "the reader is forced to accept that lawgiving occurred, that it is vitally important, but that we can never be sure precisely what it entails" (74). The Pentateuch provides for us neither univocality or clarity but argument and perplexity. Sommer distinguishes between maximalist and minimalist approaches to Sinai and clearly his view is minimalist. The final form of the Torah poses to us, as it were, the question, To what extent did the people participate in revelation? D is maximalist; P and J are minimalist; E prompts thinking regarding tensions between the two views.

Sommer's turn to Maimonides as an exemplary minimalist at this point is noteworthy. According to Sommer, "Maimonides intimates that even Moses's experience of God at Sinai could not have been verbal. Indeed, it cannot be audial in any sense, because, Maimonides insists, *speech cannot be attributed to the incorporeal God* any more than walking or eating can" (82; emphasis added). He continues:

> When the Torah describes God as talking, it does not mean that God communicated using a voice and words. Indeed, for Maimonides, it cannot and must not mean that. It refers only to volition or thought. Further, it cannot refer to an act of volition or thought that Moses could receive through some sort of extrasensory perception. For if God acted at a given moment to think a specific thought or to express a particular wish . . . *then God is not eternal and unchanging.* Whatever happened to Moses at Mount Sinai, it did not involve his ears hearing God speaking any words to him, or even his mind "hearing" God silently expressing specific volitions. Both Moses and Israel had some intellectual experience of God at Sinai; but in light of Maimonides's statement in I:65,

even Moses's deeper perception there did not involve the medium of language, even silently. (83; emphasis added)

In terms of God's commands, Sommer asserts that "to say that God commands is to say that God is the ground for the fact that a good and rational command has been perceived by a wise human; it is not to state that God literally uttered the command" (84).

Sommer argues that we find such a view not only in a rationalist like Maimonides but also in a Jewish mystic like Menaḥem Mendel of Rymanov (1745–1815), who argued that Israel only heard the first letter of the Hebrew *'ani* (I), namely the letter *aleph*. Sommer finds biblical support for such an extreme view in the narrative of Elijah in 1 Kgs 18, which polemicizes against the Baal-like view of theophany by asserting that God was not in typical theophanic phenomena but in the still, small *qol*. For Sommer, this demonstrates that Mendel's reading is not a new one.

Thus, Sommer's participatory theory of revelation means that at Sinai "God communicated with Israel and Moses but spoke little or not at all" (99). Sommer does not relinquish the event of Sinai, but he argues that revelation resulted in a "sense of commandedness, which required paraphrasing in the form of law" (101). "The moment of revelation may have included no verbal content, but what followed in its wake is full of content, both legal and theological" (101). The motif of Moses's mediation thus raises the question, How did divine laws emerge from communication without words? In response Sommer appeals to the *translation* theory of prophecy, to correlation, to a distinction between *Gebot* (divine command) and *Gesetz* (a specific law). Jewish tradition starts with Moses and his many followers who seek to "echo, amplify, and reify God's voice" (121) because God's voice delivers no content but does command! Thus "the participatory theory of revelation maintains that Jewish tradition results from the work of teachers starting with Moses who struggle to echo, amplify, and reify God's voice" (121). For Sommer, "Israel completes the sentence that begins 'God commands us to,' but God remains the subject, and the verb does not lose its basic meaning of requiring obedience" (122). In this way the centrality of law in the Jewish tradition is maintained but the content becomes mixed.

What of Moses and the question of pseudepigraphy? Claiming Mosaic authorship is a sign of humility, according to Sommer, but should not be taken literally. Most ancient texts did not have one author and the texts of the Bible crystallized over generations. Pseudepigraphy was well known in the ANE, and it became common practice among Jews to attribute new laws to Moses. For Sommer this continued a tradition that went back to Sinai through a process of telescoping. Sommer defends *ex post facto* holiness in this regard. "Israel responds to God's command at Sinai by authoring specific laws, which, having endured for generations, can be understood to have been accepted and even legislated by God" (145). God, in this way, did not accept laws that did not endure. *"Israel's observance of the law helps God to grant the law the status of divine bidding"* (145). For Sommer God's presence in the Bible is not found in its words "but in the *qol* that is not yet a word, in the *aleph* of God's presence that hovers beneath the biblical text and invites it into being" (146).

Sommer's approach leads him to equate Scripture with tradition, to privilege the Oral Torah over the Written one, and to make Scripture part of the ongoing dialogue of Oral Torah. "It follows that the distinction be-tween what rabbinic culture calls Written Torah and Oral Torah falls away entirely. Scripture is simply another form of tradition" (147).[6] In fact, there is no Written Torah but only Oral Torah, which begins in Gen 1:1. For Som-mer, Oral Torah has a conceptual and temporal priority over Written Torah since Scripture emerged from tradition and is often modified by tradition. Eliminating the distinction between Oral and Written Torah, he claims, is loyal to elements in Jewish tradition and to biblical religion. Biblical authors revise, interpret, and reject other authors, an insight that intertextuality and inner biblical exegesis has foregrounded. Indeed, to a great extent, the Bible is an interpretive anthology.

Inner biblical exegesis demonstrates that tradition is historically prior to Scripture. Further, in the ANE we find no firm distinction between written and oral sources of authority. Thus, the distinction between Scripture and tradition is misleading; both are revealed, sacred, and authoritative. The nature of oral tradition as a theological idea, following the insights of Walter Ong, is a process, interpersonal, and always revealed in the present. "Oral Torah, then, is the body of rules, attitudes, and habits of thought through

---

6. Levenson, "Do Bible Scholars Need Theology?," comments in this regard, "As I see it, the interplay of the two modes by which Torah comes to the Jews— through the scriptural canon and through authorized teachers—defines a constitut-ing dynamic of rabbinic Judaism and is a matter of concern throughout subsequent tradition. Were the Written Torah to be folded into the Oral, this dynamic would disappear. And this brings us to what I see as a paradox in Sommer's proposal: on the one hand, it champions the Oral Torah at the expense of Written, but, on the other hand, in the very process it has to redefine radically what is meant by Oral Torah."

which Jews receive, understand, and pass on revelation" (178). Oral tradition is organic and dynamic; Sommer quotes Cohen on Martin Buber and Rosenzweig with approval, referring to the "living voice of God" (181).

According to Sommer, oral tradition never ceases to evolve; it has no closed canon and is better thought of as an event that occurs in the present as part of ongoing revelation. Sommer discusses Silman's three models for God's ongoing influence of Jewish sages: the perfection model in which the Oral and Written Torah is regarded as complete; the being-ever-perfected model in which humans add contributions to Torah through the ages; and the discovery model in which heavenly Torah is perfect but our limited perception of it is constantly being perfected. Rosenzweig is closer to the second view, Heschel to the third. Sommer asserts that we find different approaches to this question in JED and P, and he utilizes D to develop a view of Sinai for every generation. He argues that D envisions divinely ordained additions to the law so that we should read Deut 4:2 and 13:1 with a grain of salt. "D is a work of Oral Torah that attempts (pretends?) to identify itself as a work of Written Torah" (198). Heschel and Rosenzweig emphasize the "today" of Torah: lawgiving must always be in the present. God's lawgiving occurs in eternity and since time does not apply to God this allows "one" to experience revelation in an eternal present.

In his answer to whether Torah changes, Sommer refers to Horowitz's view that each idea at Sinai has its appropriate moment. Rosenzweig argues that Israel stands outside of time so that all the Torah exists simultaneously in eternity. "If this is the case, then an innovation has the same venerable antiquity as a practice that goes back millennia. . . . If every Jew was at Sinai, we must reckon with the possibility that the new practice was sanctioned by God at Sinai, though it has only moved from potential torah to actual torah in our own day" (207). Not all innovations are legitimate, according to Sommer, but the eternity of Torah in heaven erases early and late as key criteria for making an evaluative distinction. As an example, Sommer refers to the ordination of lesbian women, which could, over time, turn out to be truly Torah. Time and the response of the community seem to be the key criteria for Sommer.

In all of this, Sommer attempts to articulate a modern Jewish approach to Scripture that affirms and engages fully with historical criticism. He thinks of the history of Jewish thought as "disputes for the sake of heaven," noting that biblical criticism allows us to study the earliest disputes. The Bible, from this perspective, is the earliest form of Oral Torah. "Religious readers who ignore the findings of biblical criticism, however, exclude the first Jews from our dialogue and perpetuate a new form of supersessionism that separates biblical Israel from Judaism" (209–10). "Torah in heaven" profoundly influences Sommer, who argues that "to study in a traditional Jewish setting entails the suspension of time and space" (210). Biblical criticism enables us to include the earliest sages in the discussion so that we can put biblical authors in dialogue with later sages. "I am able to trace this long-term coherence in Jewish thought only by recognizing the Pentateuch's lack of coherence. . . . In short, I read the Pentateuch for disunity in order to find a greater unity in Jewish tradition" (212–13).

Sommer references his earlier work on YHWH's bodies, in which he argues that in common with ANE ideas YHWH was conceived of as having multiple cultic bodies. P and D attempt to suppress this tradition and only hard biblical criticism enables us to retrieve it. The Bible is akin to a record of an ongoing debate. It is the first rabbinical book.

Sommer distinguishes between centrifugal and centripetal readings. The latter searches for a solid center, the former promotes diversity. Both are present in the Bible and in Jewish tradition, but in the Bible the former is more widespread. Childs's canonical approach, which privileges the final form of the text, is an example of a centripetal approach, but Sommer disagrees with him: "I cannot see why, from a Jewish point of view, the redactor of the Pentateuch should have a more important voice than the P authors or the D authors who came before him, or than various commentators on the Pentateuch who came after" (230). This does not mean that all voices are equally authoritative, as Jewish tradition has made clear in many cases.

In agreement with Jon Levenson, Sommer is clear that there can be no Jewish biblical theology, but only Jewish theology. All Torah, ancient, medieval, and modern, is a response to the Sinai event. Each generation stands, as it were, at Sinai and responds in its own way, and the responses inevitably involve innovation and continuity "within the covenant formed at Sinai" (241) and its "binding covenantal law" (246). The Torah is given to the Jews, and one has the right to alter what is one's property. Sommer draws on Bernard Levinson's work to argue that "what matters is not the specific action the law requires but the fact that the law does require" (242). As noted above, Sommer's proposed methodology is correlational. He asserts that the vectors connecting heaven and earth are not just descending ones from heaven, but also ascending ones from the Jewish community. God, furthermore, is portrayed in the Bible as fallible: "The covenant formed at Sinai is correlational, but it is not a contract between equals" (248). For Sommer, "Jews create torah" (249).

Clearly Sommer's work requires a detailed response, and in many ways it represents the sort of view engaged with critically throughout this book. For now, to recap, it should be noted that the following key elements inform Sommer's minimalist view of the Sinai event:

1. Exod 19–24 is incoherent and full of ambiguities.
2. There is not one story of the Sinai event in the Pentateuch but four—namely, those of JED and P. For Sommer intellectual honesty compels us to take historical critical readings of the Sinai accounts with utmost seriousness.
3. The ambiguities in Exod 19–24 raise the question of whether God spoke at all.
4. The Bible, including Exod 19–24, is a work of human tradition, albeit in response to a sense of commanded-ness issuing forth from Sinai. Central to Sommer's minimalist account is his setting up revelation as either participatory or stenographic, and opting for a strong version of the former.
5. The ambiguities in the multiple and conflicting accounts of Sinai also alert us to the fact that human language is inadequate to describe an event like Sinai.
6. Maimonides's theology confirms Sommer's view that Israel encountered God at Sinai but there was no content to God's speech, because God cannot speak.

Clearly, a major element in Sommer's case is that Exod 19–24 is incoherent as its stands and that, if we are intellectually honest, we should follow him and others in excavating JED and P, with their diverse accounts of the "Sinai" event, and privilege these as much as the final form of the text. Sommer argues that historical criticism aims to read the Pentateuch so as to discern how its first audience would have heard it. He seems, anachronistically in my view, to assume that they would have heard JED and P speaking, whereas JED and P is a thoroughly modern construct. The most basic reception history of the Pentateuch would, I suggest, point in a very different direction. In our final chapter, we will turn to the actual text of Exod 19–24 to see if this is indeed the case.

But there is far more to Sommer's approach than the results of historical criticism. There is his reading of the Jewish tradition, his appropriation of Rosenzweig and Heschel, his view of revelation, and, crucially, his affirmation of certain philosophical and theological viewpoints that shape his view *integrally*. We will need to attend to all these dimensions in the following chapters in order to respond to his sort of approach to the Sinai event. For now, in order to open up our view of the diverse ingredients in his participatory view of revelation, and as a link into the following philosophical chapters, I draw attention to one of the *philosophical* viewpoints informing Sommer's approach, a viewpoint that receives little critical attention by him.

Immanuel Kant and Sinai

As we noted, Sommer reaches for Rosenzweig and Heschel to support his participatory view of revelation. In the process, he has an intriguing discussion of Rosenzweig's view of *autonomy*, with his stress on our own inner power. Sommer connects Rosenzweig's view of autonomy with that of Kant and asserts, "The Kantian autonomy Rosenzweig assumes is a universal and not a personal autonomy, and for this reason it is far more enriching to traditional Jewish notions of *hiyyuv* [obligation] than many have assumed" (132).

In my view this is far from the case. Sommer quotes Seeskin on Kant's view of autonomy (131), noting that divine commands only become such when *I* accept them; the real decision rests with the individual and not with God; the will is subject to the law but also *self-legislative*; the will can be regarded as author of the law! Thus, Kantian autonomy assumes a personal and universal view and is exemplary of the anthropocentric nature of post-Enlightenment thought.

While it is certainly true that God's Torah fits with the way he made the world and thus is inherently universal, albeit historically particular, to turn this upside down and make our reason the source of the moral law is, in my view, perverse and quite wrong. It is the exact opposite of what we find at Sinai, and indeed in the HB/OT as a whole. Thus, I do *not* see Kantian *autonomy* as enriching for the Jewish or the Christian tradition. Instead, Sommer's appropriation of it shows how easily his participatory view of revelation can become a nose of wax subject to manipulation and control. Kant, for example, notes that "the concepts and principles required for eternal life cannot really be learned from anyone else: the teacher's exposition is only the occasion for him to develop them out of his own reason."[7]

---

7. *RRT*, 263. Hereafter, page references to this work are given in parentheses in the text.

Indeed, Kant's view of reason is a major source for *undermining the very notion and possibility of divine revelation in and through history*. The major source in this respect is Kant's *Religion within the Bounds of Reason*, but his anti-historical approach is also found in several other works. It surfaces repeatedly, for example, in Kant's *The Conflict of the Faculties*. Kant asks, for example, "why should we get entangled in all these learned investigations and disputes because of a historical narrative that should always be left in its proper place (among matters that are indifferent)?" (*RRT*, 266). Kant asserts, "For if God should really speak to a human being, the latter could still never *know* that it was God speaking. It is quite impossible for a human being to apprehend the infinite by his senses, distinguish it from sensible beings, and *be acquainted with* it as such" (*RRT*, 283).

Such has been Kant's influence that Jewish and Christian philosophers have struggled to come to grips with it in relation to their own traditions. One thinks, for example, of Moses Mendelssohn who struggled to be a public intellectual and remain faithful to the Jewish tradition. Mendelssohn is fascinating in his own right. For our purposes, it is intriguing that he drew a line in relation to Kant's rational religion when it came to Sinai. Kant quotes him disapprovingly when Mendelssohn says, "Until God, from Mount Sinai, revokes our law as solemnly as He gave it (in thunder and lightning)—that is, until the end of time—we are bound by it" (quoted in *RRT*, 275). Sinai is for Mendelssohn the great exception: "All the miracles that have occurred or are said to have occurred in any corner of the earth are not to be compared with this great, God-behoving appearance. Also no known testimony of any validity contradicts it."[8] This makes it a "historical matter."[9]

Clearly Kant's influence is important for historical divine action and revelation since it relegates it to insignificance. However, it also returns us to Sommer's ready adoption of historical criticism of the Bible and use of JEDP to support his participatory theory of revelation. Sommer treats historical criticism simply as neutral analysis of the Bible in the context of the ANE. However, there is far more going on here than Sommer assumes.

What is not nearly so well known as it needs to be, and which we will explore in Chapter 6, is that Wilhelm de Wette, the father of modern bib-

---

8. Quoted in Willi Goetschel, *Spinoza's Modernity: Mendelssohn, Lessing, and Hume* (Madison: University of Wisconsin Press, 2004), 130.

9. Goetschel, *Spinoza's Modernity*, 130.

lical criticism, learned deeply from Kant, and experienced a conversion to the Kantian paradigm. He spent years trying to bring biblical studies into line with that paradigm, and central to it was the view that historical reference is irrelevant in terms of the religious value of the Bible. Biblical criticism is thus far from neutral philosophically or theologically, despite Barr's and Barton's protestations to the contrary, and, while its results cannot and should not be ignored, it is essential that one considers the underdetermination of facts at this point, as explicated in the philosophy of science.[10] The sort of biblical critical analysis that Sommer assumes has been savaged in multiple ways, and time is ripe for reassessment, particularly of the critical approach to the Pentateuch *and* the philosophies of history informing it.

Philosophy and Theology

Sommer's affirmation of Kant opens one window onto his debt to certain philosophies. So too does his appropriation of Maimonides whereby God cannot speak. Indeed, throughout his book certain philosophical views are assumed without being critically interrogated. For example, he relates the "fog" of Sinai to the fact that "human language cannot encompass an event in which heaven comes to earth and the transcendent becomes immanent."[11] This is a philosophical and a theological view; the critical question is, How does Sommer know this? If God is the creator of this world and of language, why would language be so alien to God's involvement in his creation?

Utterly central to how we think about the Sinai event is the question of *God speaking*. On the surface, Exodus seems to be unequivocal in affirming the fact that YHWH speaks, and that he does so a great deal. Sommer leverages Maimonides's perfect-being, rationalist philosophy to assert otherwise. The magnitude of this move for Sommer's project *should not be underestimated*. Clearly if God cannot speak, then the Torah is a human product through and through. The Pentateuch is chock-full of content but none of

---

10. Cf. Thomas Bonk, *Underdetermination: An Essay on Evidence and the Limits of Natural Knowledge*, Boston Studies in the Philosophy of Science 261 (Dordrecht: Springer, 2008).

11. Sommer, *Revelation and Authority*, 45.

this can come from God and must be a thoroughly human product, with God somehow present immanently in the ongoing process of Oral Torah. The Written Torah is elevated to a large extent by Jews and Christians because in it we have a record of God's address, however much mediated through human agents. But, if God cannot speak then it is easy to see how reducing the Written Torah to part of the ongoing Jewish tradition is virtually inevitable. The voices we hear in the Pentateuch become equated with rabbinic or contemporary voices arguing over different interpretations of God's *unspoken* Torah/instruction. Even the relative proximity to Sinai of JED and P compared with our perspective does not count since the giving of the law is an eternal event outside of time and space, an eternal event that Sommer thinks contemporary Jews can enter into.

A range of important issues for our project thus emerge:

- Is it true that God cannot speak?
- Need we adopt Maimonides's and Sommer's sort of *perfect-being theology* with its doctrines of God's eternity, timelessness, and simplicity such that God cannot speak, but Jews can continue to experience Sinai as a timeless event? Thomas Aquinas, for example, thinks in this tradition but affirms God speaking and acting in history.
- What view of God is in play if God cannot speak but can generate a sense of obligation?
- How can Jews translate a sense of obligation that is content-less? This sounds a lot like Kant's doctrine of the categorical imperative, which Kant was able to develop apart from God, certainly apart from the living God of the Bible.
- How is our approach to the Sinai event changed if God can speak and there are no philosophical obstacles to this?
- Is historical criticism as neutral and objective as Sommer assumes, or is it itself shaped by the sort of philosophies Sommer refers to?
- How might a different, more biblical doctrine of God and a theology of revelation that includes God speaking shape an alternative account of Sinai?

Clearly there is far more philosophy—and theology—involved here than first meets the eye. In order to navigate this sort of view of Sinai, deep philosophical and theological excavations will be required. This will be evident in the chapters that follow.

Conclusion

It will be obvious from this chapter why I find Sommer such an attractive dialogue partner. He is unusual among HB/OT scholars in his ability and willingness to lay out all the elements that constitute his approach to Sinai and, to varying degrees, most of these will be taken up in one way or another in subsequent chapters.

There is truth in Sommer's advocacy of a participatory view of revelation, but to set up the contrast between a participatory and a stenographic approach is distinctly unhelpful, and may be overly Jewish in the sense of setting up a dichotomy between the Orthodox Jewish dictation view and Sommer's type of participatory view as the two main options, whereas among Christian scholars those of us who affirm the substantial Mosaicity of Exodus–Deuteronomy would eschew a purely dictation approach, and leave considerable room for human involvement in the production of the text. Indeed, for much of modernity Christian biblical scholars have rejected dictation (stenographic) theories of inspiration. We have instead argued for a range of sophisticated organic views of revelation that attempt to do justice to the divine and human aspects of the Bible, but without reducing God to a "dialogue" partner who cannot speak or act. Indeed, if God cannot speak then "dialogue" is clearly the wrong word for Sommer's "participatory" approach. If God cannot speak, then we do all the speaking and writing, leaving God's input rather nebulous and—at most—somehow immanent to the process.

CHAPTER 3

Moses Maimonides, Judah Halevi, and Michael Wyschogrod

I do not think I need to explain to you the inadmissibility of speech in reference to God. . . . Speech is attributed to Him, in so far as the word which Moses heard, was produced and brought to existence by God in the same manner as He produced all His other works and creation.

—Maimonides[1]

In the previous chapter we saw how an element in Sommer's reading of Sinai is his appeal to Maimonides's view that God cannot speak. However, in the introductory chapter, we noted Eliezer Berkovits's preference for the tradition of Judah Halevi (ca. 1075–1141) rather than the philosophically heavy approaches developed by Jews in medieval and modern times, such as that of Maimonides. For Berkovits, such approaches have culminated in our situation, in which "The entire structure that was built around the identification of religion and reason must now be seen as lying in ruins."[2]

Halevi was a close predecessor to Moses Maimonides (1135–1204), and the early Halevi shared much in common with Maimonides, who is famous for his attempt to reconcile reason with Scripture and the Jewish tradition.[3] In later life Halevi reacted strongly against the over-privileging—as he saw it—of philosophy and turned far more strongly to the Hebrew Bible and Jewish tradition as his primary sources, as we will see below. Within the Jewish

1. Moses Maimonides, *The Guide for the Perplexed*, 2nd ed. (New York: Dover, 1904), 97. Hereafter, references to this work are given in parentheses in the text.
2. Berkovits, *God, Man and History*, 12.
3. Cf. Joshua Parens, *Maimonides and Spinoza: Their Conflicting Views of Human Nature* (Chicago: University of Chicago Press, 2012), 4.

35

tradition, Halevi thus provides us with a counterpoint to Maimonides and Sommer's dependence on him.

We will begin, therefore, with Maimonides, and then move on to the later Halevi, and then on to Michael Wyschogrod's contemporary philosophy of Judaism, which shares much in common with Halevi.

Moses Maimonides

Maimonides[4] was born in Córdoba, in Andalusia, Spain, which was then under the control of the Almoravids,[5] a Berber Muslim dynastic empire centered in Morocco. Andalusia came under the rule of the Almohads, a Moroccan Berber Muslim Caliphate, some ten years after Maimonides's birth. Both powers sought to purify the Islam of the area, making life exceedingly difficult for Christians and Jews. Maimonides's family emigrated to Palestine and then to Egypt where there was a large Jewish community that benefited from the relative tolerance of the Fatimid regime.[6] Maimonides was soon recognized as an authority on *halakha*[7] and was appointed head of the Egyptian Jewish community, a position he held for one or two years in the period 1171–73 and possibly later in the 1190s. His reputation as an expert on *halakha* rested on two substantial publications, namely his *Commentary on the Mishnah* (1168) and his *Mishneh Torah* (Repetition of the Law, 1177), an orderly, comprehensive code of Jewish law. *Halakah* was in disarray at this time, and Maimonides engaged in a massive task to bring order and accessibility to it. According to Halbertal, "A code such as *Mishneh Torah*—comprehensive, exhaustive, accessible, and unambiguous—had never been written before Maimonides's time and has not been written since."[8]

4. The literature about Maimonides is immense, and there are differences of opinion about how to interpret him on many issues. For a useful introduction see Kenneth Seeskin, ed., *The Cambridge Companion to Maimonides* (Cambridge: Cambridge University Press, 2005).

5. On Maimonides's time in Andalusia see Moshe Halbertal, *Maimonides: Life and Thought* (Princeton and Oxford: Princeton University Press, 2014), 14–23. Cf. also Joel L. Kraemer, *Maimonides: The Life and World of One of Civilization's Greatest Minds* (New York: Doubleday, 2008), 23–80.

6. Maimonides's life in Egypt is known through his extensive correspondence.

7. Jewish law derived from written and oral sources.

8. Halbertal, *Maimonides*, 1.

Maimonides composed his *Guide for the Perplexed* during the years 1185–90. It is this aptly titled work that will be our major concern. As Maimonides explains in the introduction, the book is written for the religious Jew who believes in the Law, fulfills his religious duties, has studied philosophy, and "human reason has attracted him to abide within its sphere; and he finds it difficult to accept as correct the teaching based on the literal interpretation of the Law, and especially that which he himself or others derived from those homonymous, metaphorical, or hybrid expressions. Hence he is lost in perplexity and anxiety" (*Guide*, 2).

In this quote, Maimonides is, among other things, describing himself. Through his studies, he had become convinced of many of the tenets of Aristotelian and Neoplatonic philosophy, and found them difficult to reconcile with typical Jewish views. Ivry perceptively points out that "Maimonides' difficulties as a philosopher and as a theologian begin and end with his concept of God."[9] He had become convinced that through their deductive arguments the philosophers had come to a true view of God, whether as First Cause or Necessary Existent. Maimonides came to this view through the traditions of Aristotle and Plotinus via his Muslim mentors, Alfarabi and Avicenna. He says of Aristotle that he "reached the highest level of knowledge to which man can ascend, with the exception of the one who experiences the emanation of the Divine Spirit, who can attain the degree of prophecy, above which there is no higher stage."[10] Maimonides views God as the First Cause (*Guide*, 249), the unmoved mover, the necessary existent (Avicenna), while assuming also "the One" of Plotinus, from which emanate the different stages of being, from the immaterial realm of forms to the physical realm of matter.[11] This God is impersonal; he can will but not speak; and he cannot be perceived by the senses. Maimonides finds support for the latter view in Exod 3:6, and, more surprisingly, in Exod 24:10, where the purpose of the description of Moses and the elders seeing the God of Israel is, in Maimonides's view, to criticize the act of seeing (*Guide*, 18). The difference between God and all his creatures is absolute: "no definition can comprehend both; therefore His existence and that of any other being totally differ from each

---

9. Alfred L. Ivry, *Maimonides' "Guide of the Perplexed": A Philosophical Guide* (Chicago: University of Chicago Press, 2016), 226.

10. *Letters of Maimonides*, 136, quoted in Halbertal, *Maimonides*, 21.

11. But cf. Kenneth Seeskin, "Metaphysics and Its Transcendence," in Seeskin, ed., *The Cambridge Companion to Maimonides*, 82–104, for the complexity of Maimonides's thought on these issues.

other, and the term existence is applied to both homonymously, as I shall explain" (*Guide*, 49).

The *Guide* is a fabric woven from three strands: scriptural exegesis, philosophical discussions, and sections Davidson terms ideological, which embody Maimonides's efforts to construct a rationalist version of Jewish religion. "The exegesis of scriptural texts presupposes conclusions that will be reached in the strictly philosophic parts. The scriptural exegesis and the philosophical discussions contribute to the third strand, the spiritualizing and rationalizing of the Jewish religion"[12] Far from exegesis being of secondary importance to Maimonides, it is central to the book and "it remains the warp into which the other strands are woven" (334). In the Guide there is hardly a single page on which Maimonides does not quote Scripture. Overall some 1500 verses are quoted, and most are interpreted as well (334).

Scripture must not, according to Maimonides, be read by imagination but through the intellect after one has gained proficiency in the sciences and knowledge of the mysteries of prophecy. "He is taking the position that Scripture must be read through the prism of what the philosophic sciences teach regarding the phenomenon of prophecy and what they demonstrate about other matters—the incorporeality of God, His being free of all qualities, and the like" (335).

The first forty-five chapters of the *Guide* amount to a glossary dealing with some forty-plus words in Scripture that might cause perplexity to readers who fail to take homonymy seriously. A *homonym* is a word that has a variety of possible meanings. The exploration of homonyms, figurative language, and anthropomorphisms is a task central to the *Guide* since they provide Maimonides with a path through which to reconfigure traditional understandings of Scripture with his philosophy. His explanation of anthropomorphisms and rejection of the idea that God has a body will be familiar territory to most readers. However, Maimonides takes this approach much further to fit Scripture with philosophy.

Take Gen 1:26-28, for example. Maimonides locates the likeness between God and humankind in the intellect: "on account of the Divine intellect with which man has been endowed, he is said to have been made in the form and likeness of the Almighty" (*Guide*, 14).[13] For Maimonides, it follows

---

12. Herbert A. Davidson, *Moses Maimonides: The Man and His Works* (Oxford: Oxford University Press, 2005), 333. Hereafter, page references to this work are given in parentheses in the text.

13. For Maimonides (*Guide*, 15), "the fall" involves the loss of part of the intellectual faculty that humankind previously possessed.

from his view of God that God does not speak or consult with others, all of which appears to be present in these verses. As he notes elsewhere in the *Guide*, "I do not think I need to explain to you the inadmissibility of speech in reference to God, especially since our people generally believe that the Law, i.e., the word ascribed to Him, was created. Speech is attributed to Him, in so far as the word which Moses heard, was produced and brought to existence by God in the same manner as He produced all His other works and creation" (*Guide*, 97). As we saw in Chapter 2, this argument of Maimonides that God cannot speak is central to Sommer's view of Sinai. Thus, the exhortation "Let us make" must be interpreted figuratively and Maimonides understands these words as an allusion to how humankind was made. Davidson notes that,

> If I have read Maimonides correctly, the sentence "Let us make *adam* in Our image and after Our likeness" says the following when fully understood: In the course of creation God brought forth the human species, a species whose essence embodies the ability to think intellectual thoughts in a manner somewhat similar to the manner in which God consists in pure intellectual thought; and God carried out his plan through the intermediacy of the supernal incorporeal beings and other natural forces in the universe. The scriptural verse has been freed of its problematic features and reemerges in precise rationalist garb. (337–38)

In his introduction to Part 1 of the *Guide* Maimonides discusses Prov 7:6–26, the story of a young man being seduced by an adulteress (*Guide*, 7). He notes how the figure of a woman is a prominent motif throughout Proverbs, and he asserts that the lesson of Proverbs is that a man should not be guided solely by his animal or material nature, since his materiality is identical with that of brute creatures.

What must not be forgotten is Davidson's point above that Maimonides's exegesis is executed through the lens of his philosophy. Ivry states that "the overwhelming thrust of the *Guide* is to construct a view of God that is logically and philosophically persuasive, however undemonstrated."[14] Kraemer notes that, "above all, Maimonides aspired to revolutionize Judaism by transforming it into a religion of reason. Maimonides wanted to change Judaism from a religion rooted in history, in great events such as the Exodus and revelation, to a religion implanted in nature and knowledge of the

14. Ivry, *Maimonides'*, 228.

natural beings, God's works rather than God's words."[15] As with Plotinus, Maimonides denigrates the physical realm, which is the most far removed from the One, and privileges an intellectual approach to God, as we saw above in his treatment of the *imago Dei* and Proverbs. He asserts that "the corporeal element in man is a large screen and partition that prevents him from perfectly perceiving abstract ideals; this would be the case even if the corporeal element were as pure and superior as the substance of the spheres" (*Guide*, 264).[16] The revelation of God in clouds and darkness is designed to teach this lesson. Ontologically and epistemologically, Maimonides affirms belief in the key elements of Plotinus's thought: God, the different intellects of the spheres, and the heavenly bodies that they move. *Emanation* becomes the causal link between God and the world. "Maimonides understands prophecy and the entire government of the world through this process, interpreted as manifestations of the divine will."[17] Indeed, "Maimonides closes the *Guide* without sacrificing his belief in an impersonal though providential God, a being with deistic features in which divine will matches wisdom."[18]

Prophecy, Moses, and Sinai

In the HB/OT Moses is depicted as the great prophet and thus God's revelation to and through him is regularly discussed in Jewish literature under "prophecy."[19] Maimonides identifies three different views of prophecy (*Guide*, 219–21):

- The "ignorant view," which thinks that God selects any person, grants him the spirit of prophecy and a prophetic mission.
- The philosophic view that the capacity to prophesy is a faculty of the human person in the state of perfection, which can only be attained through hard study.

15. Kraemer, *Maimonides*, 18.
16. Cf. Josef Stern, "Maimonides' Epistemology," in Seeskin, ed., *The Cambridge Companion to Maimonides*, 105–33, 120.
17. Ivry, *Maimonides'*, 228.
18. Ivry, *Maimonides'*, 229.
19. On this topic cf. the important work by Howard Kreisel, *Prophecy: The History of an Idea in Medieval Jewish Philosophy* (Dordrecht: Springer, 2001).

• The view taught in Scripture, which is the same as the philosophic view with one exception; a person may do all the necessary preparation and still not prophesy. Actual prophesying depends on the will of God.

The extent to which Maimonides's view of prophecy is shaped by his philosophy is clear in his definition: "Prophecy is, in truth and reality, an emanation sent forth by the Divine Being through the medium of the Active Intellect, in the first instance to man's rational faculty, and then to his imaginative faculty; it is the highest degree and greatest perfection man can attain; it consists in the most perfect development of the imaginative faculty" (*Guide*, 225).

From Maimonides's perspective prophecy is impossible without intensive study and training. Indeed, it requires intellectual perfection attained through study and training, perfection of the imagination, and moral perfection (*Guide*, 227). The body of the prophet must also manifest such wholeness; it must not suffer from any illness. Because the imagination is a faculty of the body and imagination is the organ of prophecy, prophets, including Moses, are deprived of the faculty of prophesying when they are dejected, mourning, and so on.

In the context of his ontology, Maimonides explores the nature of the divine influence through the Active Intellect upon humans, the source of prophecy. In some it reaches only the intellect and not the imagination; with prophets it reaches both; with some it reaches only the imagination. With prophets the influence is abundant so that the prophet is compelled to teach others. All humans possess the intuitive faculty but in varying degrees. This faculty enables some to foretell future events. Prophets had high degrees of courage and intuition, strengthened under the influence of the Active Intellect. For example, Moses's courage is evident in his willingness to confront Pharaoh. Under the divine influence true prophets conceive ideas that human reason could not attain to by itself, hence Maimonides's statement above about the possibility of exceeding even Aristotle. "The prophets must have had these two forces, courage and intuition, highly developed, and these were still more strengthened when they were under the influence of the Active Intellect" (*Guide*, 229).

Most medieval philosophers saw the Active Intellect as the last—furthest from the First Cause—of the separate immaterial intellects Aristotle identified for each sphere.[20] This Active Intellect enabled the potential intellect—

---

20. Cf. Stern, "Maimonides' Epistemology," 107–15. Cf. Aristotle, *Metaphysics* 12.8 (pp. 376–81).

the "material intellect"—to become active, abstracting the universal species in nature. The result is that, "like Alfarabi before and Maimonides after him, Avicenna sees prophecy as a natural phenomenon, the Agent Intellect emanating its intelligible, universal forms upon a person with suitable imagination and intellectual endowments."[21] Intriguingly, Maimonides argues that, in principle, all humans, including Gentiles, can prophesy.

For Maimonides, the imaginative faculty is the organ of prophecy. Stern points out that in Maimonides's thought the status of the imagination is ambiguous: "On the one hand, its images provide the input to intellectual processes and the imaginative faculty is also crucial for the activity of the prophet, who, using it, translates abstract philosophical truths into figurative representations that can by grasped by the community-at-large and laws on which the community can act. . . . On the other hand, Maimonides is suspicious of the interference of the imagination with reason."[22] The highest function of the imagination is achieved when at rest. Prophecy is a perfection acquired in a vision or a dream; the prophet then sees the thing *as if* it came from without; *as if* through the bodily senses (*Guide*, 226).

Maimonides discerns eleven degrees of prophecy (*Guide*, 241–45). Intriguingly he places prophecies that begin "And the word of the LORD came to . . ." in the lowest class, whereas he places prophecies in which an allegory is seen in a dream in the highest class. In the latter, an angel speaks to the prophet in a vision. If words are spoken it is likely that they came as the vision changed into a dream. Here again we see Maimonides's wariness of divine speech. "But in a prophetic vision only allegories are perceived, or rational truths are obtained, that lead to some knowledge in science, such as can be arrived at by reasoning" (*Guide*, 245). Maimonides notes that prophets regularly omit the intermediate causes relating back to the First Cause, and then use language like "God commanded," "God said," and so on, to indicate the ultimate source. For Maimonides, any language of God speaking and saying can only mean he willed, desired, or thinks—we absolutely must not think that God used a voice or sound. "Therefore the command is figuratively ascribed to God when that takes place which He wishes, and we then say that He commanded that a certain thing should be accomplished" (*Guide*, 97).

For Maimonides, Moses's experience at Mt. Sinai was different from that of the other Israelites. He alone was addressed by God through the voice created by God, and Maimonides finds confirmation of this in the use of the

21. Ivry, *Maimonides'*, 47.
22. Stern, "Maimonides' Epistemology," 107–8.

second-person singular in the Decalogue. The Israelites heard a loud noise but not actual speech: "even where the hearing of words is mentioned, only the perception of the sound is meant" (*Guide*, 222). Moses's inspiration came directly through his intellect, and unlike the other prophets, not through the imagination. This difference alone qualified Moses to declare the Law. For Maimonides, at Sinai Israel apprehended through their intellects that God exists and is one. Kellner points out in terms of Sinai that "At the moment of its inception, therefore, Israel was constituted as such by the rational acceptance of true philosophical teachings concerning God. This is as far from an essentialist definition of Israel as one can get!"[23]

There were prophets before Moses, and Maimonides, for example, develops a rationalistic explanation of Abraham's call and response to God. He led men by training and instruction to the truth that he had perceived: "Thus Abraham taught and showed by philosophical arguments that there is one God, that He has created everything that exists beside Him, and that neither the constellations nor anything in the air ought to be worshipped" (*Guide*, 231).

Kellner notes of Abraham that

> the founder of the Jewish nation, then, is presented in both the *Mishneh Torah* and the *Guide of the Perplexed* as a philosopher who achieved knowledge of God through rational examination of the world around him and sought rationally to convince others of the truths he had discovered. This is made clear here in this passage from the Guide. Abraham received an "overflow" (i.e., emanation) from God, such an emanation, as Maimonides explains in his chapters on prophecy (II.32–48), being a consequence of intellectual perfection. As a reward, Abraham was promised that special benefits would be conferred upon his progeny. The foundation of the Jewish people as an entity defined in terms of its Abrahamic descent is itself a consequence of a philosophical appreciation of God.[24]

Maimonides finds the justification for law in the fact that humans are social beings. The law aims at the well-being of the body and of the soul, and the first of these can only be attained in society. The second "consists in

---

23. Menachem M. Kellner, *Maimonides on Judaism and the Jewish People* (Albany: State University of New York Press, 1991), 87. Cf. Kellner, "Spiritual Life," in Seeskin, ed., *The Cambridge Companion to Maimonides*, 273–99.
24. Kellner, *Maimonides*, 85.

his [man's] becoming an actually intelligent being; i.e., he knows about the things in existence all that a person perfectly developed is capable of knowing. This second perfection certainly does not include any action or good conduct, but only knowledge, which is arrived at by speculation, or established by research" (*Guide*, 313). The second objective can only be attained when the first has been acquired. The purpose of the Mosaic Law is to provide for this twofold perfection. It aims at good relations among people and, "secondly, it seeks to train us in faith, and to impart correct and true opinions when the intellect is sufficiently developed" (*Guide*, 313). And thus, for example, Maimonides interprets "for our lasting good," in Deut 6:24, as a reference to the second objective; "so as to keep us alive," in the same verse, refers to the first objective.

We are exhorted to love YHWH and this is only possible, for Maimonides, when we grasp the real nature of things and perceive the divine wisdom therein. Indeed, Maimonides begins and ends his *Guide* with two parables illustrating true human perfection: "The fourth kind of perfection is the true perfection of man; the possession of the highest intellectual faculties; the possession of such notions which lead to true metaphysical opinions as regards God. With this perfection man has obtained his final object" (*Guide*, 395). Intriguingly, Maimonides argues that with the sacrificial laws God accommodated himself to the Israelites who lived in a context of sacrifices and rituals in order to wean them off idolatry. Thus, sacrifice is allowed but confined to the Temple, and thus restricted, whereas prayers and supplications can and should be made everywhere: "the first laws do not refer to burnt-offering and sacrifice, which are of secondary importance" (*Guide*, 326). Here again we see Maimonides's intellectualization of the Jewish tradition. Cremer, by comparison, who roots our knowledge of God in his revelation in history and not in philosophy, asserts: "For it is not in the moral law but in the cultic that God's holy counteracting of sin found its actual statutory expression."[25] Maimonides is particularly wary of the sense of touch and interprets Exod 19:15, "do not go near a woman," as one of the ways in which the law seeks to suppress sensuality.

Ascending and descending are central motifs in Exod 19–24. Maimonides treats these as part of his discussion of homonyms in the opening sections of the *Guide*. We occupy a lowly position in relation to the heavens, and God is likewise much greater and higher than us, not spatially but in

---

25. Hermann Cremer, *The Christian Doctrine of the Divine Attributes*, trans. Robert B. Price (Eugene, OR: Pickwick, 2016), 27.

terms of his nature. Thus, one way in which Scripture speaks of prophetic inspiration is of God descending. Moses's ascents to Mt. Sinai are literal but God's descent on Sinai is not: "we must not imagine that the Supreme Being occupies a place to which we can ascend, or from which we can descend. He is far from what the ignorant imagine" (*Guide*, 23).[26] God is incorporeal and can have no locomotion (*Guide*, 35).

Apart from Moses, all prophets received prophecy through an angel. Moses's prophetic perfection exceeded that of all others. Moses's miracles and signs are also distinct. He alone performed them publicly among friends and enemies.

Conclusion

Maimonides was torn between philosophy and theology. In his *Commentary on the Mishnah*, he sets out Judaism's core beliefs, most of which are particular and "based on a biblical text that affirms a personal deity in close, historic association with a chosen people."[27] He could not renounce these but believed that they could be translated into a philosophical mode, and this he sets out to do in his *Guide for the Perplexed*. However, as Ivry rightly notes, the tension between the two approaches is evident throughout the *Guide*, a tension manifest between:

- the universal (philosophy) and the particular;
- an impersonal (philosophy) God and the personal God of the Bible;
- reading the Bible literally and reading it allegorically;
- validating metaphysics and questioning it;
- advocating an instrumental view of the Law and seeing it as essential.

Ivry speculates that the accidental death of Maimonides's younger brother and his resulting depression may have motivated Maimonides to try and resolve the relationship between faith and reason through writing the *Guide*.[28]

26. Cf. *Guide*, 36; no motion is involved.
27. Ivry, *Maimonides'*, 225.
28. Ivry, *Maimonides'*, 225–26. The theme of providence is central to the *Guide*, and at one point Maimonides tries to find meaning in the very sort of death his brother suffered.

Judah Halevi

"The contrast between Maimonides' view in the *Guide* of the significance of Jewish history, and of history in general, and that of his illustrious predecessor, Judah Halevi, could not be more striking. Halevi's whole philosophy can be seen as an affirmation of the centrality of Jewish history in testifying to the uniqueness and superiority of Judaism."[29] Slonimsky evaluates Halevi as "the greatest poet and one of the profoundest thinkers Judaism has had since the closing of the canon."[30] Halevi's mature thought represents a radical contrast with Maimonides.

Like Maimonides, Halevi lived in Spain during the struggle of Christians and Muslims for control. Halevi was by birth part of the upper segment of court Jewry, and for the first half of his life he shared their views. He was born in Toledo and went south for his education, where he received exposure to Jewish thought and the science and philosophy of Arab culture.[31] During this time he became part of the circle of intellectuals around Moses Ibn Ezra.[32] He returned to Toledo, which was now in Christian hands, to practice medicine. His comment on practicing medicine in this context provides evidence of a growing sense of personal dissatisfaction: "Thus we heal Babylon, but it cannot be healed."[33] Indeed, in the latter years of his life, Halevi came to reject the culture in which Spanish Jewry existed. The radical break he made with it came to expression in his *Kuzari*, completed shortly before he embarked on his pilgrimage to Jerusalem. The *Kuzari* was written between 1130 and 1140. In 1140 Halevi set off for Jerusalem.[34]

Halevi's break with court Jewry was far more than cultural. The substantial break is with a form of Judaism strongly influenced by Aristotelian philosophy mediated through the Arab scholars of the day. Halevi was a poet and sought a real, personal relationship with the living God, a relationship

---

29. Ivry, *Maimonides'*, 176.

30. Henry Slonimsky, "Judah Halevi: An Introduction," in Judah Halevi, *The Kuzari: An Argument for the Faith of Israel*, trans. Hartwig Hirschfeld (New York: Schocken, 1964), 17.

31. Cf. Raymond P. Scheindlin, *The Song of the Distant Dove: Judah Halevi's Pilgrimage* (Oxford: Oxford University Press, 2008), 13–15.

32. Scheindlin, *The Song of the Distant Dove*, 15.

33. Quoted in Slonimsky, "Judah Halevi," 20. Cf. Scheindlin, *The Song of the Distant Dove*, 17.

34. We do not know if he ever arrived there.

that would bring meaning to his life. He reacts precisely to the sort of philosophical religion we find in Maimonides. Slonimsky expresses well this disillusionment Halevi felt: "The enlightenment which came in the train of philosophical studies had led not to a higher and freer faith on the basis of pure reason, but merely to a decay of the inner sanctions of the old religion, and even to a readiness on occasion to forsake Judaism—as if Christianity were any less subject to the same rationalistic critique."[35] Halevi sought a return to God, a return to traditional Judaism with its transcendent claims, a return to revelation and election. Halevi was a physician, scholar, and a poet, but he was not a rabbi as far as we know.[36]

The *Kuzari* is a defense of the Jewish religion in which Halevi articulates a theology of history to which philosophy is made subservient. The anti-rationalist tone makes the *Kuzari*, and thus Halevi, unique among Jewish medieval thinkers. It is directed at the enemy within the gate, as Halevi perceived it. Against the influences of Arab philosophy, Halevi asserts the original historical nature of Judaism: "The great scene at Sinai puts it in possession of the truth. . . . Sinai being the one authentic event in religious history."[37]

Halevi makes revelation in history central to true knowledge of God. He is not opposed to philosophy but rejects its claims to replace religion. In its efforts to reach God, philosophy undertakes a Promethean task, seeking to reach God through humankind's unaided effort and desire to know. The real source of religious truth is, however, God's revelation of himself to his people. Contact with the living God is a gift and cannot be achieved by humankind's efforts, so that "revelation alone then establishes the true, the real religion."[38]

The *Kuzari* is a fascinating book, revolving around a dialogue between a rabbi and the king of the Khuzars. The king is devout but has had a disturbing dream in which an angel informs him that his way of thinking is pleasing to the creator, but not his way of living. The king is perplexed by this dream and seeks the advice of a philosopher, a Christian scholar, and a rabbi. Neither the philosopher nor the Christian scholar satisfies the king. The philosopher is an exponent of perfect-being theology in which God is above desire and intention; the world is eternal and God never created

35. Slonimsky, "Judah Halevi," 22.
36. Scheindlin, *The Song of the Distant Dove*, 3.
37. Slonimsky, "Judah Halevi," 24.
38. Slonimsky, "Judah Halevi," 27.

humankind. "He, therefore, does not know thee, much less thy thoughts and actions, nor does He listen to thy prayers, or see thy movements."[39] The king feels he has received a communication from God, and thus, not surprisingly, the philosopher is of no help to him. After the philosopher and the scholastic Christian scholar, the king invites a Jewish rabbi, and the rest of the book deals with their interactions, involving, among other things, the circumcision and conversion of the king to Judaism.

The rabbi is able to help the king because the king is dealing with a personal experience of revelation, and Halevi—through the voice of the rabbi—sees personal and sensory experience as at the heart of revelation. The rabbi asks the king what would convince him if he heard all sorts of things about the king of India. The king agrees that if the king of India's messenger came bearing a variety of unique gifts he would be convinced. The rabbi replies, "I answered thee as was fitting, and is fitting for the whole of Israel who knew these things first from personal experience, and afterwards *through uninterrupted* tradition, which is equal to the former" (*Kuzari*, 46–47). For Halevi, Israel came to believe that God speaks through personal, sensory experience of him speaking. As Silman observes, "The reliance on experience completely changes the meaning of God and, in parallel, of man."[40] Indeed, a reassessment of the role of human experience runs like a thread through the later work of Halevi, weaving it into a unity.

Prior to Sinai, according to Halevi, the Israelites could not imagine God speaking, but one goal of God's revelation at Sinai is to change their minds in this respect:

> The people prepared and became fitted to receive the divine afflatus, and even to hear publicly the words of God. . . . [T]hey distinctly heard the Ten Commandments, which represent the very essence of the Law. . . . Henceforth the people believed that Moses held direct communication with God, that prophecy did not (as philosophers assume) burst forth in a pure soul, become united with the Active Intellect . . . and be then inspired. . . . The people saw the divine writing, as they had heard the divine words. (*Kuzari*, 60–61)

39. Halevi, *Kuzari*, 36. Hereafter, page references to this work are given in parentheses in the text.

40. Yochanan Silman, *Philosopher and Prophet: Judah Halevi, the Kuzari, and the Evolution of His Thought*, trans. Lenn J. Schramm (Albany: State University of New York Press, 1995), 324.

For Halevi, we must avoid rejecting the implications of such revelation even though we do not know precisely how the divine speech entered the ears of the Israelites. God engraved the two tablets with his words as he created the heavens and the earth, by his will alone. The Israelites present were convinced that God had communicated to them. In this way the objections of the philosophers disappear, and the limits of reason are exposed: "Human reason is out of place in matters of divine action, on account of its incapacity to grasp them. Reason must rather obey, just as a sick person must obey the physician in applying his medicines and advice" (*Kuzari*, 141–42).

In line with his emphasis on the personal, sensory nature of revelation, Halevi distinguishes carefully between Elohim and YHWH as names of God. Elohim is a generic or common noun, whereas YHWH is a proper noun, a proper name. Elohim is associated with the generic God demonstrated by the philosophers, but

> Demonstration can lead astray. . . . Those who go to the utmost lengths are the philosophers, and the ways of their arguments lead them to teach of a Supreme Being which neither benefits nor injures, and knows nothing of our prayers, offerings, obedience, or disobedience, and that the world is as eternal as He is Himself. None of them applies a distinct proper name to God, except he who hears His address, command, or prohibition, approval for obedience, and reproof for disobedience. He bestows on Him some name as a designation for Him who spoke to him, and he is convinced that He is the Creator of the world from nought. (*Kuzari*, 199–200)

Halevi relates the name YHWH to God's influence and presence among the Israelites. "Let them search for no stronger proof than My presence among them, and name Me accordingly" (*Kuzari*, 202).

Halevi similarly interprets God's name *Adonai* as meaning that God's presence will accompany you. As with YHWH, Halevi is clear that, unlike the meaning of Elohim, philosophical speculation cannot unlock the meaning of Adonai but only prophecy. Halevi relates the presence of God to the work of the Holy Spirit, the effect of whose influence is that

> all previous doubts concerning *Elohim* are removed, and man deprecates those speculations by means of which he had endeavoured to derive the knowledge of God's dominion and unity. It is thus that man becomes a servant, loving the object of his worship, and ready to perish

for His sake, because he finds the sweetness of this attachment as great
as the distress in the absence thereof. This forms a contrast to the philosophers, who see in worship of God nothing but extreme refinement,
extolling Him in truth above all beings. (*Kuzari*, 222–23)

The king replies, "I see how far the God of Abraham is different from that of
Aristotle. Man yearns for *Adonai* as a matter of love, taste and conviction;
whilst attachment to *Elohim* is the result of speculation" (*Kuzari*, 223). This
indeed was Halevi's experience, and the intensity of his desire for God is evident in the poetry he wrote en route to Jerusalem, poems that are strongly
reminiscent of the Psalms.[41]

Halevi's understanding of Abraham forms a sharp contrast with that
of Maimonides. For Halevi, Abraham was able to bear the great trials he
went through precisely because God had come to him through love, and not
through philosophical speculation. Once God revealed himself to Abraham,
Abraham renounced philosophical speculations and strove only to please
God.

In relation to God, Halevi affirms the indispensability of *anthropomorphisms*. According to Silman, there is no other issue on which Halevi differs
so strongly from Aristotle than this one. God's sensible revelation of himself
is necessarily perceived and grasped in physical images, and the best way
to embrace the moment of revelation is to use the images rooted in the
particular experience. The king suggests that the philosophical doctrines
of God's unity, omnipotence, and omniscience may be sufficient without
anthropomorphisms, but Halevi rejects this:

This is a doctrine of philosophers. . . . Do not believe him who considers
himself wise in thinking that he is so far advanced that he is able to grasp
all metaphysical problems with the abstract intellect alone, without
the support of anything that can be conceived or seen, such as words,
writing, or any visible or imaginary forms. . . . In this way, prophets'
images picture God's greatness, power, loving kindness, omniscience,
life, eternity, government, and independence, the dependence of everything upon Him, His unity, and holiness, and in one sudden flash
stands revealed this grand and majestic figure with its splendour, its
characteristics, the instruments which typify power, etc., the up-lifted

41. See Scheindlin, *The Song*. Cf. also Silman, *Philosopher and Prophet*, 191–92,
for a liturgical poem by Halevi.

hand, the unsheathed sword, fire, wind, thunder and lightning which obey his behest, the word which goes forth to warn, to announce what has happened, and to predict. . . . Will a philosopher ever achieve the same result? (*Kuzari*, 213–14)

Halevi is not, however, opposed to philosophy; indeed, the rabbi strongly rejects the view that there could be anything in the Bible contrary to that proved by science or philosophy. Unlike Maimonides in his *Guide*, Halevi does not focus on creation in a major way in the *Kuzari*. He affirms the obscurity of the question of eternity and creation and remains open to the possible existence of eternal matter and other worlds (*Kuzari*, 54). In terms of Halevi's own philosophy, "a comparison of the philosophy of the *Kuzari* with the various Aristotelian schools known to Halevi indicates that it cannot be identified with any one of them."[42]

History is central to Halevi's view. He rejects the Aristotelian view that the human goal is ahistorical. According to Silman, for Halevi, the individual is part of the human collective and history has directionality: "With the appearance of the Jewish people on the stage of history, with their extraordinary experience of the presence of a personal God Who takes an interest in human beings, a fundamental change took place in human history, a change that cannot be negated or ignored" (255). For Halevi, the second half of the first of the ten commandments[43]—"who brought you out of Egypt"—is not secondary to the first half, but absolutely central to the whole. It disqualifies rational analysis as the means to gain true cognitive, relational, and ethical knowledge of God. Judaism will, according to Halevi, eventually become the religion of all humankind. History thus progresses, but not evenly: "Divine intervention cuts through the bonds of natural law; its results, ontologically speaking, are new creations" (256). The establishment of the Israelites as the people of God through the exodus/Sinai events is akin to an act of creation by God. "Viewed from this angle, the historical process incorporates turning points where its continuity is ruptured by sudden jumps—revolutionary changes that cannot be understood solely on the basis of previous stages in the process" (256). One-off events like Sinai are not entirely subjective. They can be compared with other similar ones and exodus/Sinai took place in the public domain.

42. Silman, *Philosopher and Prophet*, 11. Hereafter, page references to this work are given in parentheses in the text.
43. According to the Jewish way of counting the commandments.

It is thus not surprising that Halevi saw the value of the biblical narratives for authentic religion. "Just as the annals of the Jewish people are marked by Divine revelation, God's image is shaped by the history of the Jewish people. These events, including the central figures who take part in them, are constitutive elements that cannot be replaced by a mere definition of God's identity. This multifaceted drama . . . finds literary expression in the story and dialogue" (335–36). The biblical narratives form part of Jewish tradition, and the latter is vital because God's call and revelation are a gift and cannot be initiated by humans, but can be recalled through the narrative accounts.

As we saw with Maimonides, his intellectual anthropology is closely connected with his view of God and revelation. The same is true of Halevi, who develops a strikingly different view of the human person. Halevi thinks of humankind holistically. The essence of the human person is not found purely in the mind but also in the body, the soul, the emotions, reason, and imagination. The integrality of the human person is made explicit in the God–human dialogues so that "Human beings are bidden to serve God in their full concrete being—their reasons, emotions, feelings, and bodies" (232). Indeed, "Just as the dialogue between God and man leads to a new conception of the human individual, so too it gives rise to a new conception of the human collective and of humanity as a whole" (323). Action, for Halevi, is privileged over abstract truth, which acquires significance only once it is embodied. As Silman perceptively observes, "Note that the opposition between the two views of man stems from the fundamental difference in the nature of the universal bipolarity. For the Philosopher, it is a dichotomy of form and matter; for Halevi, of Creator and created. Form-and-matter dualism cuts through every manifestation of existence. By contrast, the division into Creator and created highlights what the two dimensions have in common, and this unifies all aspects of created existence" (251).

Much of the *Kuzari* deals with Halevi's view of Israel and the land and the language of Hebrew as unique and essential parts of Judaism. Some of this is strange, such as Halevi's view that the Israelites are given a special religious faculty not common to other nations, and some of it is less relevant to our concern with divine action and revelation.

Evaluating Maimonides and Halevi

Maimonides's *Guide* is fascinating, and one certainly cannot accuse him of avoiding Scripture. Indeed, the *Guide* contains far more exegesis than the

Kuzari. His exegesis is always interesting and often fresh and insightful. His attention to homonymy and anthropomorphic language is important and cannot be avoided by any doctrine of God. However, Maimonides clearly subjects Scripture to the grid of his—Aristotelian—philosophical views of God, humankind, and the world, and this generates far too much eisegesis rather than exegesis of the HB/OT.

Maimonides and Halevi deliver two quite distinct views of God. Maimonides's God is distant, impersonal, and deistic, truly the God of the philosophers, whereas Halevi's God is the living God of the Bible—personal and transcendent but immanently involved in the creation. From our examination of Maimonides, we can see how Sommer arrives at the view that God does not and cannot speak. But this is closer to deism rather than theism, and, in my view, Halevi's doctrine of God is far closer to Scripture and yields an intensely personal God who can and does speak and who acts in history.

Maimonides and Halevi develop radically different views of revelation. Maimonides privileges the intellectual in God and humankind, and revelation is to a significant extent a natural phenomenon occurring through emanation via the Active Intellect. Halevi, like Berkovits, develops a view of revelation as sensory encounter in history, while acknowledging the mystery behind how this actually takes place. Halevi's foregrounding of the role of human experience in revelation is akin to William Alston's *Perceiving God: The Epistemology of Religious Experience*.

Maimonides and Halevi embrace very different understandings of the role of philosophy in relation to religion. Religion is made subservient to Aristotelian and Neoplatonic philosophy in Maimonides's system, whereas Halevi stresses the limits of philosophy as speculative, unaided reason, and privileges revelation over reason and philosophy. In this respect Halevi approximates the Reformed epistemology developed in our day by Alvin Plantinga, Nicholas Wolterstorff, and many others.

The major differences between Maimonides and Halevi continue to frame contemporary Jewish debates. To take two prominent, contemporary Jewish philosophers, Lenn Goodman is closer to Maimonides, and David Novak is far closer to Halevi.[44] Novak concludes an essay on Maimonides

---

44. It has been a privilege to get to know Lenn Goodman through the gatherings of the Senior Fellows of Herzl Institute. The difference between Goodman and Novak is seen clearly in their very different views of Spinoza. For Novak on Spinoza see his *The Election of Israel*, 22–49.

entitled "Can We Be Maimonideans Today?" as follows: "If we cannot accept Maimonides' metaphysical paradigm, we should try to replace it with a counterpart that is more adequate and fruitful in law and theology. That would be the greatest tribute we could pay to Maimonides: to be mindfully inspired and guided by his own philosophical quest, while not succumbing to any mindless deference to his posthumous authority."[45] Novak's own work is an example of the quest for such a counterpart.

In *The Election of Israel*, Novak argues that the election of Israel is only convincing if it refers to a relationship in time. "Accordingly, election is historical, that is, it is a humanly remembered temporal event, characterized by freedom rather than by necessity."[46] Nature is the realm of causality; history that of novelty and freedom. "It is only this sort of ontology, one that sees the primacy of divine historical activity for humans followed by their practical activity in response to it, and one that sees science . . . as tertiary to them both that can enable one to retrieve philosophically the fundamental Jewish doctrine of election."[47]

Both God and Israel, according to Novak, are temporally related. Israel's time is limited (finite); the time of God as creator is unlimited (infinite). God, for Novak, is coeval or contemporary with time, whereas creatures are transcended by time. God does not transcend time in the way he transcends space. He is not eternal in the philosophical sense of being unchanging or unresponsive but is everlasting. Novak describes Ephraim E. Urbach's two models for understanding the election of Israel: the cosmic-eternal view and the historical-relative one. Novak finds neither satisfactory on their own, and suggests, unconvincingly in my view, that retroactivity offers a solution in which one considers something that happens in time as having been so beforehand. Where Novak is correct is that the "full significance [of the election of Israel] must be correlated with God's relationship with his entire creation, with the world as a whole."[48] Without the link between election–exodus–Sinai and creation in place, the comprehensive and eschatological dimensions of these events are lost. Of course, as a Christian, I would develop the eschatological dimensions differently to Novak.

45. David Novak, "Can We Be Maimonideans Today?," in *Maimonides and His Heritage*, ed. Idit Dobbs-Weinstein, Lenn E. Goodman, and James A. Grady (Albany: State University of New York Press, 2009), 192–209, at 206.

46. Novak, *The Election of Israel*, 200.

47. Novak, *The Election of Israel*, 201.

48. Novak, *The Election of Israel*, 207.

Michael Wyschogrod

In his conclusion Novak discusses more recent Jewish work on election, and specifically Michael Wyschogrod's *The Body of Faith: God in the People Israel,*[49] toward which Novak is favorably disposed. I share this favorable disposition. Novak's focus is on election, whereas ours is broader in terms of the way in which God is rendered for us in Scripture and how this relates to the doctrine of God and divine action. In his introduction, Wyschogrod sets out his presuppositions, which are a drink of cold water in a rationalistic desert! His project is a philosophy of Judaism and we will examine his thought through his presuppositions and how they are developed in *The Body of Faith.*

Wyschogrod asserts that his Judaism is *biblical.* The Oral Torah is vital, but it is dependent on the Written Torah, which is the "primary document of revelation" (xiv). As an example of how this influences his philosophy, we can think of Abraham. Wyschogrod notes that in rabbinic literature Abraham is represented as having discovered the one God through reasoning, but this is not found in the Bible. This is clearly correct, and a rationalist reading of the Abraham story is an example of eisegesis through a philosophical lens.

Second, for Wyschogrod preservation of a doctrine of *God as personal* is essential. For him Maimonides's demythologization of the doctrine of God is *unbiblical* and dangerous for Jewish faith. "Jewish faith cannot survive if a personal relationship between the Jew and God is not possible" (xiv). The legal realm can be systematized rationally, "But this is not so of the very being and personality of God, which is not revealed to man as a philosophical first principle but as a living and interacting father concerned about the well-being of his children" (34).

In chapter 3 Wyschogrod explores the issue of the personhood of God in detail. He asserts that "Jewish existence is existence for the living God" (83) and credits Martin Buber with his influential notion of the I–Thou relationship for returning this emphasis to the center of Jewish thought. However, like Berkovits, Wyschogrod ultimately finds Buber's doctrine of God unsatisfactory. Buber succumbs finally to the same problem as the philosophers, with God elevated so high that nothing can be said about him. For Buber the I–Eternal Thou relationship can never be reduced to an I–It relationship. The

---

49. Michael Wyschogrod, *The Body of Faith: God in the People Israel* (Northvale, NJ: Jason Aronson, 1996, 1983). Hereafter, page references to this work are given in parentheses in the text.

eternal Thou "cannot be experienced; . . . cannot be thought."[50] In this way
the philosophic tradition returns: God is beyond conception. Wyschogrod
notes that Buber left no prayers behind and was estranged from the Jewish
community of worship. In this respect, he forms a stark contrast with Halevi.
Wyschogrod rightly points out that to believe in God involves a psychological relationship with him, which includes the I–It relationship. "To have a
psychological relationship with someone involves getting to know his orientation, what he strives for, what matters to him and what does not" (92).

The God of the Bible is a person, and Wyschogrod points out that in the
HB/OT he is portrayed

- as a character in the biblical narratives;
- with a personality that undergoes development;
- as capable of emotions such as sorrow, anger and jealousy, burning love,
  desire and opposition, faithfulness;
- having actions that generate unexpected consequences;
- ambiguously with regard to whether he has a body (99).

For Wyschogrod, "Against this simple fact, Jewish philosophy has marshaled
all of its resources. The personality of God had to be demythologized" (84).
In Wyschogrod's view this process of depersonalizing God starts in rabbinic
Judaism by separating *halakhic* and *agadic* materials and through dehistori-
cizing Judaism. It comes to fulfillment in the sort of philosophical Judaism we find in Maimonides. In opposition to this, and in ways that parallel
Halevi,[51] Wyschogrod focuses on the Jewish notion of Hashem (YHWH),
which is the opposite of the philosophical doctrine of emanation. Of emanation Wyschogrod notes that "this is the perfect antithesis of Hashem" (94).

YHWH is located in certain places at certain times and humans can meet
him there when he so desires. He cannot be seen but is present in the highest
degree. He dwells in heaven but from time to time leaves there and descends
to the earth. Wyschogrod understands the desire to demythologize such
notions but insists that "human nearness to God must be spatial because
man is a spatial being" (101). Unlike ANE gods, YHWH knows no territorial
limitations. "There is no relation possible for gentiles with Hashem except

50. Martin Buber, *I and Thou*, trans. Walter Kaufmann (Edinburgh: T&T Clark,
1970), 161. Wyschogrod, *Body of Faith*, 89.
51. I have found only one reference to Judah Halevi in Wyschogrod's *Body of
Faith* (53).

in the context of their relation with the Jewish people" (103). For Wyschogrod it is loneliness that causes YHWH to create humankind and YHWH's relationship with humankind is consequently ambivalent. Israel's love for YHWH cannot be separated from YHWH's love for Israel.

On the whole, Wyschogrod's biblical portrayal is stimulating and full of insights. There are places where I disagree with him but he is surely right that, "if we are to talk about the real God of Israel who has revealed himself in the Bible, then we must take seriously what we find in that book, and we find in it a passionate and concerned God who is a real rather than imaginary person and who stands in personal relation with many human beings" (104). For Wyschogrod "God must not be subject to necessity or to a good not of his making, and must not be judged by standards external to him" (58).

The philosophical approach to God that Wyschogrod engages with critically has become known as perfect-being theology. This way of thinking about God goes back to Plato and Aristotle,[52] and is also found in the thought of the Stoics Zeno and Cicero. In Christian thought it is most associated with Anselm (1033–1109). Leftow helpfully explains perfect-being theology as follows: "Philosophy and theology both ask what sort of being God is. One way toward an answer begins from the idea that God is in all respects perfect, and fills out the concept of God by reasoning about what a perfect being would be like."[53] Of course, different Jewish and Christian thinkers fill out the concept of God as perfect being in significantly different ways and Wyschogrod has Jewish thinkers like Maimonides in view in his critique of this approach.

In his extensive chapter 4, Wyschogrod engages this approach in detail, much of which we cannot explore in this chapter. The main points are, however, clear. Wyschogrod is admirably concerned to reverse the depersonalization of God and notes that attention to philosophy of being is central to any such attempt: "The question of being is *the* question that seems to be the archetype of all questions about God" (127). Intriguingly, as a Jew Wyschogrod engages substantially with Martin Heidegger, who moved the problem of being back onto philosophical agendas in the twentieth century. The problem with a "being-approach" to God is that it establishes a concept above God that would embrace all entities, including God. In contrast,

52. Aristotle, *Metaphysics* 12.7 (Book 12, chapter 7).
53. Brian Leftow, "Anselm's Perfect-Being Theology," in *The Cambridge Companion to Anselm*, ed. Brian Davies and Brian Leftow (Cambridge: Cambridge University Press, 2004), 132–56, at 132.

Wyschogrod argues that YHWH is Lord of being. He is beyond being and nonbeing. Being is created and is not its own foundation: "Only in the light of creation and therefore of being can we speak and think" (165). YHWH bounds being but is not the foundation of being. "He is the space in which the world is enveloped" (168). He is also the Lord of language so that "we learn what language can say about Hashem by listening to what Hashem says about himself in and through language" (171).

Wyschogrod does not explore the Sinai event but notes that "The carnal election of Israel is intimately related to the historicity of Judaism" (177). The election of Israel involves the sanctification of a natural, corporeal family. Ethics is central to Judaism, but it is decidedly not an autonomous ethics: "It is rooted in the being and command of God, without which no obligation is conceivable" (xv). Israel's faith is a "carnal faith" and redemption must occur in this world in which we live. If death is overcome, it is by the resurrection of the whole person.

Wyschogrod notes of his presuppositions that in modernity many Jews have been attracted to universalistic philosophers like Spinoza, but, if a philosophy is to be anchored in human reality it must attend not only to geometry (Spinoza) but also to poetry, "which is reflective of the particularity of the national consciousness and destiny" (xvi). While noting his tainted associations with Nazism, Wyschogrod invokes Heidegger in this respect. Halevi is not referred to in this work but it is hard not to recall his profound poetry deeply expressive of his religious and national longing.

Wyschogrod is himself a philosopher and by no means an opponent of reason but refers intriguingly to biblical reason and to Talmudic rationality. He, rightly in my view, notes that the interpretation of the *imago Dei* in terms of reason is the contribution of Greek philosophy, but it is not biblical. "Man's fundamental project is not understanding but obedience to the divine command" (5). Indeed, the Greek focus on rationality is incompatible with the biblical view because it lacks historical contingency. Rather than "reason," which is a philosophical construct, Wyschogrod prefers to speak of intelligence.

Wyschogrod speaks of human reason as a dark reason: it is rooted in soil which is not of its own making and it comes up against God who reveals and withdraws himself in the character of *tsimtsum*.[54] In this way reason rep-

---

54. A Jewish Kabbalistic notion of God contracting or withdrawing himself. Cf. Arthur Green, *These Are the Words: A Vocabulary of Jewish Spiritual Life*, 2nd ed. (Woodstock, VT: Jewish Lights, 2012), 37–38.

resents people's humanity. "But God does not desire that man be so pleased with what God has bestowed on him that he forget the source of the gift and use it to establish his sovereignty, as philosophy, by and large, has done. The human reason that God approves is reason within rules or bounds that are beyond reason" (8). For Wyschogrod the rationality of theology is thus an embodied one.

Novak welcomes much of Wyschogrod's approach. In terms of election he insists on the total historicity of the law and observes: "I criticize Herman Cohen for slighting election for the sake of universal revelation and Michael Wyschogrod for slighting revelation in its universality for the sake of the singularity of election."[55]

Conclusion

My hope is that the reader will now start to see why attention to philosophy and theology might be important for biblical studies. When Sommer draws on Maimonides to argue that God cannot speak, we will not grasp the import of this move or be in a position to evaluate it unless we have some background in Maimonides's doctrine of God and the profound extent to which it is shaped by Aristotle and other ancient and medieval philosophies.

We began this chapter with a reference to Berkovits's assertion that "the entire structure that was built around the identification of religion and reason must now be seen as lying in ruins."[56] Our examination of Maimonides enables us to see how a reading of Scripture through a particular philosophical lens renders it simply impossible to develop a *biblical* understanding of divine action. If we pursue this route then, with Sommer, we would have to conclude that God cannot, and therefore did not, speak at Sinai. In this respect Berkovits is correct.

Berkovits is also right in seeing a fertile, alternative tradition in the work of Halevi. Where we are in a better position today is that we have the work of scholars like Novak and Wyschogrod, who develop Jewish philosophy along lines that fit with Halevi's and Berkovits's concerns.

Where Maimonides remains important is that we do need to attend closely to the nature of religious language in the Bible. It is true that we can only speak of God within the creation and as creatures, and only in response

55. Novak, *The Election of Israel*, 249.
56. Berkovits, *God, Man and History*, 12.

to God's revelation of himself. But integrity demands that we are conscious of what we are doing when we use biblical language. The issue of anthropomorphisms, metaphors, and figurative language will not go away, and any attempt to answer the question of the nature of God, a legitimate and important question, will need to probe these linguistic issues philosophically and theologically. In the following chapter, which parallels this one, we will explore these issues through an examination of Thomas Aquinas, a great, Christian representative of perfect-being theology.

CHAPTER 4

Thomas Aquinas and Classical Theism

It belongs to an especially high form of prophecy to see God represented as something speaking, even though it is only in a vision of the
imagination, as I shall later show.

—Thomas Aquinas[1]

We have seen how Sommer leverages Maimonides's perfect-being theology
to argue that God cannot speak, and therefore did not speak, at Sinai. However, there are different versions of perfect-being theology and we live amidst
a renaissance of interest in it, or, as it is more commonly referred to, classical
theism,[2] among evangelicals, Catholics, and others. An important question is
thus: might versions of perfect-being theology such as that of Thomas Aquinas (1225–74) provide a far better philosophical and theological paradigm
within which to approach the Sinai event? If philosophy and the doctrine of
God are important elements in how we read the Sinai event, then it behooves
us to attend to Aquinas as the great representative of classical theism.

In the thirteenth century, theology acquired the status of a professional
discipline in separate faculties of theology at the universities of Oxford and

1. *ST* 1.12.11. Quotations from the *ST* come from Thomas Aquinas, *Summa Theologiae: Questions on God*, ed. Brian Davies and Brian Lewftow (Cambridge: Cambridge University Press, 2006).
2. On classical theism see Brian Leftow, "Classical theism," in "God, concepts
of" (1998), *Routledge Encyclopedia of Philosophy* (Taylor and Francis), doi:10.4324
/9780415249126-K030-1, https://www.rep.routledge.com/articles/thematic/god
-concepts-of/v-1/sections/classical-theism. In his article Leftow has separate sections on perfect-being theology and classical theism. There is considerable overlap
between the two, and for our purposes I am using them as synonyms.

Paris. Central questions related to this development were: Is theology a science? How is theology related to other disciplines? What is the role of logic and natural philosophy in relation to theology? Grant notes that in asking these questions theologians wanted to know if theology was a science in the Aristotelian sense of "demonstrative knowledge derived from premises that are 'true, necessary, certain, immediate, and appropriate to the phenomenon to be explained.'"[3] Most theologians did not think that theology was a science in this strict sense, not that it was inferior—indeed it was the "queen of the sciences"—but it was different from the other sciences in that it relied on revelation. Courtesy of Muslim philosophers, this was the time of the great rediscovery of Aristotle in the West so that the extent to which such questions motivated theologians and Christian scholars should not be underestimated.

Aquinas on Theology

Not surprisingly, therefore, Thomas Aquinas begins his *Summa Theologiae* (*ST*) by attending to a range of related issues in Question 1, namely:

- Humans do need more than philosophy; they need divine revelation and thus the theology of sacred doctrine differs from the theology that is part of philosophy. In the articles that follow in Question 1, Aquinas always refers to "sacred doctrine" and thus his focus in the *ST* is clearly theology as sacred doctrine, which we will refer to simply as theology.
- Theology is both a theoretical and a practical science, but it is more the former than the latter. Because it is both, it ranks above other sciences. The criteria for ranking sciences are certitude and the dignity of their subject matter. Theology ranks higher on both accounts: it is developed in the light of God's own knowledge (revelation), which is infallible, and it reaches to heights beyond the limits of reason. As a practical science theology's goal is eternal happiness, which is the final goal of all the other practical sciences.
- In Question 1, Aquinas repeatedly states that theology's first principles come not from philosophy, but from revelation: "Sacred science can borrow from philosophical disciplines, not from any need to beg from them, but in order to make itself clearer. For it takes its first principles directly from God through revelation, not from other sciences, and it

3. Edward Grant, *God and Reason in the Middle Ages* (Cambridge: Cambridge University Press, 2001), 207.

therefore does not rely on them as though they were its superior" (*ST* 1.1.5).[4] Aquinas is unequivocal about the superiority of theology to other sciences; its role is not to establish the first principles for the other sciences, but to judge them by condemning as untrue anything in them that is contrary to the truth of theology (*ST* 1.1)! As a science theology makes arguments and employs reasoning and philosophy in this respect. Aquinas invokes his paradigm of *grace perfecting nature*[5] at this point, which Lane explains as follows: "Revelation does not basically oppose human philosophy (though it will oppose *false*, incorrect philosophy), but rather supplements it and brings it to completion and perfection. Thomas's system is like a two-storey house: Aristotelian philosophy provides the foundation and the first storey; Catholic theology perfects and completes it by adding the second storey and the roof (with the assistance of philosophy)."[6] Aquinas notes that theology makes use of philosophers who have come to know the truth through natural reason, but "when it [theology] argues conclusively, its own proper authority is canonical Scripture" (*ST* 1.1.8).[7] In relation to Scripture and theology Aquinas defends the role of figurative language and the medieval hermeneutic of the quadriga, which reads the Bible according to four senses: the literal, the allegorical, the moral, and the anagogical.

• For Aquinas, God is indeed the subject that theology studies; while we cannot know "what God is" we can use divine effects whether of nature or grace (revelation) to study and develop a science of God.

So far so good. Thomas sees theology as a science, indeed as the science of sciences,[8] and one that draws its first principles from revelation. One might expect, therefore, that having dealt with prolegomena-type

4. Cf. *ST* 1.1.5.

5. See Craig G. Bartholomew and Michael W. Goheen, *Christian Philosophy: A Systematic and Narrative Introduction* (Grand Rapids: Baker Academic, 2013), chap. 6, for Aquinas's paradigm of grace perfecting nature.

6. Tony Lane, *The Lion Concise Book of Christian Thought* (Herts, UK: Lion, 1984), 94–95.

7. Aquinas (*ST* 1.1.8) asserts of Scripture that "none of their authors have erred in composing them."

8. Grant, *God and Reason*, 208, argues that it remains unclear whether or not theology really was a science for Aquinas. Grant refers in particular to Brian P. Gaybba, *Aspects of the Medieval History of Theology: 12th to 14th Centuries* (Pretoria: UNISA, 1988), 135–41.

issues in Question 1, Thomas would then engage directly with Scripture to show how his first principles are derived. However, as a cursory glance at Questions 1–26 shows, what follows is nothing of the kind, but rather a deeply philosophical explication of the case for God's existence—Thomas's five ways—followed by explications of God's simplicity, perfection, goodness, limitlessness, immutability, eternity, oneness, ideas, life, will, providence, and so on. It is only in Questions 27–43 that Thomas deals with God as Trinity.[9]

How are we to explain this? Thijssen argues that by the thirteenth century at the University of Paris, theology's "method now involved more than ever before intellectual, speculative investigation. . . . The scales had been definitively tipped in favor of a rational conception of theology, as faith seeking understanding, as an investigation of the data of revelation with the help of the sources of reason."[10] Thomas was a theologian, but he saw the need to come to grips with Aristotle as the latter's influence swept across academic circles in Europe. As is well known, he became an expert on Aristotle, wrote commentaries on Aristotle's works, and developed a synthesis between Aristotle's philosophy and the gospel. As we will see below, Thomas's relationship to Aristotle was more complex than this, but it is indisputable that his theology is deeply philosophical and that his paradigm of grace perfecting nature allows philosophy to set the theological agenda in major ways.[11] The crucial question, as Chesterton articulates it, is, Did Aquinas bring Aristotle to Christ or Christ to Aristotle? Or, to uses Thomas's analogy, Does he turn water into wine or mix water with wine?[12]

In terms of medieval theology, including Thomas, Grant points toward the latter answer: "Medieval theologians seem to have been compulsively driven to explain all aspects of their faith in rational terms. In so doing, they

9. Cf. Rowan Williams, "What Does Love Know? St. Thomas on the Trinity," The Aquinas Lecture (Oxford, Jan. 24, 2001), for the argument that Aquinas's doctrine of the Trinity is nuanced and biblical (http://people.bu.edu/joeld/love-know .pdf).

10. J. M. M. H. Thijssen, *Censure and Heresy at the University of Paris, 1200–1400* (Philadelphia: University of Pennsylvania Press, 1998), 113.

11. See Giles Emery and Matthew Levering, eds., *Aristotle in Aquinas's Theology* (Oxford: Oxford University Press, 2015) for the different views on Aristotle's influence on Aquinas.

12. Jan A. Aertsen, "Aquinas's Philosophy in Its Historical Setting," in *The Cambridge Companion to Aquinas*, ed. Norman Kretzmann and Eleonore Stump (Cambridge: Cambridge University Press, 1993), 12–37, 58n9.

seem to have emptied theology of spiritual content."[13] For Grant, theologians of the medieval era so injected natural philosophy and logic into theology that, in effect, they secularized it.[14]

Such points are, of course, controversial. In order to assess them we will need to examine the indebtedness of Thomas's first principles to philosophy, especially since they do *not* obviously proceed from Scripture. Readers should note that we cannot, of course, engage in a wide-ranging exploration of classical theism but will keep our attention focused on divine action, asking, What kind of view of divine action does Thomas's theology yield and how would this relate to the Sinai event?

Thomas held Maimonides in deep respect, and it will be obvious from our previous chapter that we employ Thomas as a Christian parallel to Maimonides. The *Guide* was translated into Latin by the 1220s and Burrell points out that "with Maimonides and Avicenna his [Thomas's] relationship was more akin to that among interlocuters, and especially so with Rabbi Moses [Maimonides], whose extended dialectical conversation with his student Joseph in his *Guide of the Perplexed* closely matched Aquinas's own project: that of using philosophical inquiry to articulate one's received faith, and in the process extending the horizons of that inquiry to include topics unsuspected by those lacking in divine revelation."[15]

The Classical Theism of Thomas Aquinas

If grace perfects nature, even—especially—when it comes to our doctrine of God, then how we know nature is of fundamental importance for understanding Thomas's doctrine of God. Like Aristotle, Thomas rejects a doctrine of innate ideas; the basis of knowledge is found in sense experience: "Now it naturally belongs to us to reach intelligible things through sensible ones, for all our cognition originates from the senses" (*ST* 1.1.9). Importantly, Thomas rejects Augustine's view of *illumination*, asserting that the human intellect has a natural light through creation that enables it to arrive at truths by unaided human reason.[16] The intellect is able to

---

13. Grant, *God and Reason*, 279.

14. Grant, *God and Reason*, 289.

15. David B. Burrell, "Aquinas and Islamic and Jewish Thinkers," in Kretzmann and Stump, eds., *The Cambridge Companion to Aquinas*, 60–84, 60.

16. There are different views on this issue. Cf. Lydia Schumacher, *Divine Illumi-*

abstract intelligible content from sensory images leading to the acquisition of knowledge. Aristotle asserts at the outset of his *Metaphysics* that "by nature all men long to know."[17] Humans thus aim at knowledge as their end. Aquinas develops Aristotle's thought by providing three reasons for this:[18]

- Each entity naturally aspires to its perfection, that is, for its potentialities to be fully actualized.
- With Maimonides he argues that "that by which a human being is human is intellect" but, since humans posses no innate knowledge of things, this potential that is central to being human only becomes actual through the acquisition of knowledge. Knowledge is thus preeminently the actualization of the natural human potentialities.
- Thus, science is inherently good.

Humans only progress gradually in their acquisition of knowledge, and Aquinas traces the progress of philosophy from the pre-Socratics through to his day. Aertsen identifies two significant features in Thomas's understanding of the history of philosophy: first, that philosophy develops from a particular to a universal understanding of *being*, and second, that "the idea of creation appears as the result of the *internal* development of thought, independent of the external aid of revelation."[19] Unaided reason can thus prove that the world had an origin, but not that it has a temporal beginning. As the creator, God is the immediate origin of all things and only humankind with its intellect has the ability to turn to its origin "expressly."[20] This turn is worked out through the human desire for knowledge. Humans naturally desire to know the cause of what they see, and this search only ceases with the first cause: "perfect knowledge is knowledge of the *first* cause,"[21] namely God. Our ultimate end is to know God through the contemplation of his essence, a knowledge that transcends philosophy. Our complete happiness cannot, therefore,

---

nation: *The History and Future of Augustine's Theory of Knowledge* (Oxford: Wiley-Blackwell, 2011).

17. Aristotle, *Metaphysics*, trans. Hugh Lawson-Tancred (London: Penguin, 1998, 2004), 4.

18. Aertsen, "Aquinas's Philosophy," 27. Hereafter, page references to this work are given in parentheses in the text.

19. Aertsen, "Aquinas's Philosophy," 30.

20. Aertsen, "Aquinas's Philosophy," 31.

21. Aertsen, "Aquinas's Philosophy," 31.

consist in theoretical knowledge. Owens observes that for Thomas, as for Aristotle, this supernatural goal consists in "intellectual contemplation."[22] In the beatific vision God will indeed be seen in his essence and this will be the perfection of our intellectual powers.

Thomas was a highly original thinker and there is no question that he felt compelled to follow Aristotle slavishly. Owens locates a fundamental difference between Aristotle and Thomas in their views of *being* and *essence*. For Aristotle, in each instance they are the same. "In Aquinas, on the other hand, there is an explicit claim that in all creatures there is a real distinction between a thing and its being. Being and essence were known by radically different acts. In fact, the real distinction between essence and existence could be regarded in neothomistic circles as the fundamental truth of Christian philosophy, which pervaded the whole of Thomistic metaphysics" (39). How did Thomas come to this view? Above all through his reading of Exod 3:14 and its explanation of the name of God, YHWH, which the Vulgate translates as "ego sum qui sum" (I am who I am). "That was, for Aquinas, the 'sublime truth' that the Christian knew about being. It was the very name and nature of God" (46). This was not Aristotle's view, but Thomas thought Aristotle's concepts sufficiently flexible to hold this insight from revelation. God is thus the primary instance of being and the efficient cause of everything. Owens notes:

> Some modern interpreters, it is true, find the union of the two incomprehensible. They claim that they are unable to see how the Aristotelian separate substance as primary mover can coincide with the loving and provident God of the Scriptures. The remote detachment and the aloofness of the Aristotelean prime mover remains irreconcilable with the Judeo-Christian God. But Aquinas experienced no difficulty whatever in this regard. He approached the problem from the standpoint of the notion of being that he had found in Exodus. (46)

Owens asserts that "there is neither coldness nor insensitivity in this relationship of the primary being to his creatures. From the viewpoint of existence and activity the relationship is extremely close and intimate" (47).

Owens notes that both Aristotle and Thomas start with the things of the

---

22. Joseph Owens, "Aristotle and Aquinas," in Kretzmann and Stump, eds., *The Cambridge Companion to Aquinas*, 38–59, 44. Hereafter, page references to this work are given in parentheses in the text.

sensible universe. Aristotle sees in them finite form, the form that actuates their matter, and reasons from that to pure forms that are finite. Aquinas starts from the existential actuality that sensible things receive from something else, actuality that is grasped through judgment. For Thomas, the existence thereby grasped is limited by the nature it actuates but in its own notion it contains no limiting factor; indeed, when it is reached as pure actuality it is infinite. There is thus continuity and radical difference between the two metaphysics: "Aquinas was led by religious belief to look upon *being* as the proper name and nature of a creative and provident God" (54).

Now if, following Aristotle and Thomas, there are no innate ideas in the human mind, and knowledge derives from sensory experience, then it becomes telling when a religious idea results in Thomas seeing things differently to Aristotle. Owens seeks to defend the naturalism at stake: "These differences are being judged on grounds that may be observed by all in external sensible things. That is the final court of appeal. . . . Aristotle saw finite form as the highest actuality in sensible things; Aquinas saw existence as that actuality. The difference in the starting points of the two ways of thinking is clear-cut and is based on external things" (56). Owens argues that both approaches remain valid today for understanding our world. It is precisely this observation available to all in external things that has come under scrutiny in modern and postmodern philosophy, and, as we will see below, renders the naturalistic cast to Aristotle's and Thomas's philosophies so problematic.

To summarize Thomas's view of the relationship between philosophy and theology:

- They are in harmony with each other since truth is one.
- "Natural knowledge is first and fundamental, because the gifts of grace are added to nature."[23]
- Faith (theology) perfects nature (philosophy).

Thomas is clearly deeply indebted to Aristotle. However, he is by no means solely indebted to Aristotle. For example, he uses the Neoplatonic scheme of *exitus* and *reditus* as an organizing principle in his thought whereby all things come from and return to God. Thomas utilizes the concept of *participation* to articulate the relationship between created being and God, a concept taken from Plato who used it for the relationship between concrete reality and the

23. Aertsen, "Aquinas's Philosophy," 35.

Forms, and one that was sharply criticized by Aristotle.[24] For Thomas, all creatures are characterized by the nonidentity of their essence and their *esse*.

Aquinas on God

In contrast to Calvin, who argues for the *sensus divinitatis*, an innate sense of God within humans, Thomas argues that it is not self-evident that God exists because, philosophically, according to Aristotle, the nature of something that is self-evident is that one cannot think the opposite, whereas clearly one can think the opposite of "God exists." "Knowledge that God exists is not implanted in us by nature in any clear and specific way" (*ST* 1.2.1). "God exists" is self-evident in itself, according to Thomas, but not to us because we do not know what God is, which Aquinas defines as "that than which nothing greater can be thought" (*ST* 1.2.1). Thus, the existence of God needs to be demonstrated philosophically from God's effects (Rom 1:19–20). We must be able to demonstrate that God exists from effects to cause; in this way "God's effects can serve to demonstrate that God exists, even though they cannot help us to know him comprehensively for what he is" (*ST* 1.2.1). Thus "we can at least be lead from them [God's effects in the creation] to know of God that he exists and that he has whatever must belong to him as the first cause of all things, a cause that surpasses all that he causes" (*ST* 1.12). Our knowledge of God by grace is more perfect than the one we have by natural reason, but it is crucial to note how Thomas develops his view of God in the light of his paradigm of grace perfecting nature. One starts, and proceeds a considerable way, dependent on unaided reason and nature alone, and then in this context moves to truths about God that cannot be known by nature alone. As Thomas says, "the light of grace strengthens the intellectual light" (*ST* 1.12.12).

Thomas argues for the existence of God on the basis of his famous five ways. The First Way is deeply indebted to Aristotle. In the world things are regularly undergoing change and change is always caused by something else. Not all chains of causes must end in a First Cause but, for Thomas, changes of the per se (intrinsic) kind must, and the First Way deals with one such change of this type. We inevitably come to a First Cause of change and this is what "everybody takes God to be" (*ST* 1.2.3). The Second Way relates to efficient causation: we have to posit a First Cause, which is what everyone

24. Aertsen, "Aquinas's Philosophy," 22.

calls God. The Third Way is related to possibility and necessity: somethings are able to be or not to be whereas other things must be. We have to stop somewhere in the chain of things that must exist and owe this necessity to something else, and thus we are forced to posit something that is intrinsically necessary, owing its necessity to nothing else, and this is God. The Fourth Way attends to gradations: there is something that causes in all other beings their being, goodness, and their other perfections. We call this God. The Fifth Way relates to governance and design: things lacking intelligence are nevertheless directed toward a goal only by being directed by an intelligence. Thus, there is a being with intelligence who directs all natural things to ends, and this is God.

Having "proved" that God exists, Aquinas begins Question 3 by asserting that "we cannot know what God is, only what he is not" (*ST* 1.3). By this statement Aquinas means that we cannot intellectually grasp the property of "Deity." As Davies points out, we should take this statement by Thomas very seriously. The *Summa*'s "treatment of the divine nature is very much an essay in what is sometimes called *negative* or *apophatic* theology—theology that strongly distinguishes between God and things in the world of which we can have what Aquinas calls *scientia*."[25] This negative way dominates the characteristics of God Thomas defends in Questions 3–26.

God is not a body; there is no potentiality (liability to change and develop) in him; he is composed of no parts and is thus *simple*, in the philosophical sense of being without parts. Humans are in God's image because of their intellect and reason, which are incorporeal, and decidedly not because of their bodies. God is essentially form, and not form and matter. As simple, God contains no accidents (attributes that are not a part of the essence of a thing), which cannot exist in God because accidents realize potentialities. God is the absence of all imperfection. As the First Cause he has to be *the most perfect of things* since the perfections of everything exist in God. Creatures, we can say, resemble God analogically, but we may not say that God resembles creatures.

Goodness means being desirable; goodness and being are the same since things that participate in being always desire their perfection. Being is, however, more fundamental than goodness. Because God is the First Efficient Cause of everything, goodness and desirability belong to him, and thus God is *the absolutely supreme good*; only God is essentially good. Because God's

25. Brian Davies, *Thomas Aquinas's* Summa Theologiae: *A Guide and Commentary* (Oxford: Oxford University Press, 2014), 51.

70

existence is not "acquired by anything" (*ST* 1.7.1) he is limitless. He is not bound by place but is omnipresent. God is in everything, not as part of everything's essence, but as an efficient cause is present to that in which its action is taking place. God contains things and acts in everything without intermediary causes. Thus God is everywhere and gives every place its existence. He fills all places, not as bodies do, but with his power, presence, and essence.

God is not subject to change. He is immutable and pure actuality, having no potential that is not already actualized. As such he is eternal, here understood as referring to an unending and instantaneous whole lacking successiveness. Time involves change, but God does not change and is not subject to time as are we. He is thus eternal. God is his own eternity so that eternity and God are the same thing. His eternity comprehends all phases of time. In the true sense eternity belongs only to God but some things may share in his eternity/immutability. "Yet others share eternity still more fully, by possessing unchangeableness of existence and even of activity. Such are the angels and saints enjoying sight of the divine Word" (*ST* 1.10.3). God is necessarily and supremely one. God's simplicity, his limitless perfection, and the oneness of the world demonstrate that there is only one God.

In Question 12 Thomas moves on to how God's creatures know him. He asserts that in himself God is supremely knowable. The created mind can see God's essence because of its incorporeal nature. "Those who see God's essence do not see it through a likeness but through God's essence united to their minds" (*ST*, 1.12.9). Because "God is not corporeal . . . he cannot be seen either by sense or imagination but only by the mind" (*ST*, 1.12.3). Thomas stresses that the divine essence cannot be known through the natures of material things and argues that "the more the soul is abstracted from material things the greater is its capacity for understanding abstract intelligible things—which is why divine revelations and visions of the future come more often during dreams and ecstasies" (*ST* 1.12.11). However, divine illumination of the mind *is* required for the mind to be raised, in this way, beyond its nature. The infinite cannot be contained in the finite, but the blessed do see God, possess him, hold him forever in their sight, and enjoy him. Thomas asserts that through grace we acquire a more perfect knowledge of God than by natural reason. For example, through the visions of the prophets God provides us with images that are better suited for expressing the divine than the images we take from the natural world. However, as Thomas says of the images from the natural world, we develop abstract, intellectual concepts from them. What Thomas appears to give with one hand to knowledge by revelation, he seems to take back with the other. At the end of Question 12 he says that "in this life revelation does not tell us what God is and so joins us to him as if to an unknown" (*ST* 1.12.13), although it does help us to know him better, shows us his works and teaches us things like the Trinity that we could never arrive at by natural reason.

We saw in the previous chapter how Maimonides struggled with the question of God speaking. Thomas notes that "it belongs to an especially high form of prophecy to see God represented as something speaking, even though it is only in a vision of the imagination, as I shall later show" (*ST* 1.12.11). When Jacob says, "I saw God face to face," he is not, according to Thomas, referring to God's essence, but to an image. God "may raise up certain minds to see his essence in this life, but not by making use of their bodily senses" (*ST* 1.12.11). Augustine, according to Thomas, says this in relation to what took place with Moses and Paul. Thomas is here referring to Augustine's discussion in Book 12 of his *The Literal Meaning of Genesis*,[26] which illustrates well just how strongly Thomas's view of knowing God is intellectual. In Book 12 Augustine discusses the heavenly paradise and the different types of vision. He is particularly focused on Paul's comment that he was caught up into the third heaven (2 Cor 12:2-4) but draws Moses into the discussion.

Augustine identifies three types of vision: bodily, spiritual, and intellectual, in ascending order. They are like a ladder by which one can climb up from the lower to the higher. For Augustine the intellectual vision is the most excellent. "Now anything that is seen not in images but as it is properly in itself, and is not seen through the body, is seen with a kind of vision that surpasses all the other kinds" (12.6.15). Mind, according to Augustine, can only be seen by mind. In the intellectual realm, "there, without any bodily likeness the pure transparent truth is perceived, overcast by no clouds of false opinions" (12.26.54). Augustine argues that we can work to attain this state:

There the glory of the Lord is to be seen, not through some significant vision, whether of the bodily kind such as was seen on Mt. Sinai, or the spiritual such as Isaiah saw or John in the Apocalypse, not in code but

26. In Augustine, *On Genesis*, trans. Edmund O. Hill (New York: New City Press, 2002). Hereafter, references to this work are given in parentheses in the text. On this work by Augustine see M. M. Gorman, *The Unknown Augustine: A Study of the Literal Interpretation of Genesis (De Genesi ad litteram)* (dissertation, University of Toronto, 1975).

clearly, to the extent that the human mind can grasp it, depending on God's grace as he takes it up, so that God may speak mouth to mouth with any whom he has made worthy of such conversation—the mouth of the mind not the body, which is how I consider we have to understand what is written about Moses. (12.26.54)

Augustine has Num 12:7–8 in mind here:

> Not so with my servant Moses;
> he is entrusted with all my house.
> With him I speak face to face—clearly, not in riddles;
> and he beholds the form of the LORD.

When Paul speaks of being caught up into the third heaven he is speaking of the intelligible realm, and not some bodily sign like the cloud of God's glory, which would stand at the door of the tabernacle when Moses went in to speak with God face to face (Exod 33:7–11). Indeed, for Augustine, Moses was so conscious of the difference between the very substance of God and the visible creatures in which God used to show himself to people and their bodily senses that he made a request: "Show yourself to me!" (Exod 33:13, 18).[27] Moses longed to see God not as he had on the mountain or in the tabernacle "but in his very substance as God, without any bodily creature being assumed which could be presented to the senses of mortal flesh, and not either in spirit in figurative bodily likenesses, but clearly in his very self, insofar as a rational and intellectual creature can grasp that, withdrawn from every sense of the body, from every coded symbol of the spirit" (12.27.55).

Thomas asks if we can predicate any term of God substantially. The problem here is that we can designate God from creatures, but such words do not express the divine essence as it is in itself. In his essence God is beyond naming. This problem is not relevant to negative terms or for words that express the relationship of God to creatures since these express what God is not. As is well known, Thomas defends the view that we can speak of God analogically, but how do such different words relate to God as he is? Thomas argues that words about God are not synonymous but do correspond to something altogether simple. "God is more distant from any creature than any two creatures are from each other" (*ST* 1.13.5). In relation to positive affirmations about God, Thomas notes that "although we can think

27. NRSV translates in v. 13 "show me your ways" and in v. 18 "Show me your glory."

of him in these different ways we also know that to each corresponds a single simplicity that is one and the same for all" (*ST* 1.13.12).

According to Thomas, God's understanding is his substance, an idea in God is simply God's essence; God's life is his understanding, and just as there is intellect in God so there is will.

"The God of the Bible and the God of the Philosophers"

When it comes to Thomas and divine action an obvious focus would be his treatment of the incarnation.[28] However, the heading for this section is the evocative title of Eleonore Stump's Aquinas Lecture, which I heard her give in Jerusalem in December 2015. Intriguingly, Stump uses the small book of Jonah to explore the biblical representation of God in relation to classical theism, and this fits with our exegetical focus on an HB/OT text. Stump notes that the view of God as set out in classical theism is often seen as in stark contrast to the biblical portrayal of God. She says, "in this book, I try to lay out the case for the rejection of this inconsistency as fully as possible in order to show, with as much evidence and reason as can be mustered in one short book, that the God of classical theism is the engaged, personally present, responsive God of the Bible."[29] Stump attends to the classical theism of Aquinas, the proponent she knows best, and she focuses on the three attributes of God that are central to the supposed inconsistency between the Bible and classical theism, namely immutability, eternality, and simplicity.

Stump references critics of these attributes of God and readers are referred to her lecture for details. Some argue that an immutable God could not answer prayer since what an immutable God knows or wills cannot be dependent on what a human being does. Eternality means that God does not change; he is timeless. Change requires succession, which is associated with time, and such a God could not engage in second-person dialogue with humans. As regards God's simplicity, it is argued that humans can have no positive knowledge of God or, even more strongly, that he is unknowable. An example of the critique of the doctrine of simplicity is found in Alvin

28. Cf. Eleonore Stump, *Aquinas*, Arguments of the Philosophers (London: Routledge, 2003), 407–26.

29. Eleonore Stump, *The God of the Bible and the God of the Philosophers*, The Aquinas Lecture, 2016 (Milwaukee: Marquette University Press, 2016), 18–19.

Plantinga's *Does God Have a Nature?*, his Aquinas Lecture.[30] Plantinga notes that "historically the most widely accepted answer to our question is Yes. God does have a nature; but he is identical with it. God is somehow simple, utterly devoid of complexity. He has a nature; but he and it are the very same thing."[31] This doctrine has its roots in antiquity, as far back as Parmenides, and has been affirmed by thinkers as diverse as Duns Scotus and Herman Bavinck, and is found in the ancient creeds as well as in the Belgic Confession. Plantinga explores Aquinas's doctrine of simplicity but concludes that "divine simplicity, therefore, is not the way out: for while it does indeed have a certain intuitive grounding, it scouts intuitions much firmer than those that support it."[32]

Stump notes that Augustine and Thomas held to the classical theist view of God and yet wrote biblical commentaries without showing any unease with combining classical theism and biblical narrative. In his *Confessions*, for example, Augustine manifests an intensely personal relationship with God. Stump approaches her answer to the critiques of classical theism via a detour dealing with Thomas's view of the Holy Spirit, concluding that, "according to Aquinas's account of the indwelling Holy Spirit, for every person of faith, the immutable, eternal, simple Holy Spirit, who is God, is present, with mutual knowledge, mutual speech, and mutual love. It is evident, then, that the God described in Aquinas's account of the Holy Spirit could deal with a person such as Jonah in the ways that the biblical story portrays."[33]

According to Stump, Aquinas understands eternity to refer to a life without succession but with atemporal duration, with "duration" defined analogically in relation to temporal duration. The relationship between an eternal God and time is one of simultaneity, which Norman Kretzmann and Stump call ET-simultaneity. For Stump, there is nothing about such a view of eternity that rules out God responding to his creatures. In terms of God's personal presence, what needs to be added to this account is the notion of "shared attention." Stump argues that God's eternity in fact allows for a

30. Alvin Plantinga, *Does God Have a Nature?* The Aquinas Lecture, 1980 (Milwaukee: Marquette University Press, 1980).

31. Plantinga, *Does God Have a Nature?*, 26–27.

32. Plantinga, *Does God Have a Nature?*, 61.

33. Stump, *The God of the Bible*, 54. Hereafter, page references to this work are given in parentheses in the text.

richer account of God's engagement with Jonah since God in his timeless eternity "is present at once to every time of Jonah's life" (75).

In terms of God's immutability, Stump argues that an immutable God can act because of something that takes place in time: "the plan of God is changing but God is not changing" (76). Thus God's immutability does not for a moment prevent him from conversing with Jonah and acting as he is portrayed in Jonah.

As regards simplicity, Stump argues that Thomas does not regard God as *being* alone, but somehow as being and a being, as *esse* and *id quod est*. Stump asserts that "similar things have to be said about God's acts. As Plantinga rightly claims, nothing that is only an abstract universal could act. But because it is also right to say that God is an *id quod est*, it is right to hold that God has the power to act and does act. God can do other than he does and he exercises choice in how he acts." Stump acknowledges that further discussion of the doctrine of divine simplicity is required.

Stump thus concludes that classical theism gives us a strong intellectual foundation for the biblical portrayal of God, and she maintains that any attempt to do without it will soon run aground in insoluble problems or serious challenges. She further elaborates on divine *impassibility*, relating it to the two natures of Christ. If God is eternal, then it is always true of God that he has assumed human nature. Thus "it is not only not true that God is able to suffer but it is also true that God knows a great many human emotions and human afflictions from his own experience of them" (101). For Stump, "what the melding of classical theism and biblical theism yields is a God who is personally engaged, personally present and interactive with everything that God has made" (105).

This leads Stump to an intriguing and insightful view of biblical anthropomorphisms. The *imago Dei* implies resemblance, and this makes it reasonable that in the Bible God so often appears human. "Anthropomorphism is wrong-headed only if it is stupid. Philosophically literate anthropomorphism is exactly what one would expect of any worldview which affirms that human beings are made in the image of God" (107). Pascal famously had sewn into his jacket a note with the statement, "Not the god of the philosophers, but the God of Abraham, Isaac, and Jacob." Stump concludes that the God of the philosophers and the biblical God are one and the same. "As the story of Jonah illustrates, the humanity of human persons has its correlative image in the responsive and personally present God of the Hebrew Bible. There is a rich anthropomorphism here that the stories underscore and approve" (14).

Jonah: An Initial Evaluation

Plantinga notes the complexity of the arguments involved in classical theism, and the literature on these issues continues to pour forth so that it is not possible in a book of this size to attempt to resolve them, even if I were able to do so! My strategy will therefore be as follows.

Even if one concedes that Stump is right about Thomas and classical theism, it seems to me that at best she shows that classical theism *can fit* with the portrayal of God in the Bible. She certainly has not shown that classical theism emerges *from* Scripture and its portrayal of God and divine action. Thus, my first engagement with her fascinating argument will be to inquire what about God in Jonah it sees, and more importantly what it misses. Second, I will argue that in Augustine and Aquinas's biblical interpretation we do find troubling ways in which their philosophy makes it nigh impossible for them to interpret Scripture according to its literal—not literalistic—meaning. Third, I will raise critical questions about the viability of the largely Aristotelian framework that informs the entire edifice of Thomas's classical theism in the context of grace perfecting nature.

While writing this book I have been finishing off a book with a colleague on the Minor Prophets. It fell to me to write on Jonah, and I have found immersion in this short narrative rich and rewarding.[34] As Stump notes, God is portrayed as intensely personal in Jonah: he talks to Jonah and commissions him; he casts a violent storm into the sea; he works so that the casting of lots leads to Jonah as the culprit; he calms the sea once Jonah is thrown overboard; he prepares a rescue for Jonah; he responds to the Ninevites' repentance by not bringing judgment upon them; and he teaches Jonah a lesson in mercy.

For Stump, none of these actions depicted of God is problematic for classical theism. God is responsive to creatures; he is capable of having effects in time; he does manifest the personal presence of shared attention; he can and does enter into engaged and personally present conversations. Indeed, as noted above, for Stump God can be more personally present to Jonah than any human contemporary of his. As with Nineveh, God's plan can change without God changing. God has the power to act and does act. Because of God's assumption of humanity in Christ, God knows human

---

34. Craig G. Bartholomew and Heath A. Thomas, *The Minor Prophets: A Theological Introduction* (to be published by IVP Academic).

emotions and is able to empathize with them. God is personally engaged, personally present, interactive with everything he has made. It even makes sense for God to say "you" to the sea!

Stump's creative use of Jonah is not, of course, intended to be complete or exhaustive. She does indeed attend to themes that are central to Jonah. Clearly in Jonah YHWH is a God who speaks: the book begins with his word of commission (Jonah 1:1) and ends with his two questions (Jonah 4:9–11). However, it is insightful to reflect further upon the representation of God in Jonah to see if perspectives on God occur that tend to be ignored by classical theism, and indeed there are.

First, the name used for God is YHWH, even by the sailors in Jonah 1:14–16. We have seen above how Thomas's Greek reading of YHWH is related to his notion of God as being. There is nothing like that here in Jonah. It is YHWH who speaks to, commissions, and interacts with Jonah; causes a disturbance in the sea and then calms it; and so on.

Second, there is the local, real presence of YHWH in Zion in the "holy temple" (Jonah 2:7), an aspect of God that, as we saw in the previous chapter, Wyschogrod draws attention to. It is from this presence that Jonah hoped he could escape by fleeing from Israel to Tarshish (Jonah 1:3). Jonah has to discover that while YHWH is really present in the Temple, he is by no means confined to that locale.

Third, although the word is not used in Jonah, implicit throughout is God's holiness and opposition to "wickedness" (Jonah 1:2, 14). As we will see in a later chapter, Colin Gunton observes that the absence prior to the Reformation of serious treatments of God's attribute of *holiness*, which, it could be argued, is central to a biblical account of the divine attributes, is symptomatic of the incompleteness of classical theism.

Fourth, three attributes of God emerge very clearly in Jonah, namely YHWH's patience, compassion, and mercy (Jonah 4:2). God is patient with his rebellious prophet and patient with Nineveh too. Patience is not commonly identified as an attribute of God by classical theists. Refreshingly Barth discusses God's patience and wisdom together, and he says this of God's patience:

> We define God's patience as His will, deep-rooted in His essence and constituting His divine being and action, to allow to another—for the sake of His own grace and mercy and in the affirmation of His holiness and justice—space and time for the development of its own existence, thus conceding to this existence a reality side by side with His own,

and fulfilling His will towards this other in such a way that He does not suspend and destroy it as this other but accompanies and sustains it and allows it to develop in freedom.[35]

Cremer comments that "the history of the world moves forward under the patience of God,"[36] and Barth rightly notes that God's patience is central to the message of Jonah.[37] Intriguingly, Barth finds the "decisive moment of the biblical testimony to God's patience" in Hebrews 1:3, according to which God sustains all things by his powerful word.[38] This holding of creation in existence against the background of human rebellion and repentance cannot depend ultimately upon our action but on God's patience. "The abyss in the heart of God is so deep that in it the other, the reality distinct from God, can be contained in all its wretchedness."[39]

Barth is insightful in connecting God's patience to the doctrine of creation. This connection is affirmed in Jonah with the king of Nineveh calling all of Nineveh, including the animals, to fast and repent, and in God's final question in which he articulates his concern for humans and animals. God's concern extends beyond the citizens of Nineveh to their "many animals" (Jonah 4:11).

God is thus portrayed in Jonah in an intensely personal way. To use traditional language, he is clearly both transcendent and immanently involved with his creation and his people. It will be obvious from this chapter and our previous one that any view of divine action *will depend upon what we think of God.* Jonah portrays a God who is without question deeply engaged with and active in his creation. This matters. For example, as I have argued elsewhere, Jonah is a profound source for instruction in spiritual formation, and such formation depends upon a God who is transcendent but deeply engaged with our lives. Stump, of course, affirms this, but I argue above that her classical theism obscures, or at the very least does not foreground, certain elements of the doctrine of God that are central to Jonah.

35. *CD* 2/1, 409–10.
36. Hermann Cremer, *The Christian Doctrine of the Divine Attributes*, trans. Robert B. Price (Eugene, OR: Pickwick, 2016), 50.
37. *CD* 2/1, 413–14.
38. *CD* 2/1, 416.
39. *CD* 2/1, 411.

Philosophical Frameworks

We noted above that Thomas was not just indebted to Aristotle, but also to Plato, Neoplatonism, Augustine, and many others, and we should never lose sight of his own originality and the impact of his deep Christian faith. Nevertheless, Aristotle is a major influence upon him philosophically. Every philosophy has its own technical vocabulary, its series of concepts that are its workhorses in the acquisition of knowledge. This is simply unavoidable. However, conceptual frameworks are not neutral and Thomas's deep indebtedness to Aristotle is evident in his concepts of being, substance, accidents, causality, potentiality, actuality, and so on. This framework and these concepts are built deeply into his theology and philosophy, especially in the light of his *grace perfects nature* paradigm. The critical question is, What are we to make of them? Can we appropriate them today, and if not, how do they shape or skew Thomas's doctrine of God and divine action? Once again, these are contested and complex issues, but at least in general they must be attended to.

Plato was Aristotle's teacher and for Plato the world of everyday reality with its flux and impermanence could never be the *source* of truth. It was like a world of shadows[40] and one needed to move through it to contemplate the transcendent realm of forms and ideas and only then could you discern the nature of justice, truth, and beauty in everyday life. Aristotle took a very different approach to his master, an approach that is rightly described as "Plato brought down to earth." For Aristotle, it was precisely in the observable realm of everyday life that truth was to be found. In contrast to Plato, Aristotle developed his conceptual framework of *being* and *categories*. Everything that exists is a manifestation of being and it can be classified through the categories. The first category "substance" refers primarily to the individual entity; secondarily it refers to the form that gives the entity its particular character. The form is not, as with Plato, located in the transcendent realm but in the particular entity. The remaining nine categories are quantity (e.g., 95 kg); quality (e.g., red, cold, good); relation (e.g., dependent upon technology); place (e.g., in the city); time (e.g., 2008); position (e.g. sitting); condition or state (e.g., running, sitting); possession (e.g., bald, i.e., being without hair); and action (e.g., plowing, becoming hungry).

40. See Plato's well-known parable of the cave in his *Republic* 7.

For Aristotle entities become intelligible as they are placed within the framework of the categories. This is because things are formed in nature according to these categories, and our minds are designed to perceive things according to the categories. Aristotle's philosophy is thus that of a thoroughgoing *realism*. He argued that our minds are such that we can extract the forms found in individual things and, using our reason, we can establish the relationship between forms. In this way, the mind is able to represent reality as it is.

Aristotle's philosophy was foundational for Western thought in a multitude of disciplines, such as science and biology, logic and language, and metaphysics and ethics. Prior to the Middle Ages many of Aristotle's works were nearly lost but re-emerged in Western thought thanks to Jewish and Muslim thinkers, as noted above, leading to a massive resurgence of Aristotelianism in the Middle Ages, and Thomas's heroic attempt to synthesize Aristotle with the gospel.

At the end of her detailed examination of Aristotle's philosophy, in the concluding chapter to her *Portrait of Aristotle*, Marjorie Grene explains why Aristotle's philosophy is no longer viable today while attending to ways it should still enrich our philosophical work. Aristotle's basic emphasis on their being patterns in the world and of comprehension in our knowledge of them remains valid. Grene provides two major reasons for her negative conclusion. First, "We live for better or worse in an evolutionary universe, and, in the last analysis, evolution and Aristotelian science will not mix."[41] Within Christian thought, responses to the theory of evolution vary but it is hard to see how Christians could affirm evolutionary naturalism.[42] If one affirms a doctrine of creation order, as do I, or a Catholic notion of natural law, then there is certainly more room for realism philosophically. Indeed, it is hard to see how Christians cannot espouse some form of realism.

From my perspective, Grene's second major criticism is the really telling one. She notes that Aristotle's emphasis on literal scientific language is possible because it is built on real definitions. His definitions can be real because "in them the mind is understanding face to face the being-what-it-is of definite, limited unique, eternal kinds of things" (238). It cannot be so for us, according to Grene, for ever since Descartes separated out the mind as

---

41. Marjorie Grene, *A Portrait of Aristotle* (London: Faber and Faber, 1963), 232. Hereafter, page references to this work are given in parentheses in the text.

42. Cf. Alvin Plantinga's several works in this area.

knower from the spread of things in space it is condemned to try and know, we have a much stronger sense of the input of the mind in the process of acquiring knowledge. Grene asserts:

> Things *are* somehow, but *we* categorize. For Kant and the Enlightenment, indeed, this categorization was common to all men in all ages; that uniformity once lost, the probabilism of modern epistemology was bound to follow in its turn. . . . We, as Kant showed us, must by our categorizing contribute to the making of the world we know. We must construct our world, a hazardous, never completed venture. This means for us science is in part *poetic*. It depends on imagination as well as accuracy, persuasive analogy as well as explicit proof. . . . Every scientific theory . . . rests ultimately on analogy and metaphor. . . . Every scientific theory . . . rests in the last analysis as much on poetic vision as on hard fact. (238–39)

Contrary to Aristotle's view that *nous* "is the peculiar substance of each kind of thing there for us to grasp, vaguely in perception, step by step through induction, directly and luminously through rational, necessary intuition" (242), *we* in fact "put the questions we put to nature; the answers are nature's, but also partly ours" (242).

Especially in philosophy of science,[43] but also in philosophy of language, awareness has grown of the importance of the paradigm within which the creation is studied, and the important role of metaphors in theory construction.[44] Aristotle's privileging of literal language is well known, as is his view of metaphor as ornamental. Shifts in these areas radically alter any ready acceptance of Aristotle's categories and raise in an acute fashion how a paradigm of grace perfecting nature might operate *today*. Postmodernism certainly successfully undermines any kind of naïve realism and has also alerted us to the plurality of worldviews and paradigms within which we work. It is thus extremely difficult—nigh on impossible, I would say—to assert in any discipline that we simply affirm the regnant paradigm and work with it as the approach of unaided human reason to nature. If this is true of natural knowledge, how much more so of knowledge of God. Of course, as Wolterstorff notes, it is one thing to

---

43. Thomas S. Kuhn, *The Structure of Scientific Revolutions*, 50th anniversary ed. (Chicago: University of Chicago Press, 2012).

44. Cf. the works by Mary Hesse, M. Elaine Botha, Lakoff and Johnson, etc.

raise problems with classical theism, and quite another to propose strong alternatives.[45] However, in my view Karl Barth and Colin Gunton have made major strides in this direction, and we will move on to Gunton in a later chapter.[46]

Finally, it should be noted that too often classical theism is not nearly as congruent with the interpretation of Scripture as Stump suggests. There is a very strong intellectual emphasis in Aristotle's and Thomas's thought, and we explored Thomas's reference above to Augustine and how God communicated with Moses in some detail to draw this out. In their discussion of God and Moses we see a privileging of the intellectual in abstraction from the material, sensory world in a way that denigrates the extraordinary depictions in Exodus of God meeting with and speaking to the Israelites, let alone God's intimate engagement with Moses.

A search of the Kindle edition of the *ST* reveals some two hundred references to Moses,[47] and it is fascinating to work through the *ST* looking at all Thomas's references to Moses.[48] Elsewhere I have noted how I find Thomas's commentary on Job more helpful than that of Calvin. Thomas is a fine exegete, and below we will flag some of his many insights as well as pay attention to how and where his philosophy gets in the way of his exegesis of Scripture:

1. God speaking to Moses mouth to mouth (Num 12:8) is interpreted as Moses seeing God's essence, whereas the verse refers to God speaking "face to face," that is, directly, with Moses.
2. For Thomas the name YHWH, given through Moses, signifies existence itself; it is universal, and the less specific or particular and the more absolute the names of God are the more they approximate his essence; it

45. Nicholas Wolterstorff, *Inquiring After God*, vol. 1 of *Selected Essays*, ed. Terrence Cuneo (Cambridge: Cambridge University Press, 2010).

46. See also Nicholas Wolterstorff's fine work, *The God We Worship: An Exploration of Liturgical Theology* (Grand Rapids: Eerdmans, 2015).

47. See Franklin T. Harkins, "*Primus Doctor Iudaeorum*: Moses as Theological Master in the *Summa Theologiae* of Thomas Aquinas," in *Illuminating Moses*, ed. Jane Beale Commentaria 4 (Leiden: Brill, 2014), 237–62. On Aquinas and the Old Testament see Matthew Levering, "Ordering Wisdom: Aquinas, the Old Testament, and *Sacra Doctrina*," in *Ressourcement Thomism: Sacred Doctrine, the Sacraments, and the Moral Life*, ed. Reinhard Hütter and Matthew Levering (Washington, DC: Catholic University of America Press, 2010), 80–91.

48. Quotations from the *ST* below come from Thomas Aquinas, *The Summa Theologica: Complete Edition* (London: Catholic Way Publishing, 2014).

signifies present existence and therefore is properly applied to God who knows neither past nor future. This is eisegesis of an unhelpful sort.[49] We do not know what YHWH means but "I will be what I will be" is a preferred interpretation. Furthermore, as Maimonides, Halevi, and many others rightly note, YHWH is a proper, particular name. Elohim is the generic, universal name for God; hence the important juxtaposition of Elohim and YHWH in Genesis 2-3 where God is unusually named YHWH Elohim. Thus, in terms of the names of God in Scripture, Thomas turns the data upside down, and for Thomas, it turns out, the particular, revelatory names for God are in fact less applicable to God.

3. Thomas is very helpful on the Law in the HB/OT, regularly engages with Maimonides, and often presents insights that are fresh today. He affirms unequivocally the goodness of the Law. However, "just as a doctrine is shown to be good by the fact that it accords with right reason, so is a law proved to be good if it accords with reason. Now the Old Law was in accordance with reason" (*ST* 2a.98.1). Strangely, the criterion here for doctrine and law seems to be natural reason.

4. We find repeated the discussion about Moses seeing God's essence. Moses's request to see God's glory indicates, for Augustine and Aquinas, that he had not seen God's essence before. "Accordingly when Scripture states that 'He spoke to him face to face,' this is to be understood as expressing the opinion of the people, who thought that Moses was speaking with God mouth to mouth, when God spoke and appeared to him, by means of a subordinate creature, i.e. an angel and a cloud. Again we may say that this vision 'face to face' means some kind of sublime and familiar contemplation, inferior to the vision of the Divine Essence" (*ST* 2a.98.3).[50]

5. Thomas follows Maimonides in noting that the HB/OT lessened bodily worship. He also follows Maimonides in arguing that the specified manner for slaying animals in the cultus of Israel aimed intentionally at the least distress for the animals. He also refers to Maimonides's point that the greater the sin, the lower the species of the animal that was offered.

6. Thomas is attentive to the politics of Israel and says that "such was the form of government established by the Divine Law. For Moses and his

---

49. Cf. the discussion of YHWH in Chapter 9.

50. Cf. Harkins, "*Primus Doctor Iudaeorum*," on apparent contradictions in Thomas's discussion of this issue.

successors governed the people in such a way that each of them was ruler over all; so that there was a kind of kingdom" (*ST* 2a.105.1).

7. Thomas has an extensive discussion of prophetic revelation and abstraction from the senses. He asserts that prophetic revelation occurs in four ways:
   - through the infusion of an intelligible light;
   - by the infusion of intelligible species;
   - by impression or coordination of pictures in the imagination;
   - and by the outward presentation of sensible images.

8. There is no abstraction from the senses when something is presented to the prophet's mind by means of sensible species—whether these be divinely formed for this special purpose, as the bush shown to Moses (Exod 3:2), and the writing shown to Daniel (Dan 5)—or whether they be produced by other causes.

9. Thomas affirms that Moses was greater than the other prophets. First, in terms of intellectual vision because he saw God's very essence, just as did Paul in his being caught up into the third heaven. Second, in terms of imaginary vision, which he experienced at the burning bush; he heard words but saw one speaking to him under the form of God while he was awake. Thomas compares Moses and David and notes that "the prophecy of David approaches near to the vision of Moses, as regards the intellectual vision, because both received a revelation of intelligible and supernatural truth, without any imaginary vision. Yet the vision of Moses was more excellent as regards the knowledge of the Godhead; while David more fully knew and expressed the mysteries of Christ's incarnation" (*ST* 2b.174.4).

Conclusion

Thomas Aquinas is our Christian parallel to Maimonides. Thomas knew Maimonides's work well and drew on it creatively. Clearly, what they have in common is a commitment to Aristotelean philosophy, however much that is nuanced and complemented by additional resources. Despite what Thomas says at the outset of his *ST* about needing revelation even in relation to topics addressed by natural philosophy, with Maimonides he shares a commitment to the insights of Aristotelean philosophy formed on the basis of unaided reason, and grace follows and perfects such insights. The result is that, as with Maimonides, Thomas's conceptual framework develops not from Scripture but from the largely accepted philosophy of his day. This is one reason why biblical scholars not trained in classical theism find it so alien to their work; the connections are not obvious because they are, in fact, positioned far apart and their vocabularies have little in common. Thomas is, of course, concerned not to contradict Scripture or the Christian tradition, and his classical theism *bends* far more toward traditional biblical insights than does Maimonides. Thomas is a fine exegete, and we have noted how useful his biblical commentaries remain today. He privileges the literal sense of Scripture and thus takes history seriously, but time and again we see how his philosophical views sit uneasily with the plain sense of the Bible, most obviously and strategically in relation to God's name YHWH.

Readers might well ask, Is it not inevitable that some philosophical framework is required from outside of Scripture for theology? Even if this were the case, as Colin Gunton notes, "the supposition that one particular philosophy—for that is in effect what is being claimed—is necessary for Christian theology is an odd one, and has been decisively refuted by Robert Jenson."[51] However, I am reminded in this respect of Oliver O'Donovan's *Desire of the Nations*, in which he rightly asserts that in the development of a political theology, *sola narratione* is insufficient. A conceptual apparatus is required.[52] Similarly, David Kelsey has noted that in order to take hold of Scripture in its totality a *discrimen* is required, and Kelsey explores whether or not this emerges from Scripture for theology.[53] O'Donovan rightly, in my view, argues that the concepts for (political) theology need to be normed by Scripture and to emerge from Scripture. Thomas claims to follow this line of argument but, in practice, he diverges significantly.

I have not sought to engage Thomas's classical theism in the detail that abounds in the academy today. Readers are referred to the extensive literature that continues to grow amidst the contemporary retrieval of classical theism. What I have proposed is that we should be conscious of the paradigm with which Thomas is working in the development of his philosophical theology—the paradigm of *grace perfecting nature*. This is inseparable from the view that the fall affects the will but not reason. In my view the philo-

---

51. Colin E. Gunton, *Act and Being: Towards a Theology of the Divine Attributes* (London: SCM, 2002), 5.

52. Oliver O'Donovan, *The Desire of the Nations: Rediscovering the Roots of Political Theology* (Cambridge: Cambridge University Press, 1996).

53. David Kelsey, *The Uses of Scripture in Recent Theology* (London: SCM, 1976).

sophical realism he embraces and the indebtedness to Aristotle are today indefensible, which is not to say for a moment that his many insights should be jettisoned. My interest, rather, is what Thomas's insights and the doctrine of God and divine action look like in the context of a *grace restores nature* paradigm, which I would argue is the more biblical one.[54] This Reformed paradigm sees the will and reason as fallen and in need of grace—and thus revelation—in order to function properly.

Few theologians have attended to this issue as closely as the British theologian Colin Gunton, and in a later chapter we will explore his approach to the doctrine of God. Centuries lie between Aquinas and Gunton, and next we will attend to Spinoza and then to Kant, two modern philosophers whose influence on the very possibility of divine action continues to be felt today.

54. See Craig G. Bartholomew, *Contours of the Kuyperian Tradition: A Systematic Introduction* (Downers Grove, IL: IVP Academic, 2017).

CHAPTER 5

Baruch Spinoza and the Problematizing
of Divine Action

The chief aim of the *Treatise* [Spinoza's *Tractatus Theologico-Politicus*]
is to refute the claim which has been raised on behalf of revelation
throughout the ages; and Spinoza succeeded, at least to the extent that
his book has become *the* classic document of the "rationalist" or "sec-
ularist" attack on the belief in revelation.

—Leo Strauss[1]

Above all, if the truth of Judaism is the religion of reason, then what was
formerly believed to be revelation by the transcendent God must now
be understood as the work of the human imagination in which human
reason was effective to some extent; what has now become a clear and
distinct idea was originally a confused idea.

—Leo Strauss[2]

Sommer mentions Baruch Spinoza (1632–77) as a key figure in the development of historical criticism.[3] However, he does not examine Spinoza's
philosophy in any detail and it is to that subject that we now turn in order
to open up the philosophical influences shaping historical criticism as it
emerged.[4] Hundreds of years separate us from Maimonides and Aquinas, and

1. Leo Strauss, *Jewish Philosophy and the Crisis of Modernity: Essays and Lectures
in Modern Jewish Thought,* ed. Kenneth H. Green (Albany: State University of New
York Press, 1997), 181.
2. Strauss, *Jewish Philosophy,* 145.
3. Sommer, *Revelation and Authority,* 15. Cf. Levinson, *"The Right Chorale,"* 4, 11–14.
4. The relationship between Maimonides and Spinoza remains controversial.
See Seymour Feldman, "Maimonides—A Guide for Posterity," in Seeskin, ed., *The*

in the Enlightenment tradition major philosophies developed that played a key role in the emergence of historical criticism. In this chapter we will focus on Spinoza, and in the following one on Kant.

The uproar that resulted from the anonymous publication of Spinoza's *Tractatus Theologico-Politicus* (*TTP*) in January 1670 in the Netherlands signaled a seminal event in Europe's intellectual history at the outset of the Enlightenment.[5] According to Nadler it is also "one of the most important books of Western thought ever written"[6] *because of the view of the Bible enshrined in it.*

Spinoza's *TTP* was published before his *Ethics*, but most of his *Ethics* was written in the decade before his *TTP*, although it was only published after his death in 1678. This is important, since in his *Ethics* he sets out in logical detail his view of God, of the mind, and of virtue and morality. Thus "Ethics" is something of a misnomer because the work includes his metaphysics. The titles of the two books might suggest to the reader that the connections between them are loose, whereas in fact Spinoza's *Ethics* provides indispensable background to understand what he is doing in his *TTP*. Both Spinoza's *TTP* and his *Ethics* provide a critique of religion; the latter a metaphysical and moral one, the former a theological, historical, and political one. It is vital to note that Spinoza's conception of God and the world in the *Ethics* integrally shapes his view of God, Scripture, religion, morality, and providence in the *TTP*.[7]

According to Nadler "Spinoza's *Theological-Political Treatise* . . . was all but ignored by philosophers in the twentieth century. The neglect came not only from those working in metaphysics and epistemology but also, and

---

Cambridge Companion to Maimonides, 324–59, esp. 349–54; Joshua Parens, *Maimonides and Spinoza: Their Conflicting Views of Human Nature* (Chicago: University of Chicago Press, 2012). There are clearly important differences between the two but what, in my view, they share is the privileging of the philosophies of the day and their making Scripture subservient to such philosophies.

5. Jonathan Israel, *Radical Enlightenment: Philosophy and the Making of Modernity, 1650–1750* (Oxford: Oxford University Press, 2001), explores in detail the profound influence of Spinoza.

6. Steven Nadler, *A Book Forged in Hell: Spinoza's Scandalous Treatise and the Birth of the Secular Age* (Princeton: Princeton University Press, 2011), xi.

7. Leo Strauss, "On the Bible Science of Spinoza and His Precursors," in Strauss, *The Early Writings (1921–1932)* (Albany: State University of New York Press, 2002), 175, rightly notes that "the ultimate presuppositions of Spinoza's critique of religion are identical with the definitions and axioms of the *Ethics*."

more surprisingly, from scholars of political theology and of religion."[8] This is an overstatement in terms of biblical studies and hermeneutics where some have indeed paid close attention to Spinoza.[9] Nevertheless, Nadler, who has written extensively and with great clarity on Spinoza, is right to draw our attention to Spinoza's corpus *as a whole*, and to his *TTP* in particular.

In his insightful book, *The Stillborn God: Religion, Politics, and the Modern West*, Mark Lilla explains the effect of the Enlightenment as follows:

> By attacking Christian political theology and denying its legitimacy, the new philosophy simultaneously challenged the basic principles on which authority had been justified in most societies in history. That was the decisive break. The ambition of the new philosophy was to develop habits of thinking and talking about politics exclusively in human terms, without appeal to divine revelation or cosmological speculation. The hope was to wean Western societies from all political theology and cross to the other shore. What began as a thought-experiment became an experiment in living that we inherited. Now the long tradition of Christian political theology is forgotten, and with it memory of the age-old quest to bring the whole of human life under God's authority.[10]

Now we find ourselves in the unforeseen situation in which "The Twilight of the idols has been postponed."[11] Religion has made a major comeback, and the West is badly unprepared to deal with it. Lilla says in *The*

8. Nadler, *A Book Forged*, xiii.

9. R. M. Grant with D. Tracy, *A Short History of the Interpretation of the Bible*, 2nd ed. (Minneapolis: Fortress, 1984), devotes four pages to Spinoza and notes that "Spinoza's method is very much like that followed in modern introductions to the Bible. It is clear and rational. It avoids all the theological questions involved in the interpretation of scripture; for scripture has no authority over the interpreter's mind" (108). R. A. Harrisville and W. Sundberg, *The Bible in Modern Culture: Theology and Historical-Critical Method from Spinoza to Käsemann* (Grand Rapids: Eerdmans, 1995), 32–48, contains a useful chapter on Spinoza. Scott W. Hahn and Benjamin Wiker, *Politicizing the Bible: The Roots of Historical Criticism and the Secularization of Scripture, 1300–1700* (New York: Herder and Herder, 2013), 339–93, contains a full and rigorous treatment of Spinoza. See also Travis Frampton, *Spinoza and the Rise of Historical Criticism of the Bible* (London: T&T Clark, 2006).

10. Mark Lilla, *The Stillborn God: Religion, Politics, and the Modern West* (New York: Vintage, 2007, 2008), 5.

11. Lilla, *The Stillborn God*, 3.

Stillborn God that the "story reconstructed here should remind us that the actual choice contemporary societies face is not between past and present, or between the West and 'the rest.' It is between two grand traditions of thought, two ways of envisaging the human condition. We must be clear about those alternatives, choose between them, and live with the consequences of our choice. That *is* the human condition."[12]

Contrary to the view that Spinoza had little influence, his work was of seminal importance in helping the West to "cross to the other shore." Israel asserts that "in fact, no one else during the century 1650–1750 remotely rivalled Spinoza's notoriety as the chief challenger of the fundamentals of revealed religion, received ideas, tradition, morality, and what was everywhere regarded, in absolutist and non-absolutist states alike, as divinely constituted political authority."[13] At this time of a global resurgence of religion, we would do well to attend closely and critically to how he contributed to that move to the other shore, and not least in relation to political theology and the Bible, central concerns of Spinoza. In the process our focus will be on the implications of Spinoza's philosophy and approach to Scripture for divine action, and Sinai in particular. But, before we get there, we need to attend to the contours of Spinoza's metaphysics, his view of the basic nature of reality.

Spinoza's View of God

Spinoza's *Ethics* lays out Spinoza's own system of thinking as he had done previously in relation to Descartes in his *Principles of Philosophy*, modeled on Euclidean geometry. In this way, however unsuccessful it ultimately is,[14] he sought to demarcate the contours of his philosophy with crystal clarity.

Spinoza's philosophy is *a theory of substance*; for him the world is a single, unique, infinite, eternal, necessarily existing *substance*. For Descartes, there were two substances, the mental and the material, whereas for Spinoza, there is only one, which can be referred to as God or Nature. He says, "by substance I understand what is in itself and is conceived through itself,

---

12. Lilla, *The Stillborn God*, 13.

13. Jonathan Israel, *Radical Enlightenment: Philosophy and the Making of Modernity, 1650–1750* (Oxford: Oxford University Press, 2001), 159.

14. Anthony Kenny, *The Rise of Modern Philosophy*, A New History of Western Philosophy 3 (Oxford: Clarendon, 2006), 66, judges that "the geometrical method cannot be regarded as a successful method of presentation."

i.e., that whose concept does not require the concept of another thing, from which it must be formed" (*CWS* 1:408). Substance possesses two attributes: thought and extension. Spinoza notes that "by God I understand a being absolutely infinite, i.e., a substance consisting of an infinity of attributes, of which each one expresses an . . . eternal and infinite essence" (*CWS* 1:409).

For Spinoza, God necessarily exists; he finds the ontological argument for God's existence compelling. Two or more substances with the same nature or attribute cannot exist in the universe so the world, or Nature, and God are one and the same, as is clear in Proposition 11: "*God, or a substance consisting of infinite attributes, each of which expresses . . . eternal and infinite essence, necessarily exists*" (*CWS* 1:417). Spinoza's philosophy is thus a form of *monistic pantheism*: God is all, and all is God. However, he does distinguish between active nature and passive nature. The attributes of the divine substance belong to active nature; the modes constituting finite nature belong to passive nature. Neither, however, can be conceived of without the other. Intellect and will belong to passive nature so that Spinoza's God is not the personal God of Jews and Christians.[15] God is the one, infinite substance of reality, the first cause of all things—in explanation but not in time, since for Spinoza the world is eternal—but decidedly not the God who speaks, commands, judges, and enters into covenants like that at Sinai. "*Whatever is, is in God, and nothing can be or be conceived without God*" (*CWS* 1:420). God acts solely according to the laws of his own nature and is not constrained by anyone.

A central motif in Spinoza's thought is God's power, his omnipotence. This sounds like orthodox theology but, as is so often the case, Spinoza uses familiar terms but fills them with radically different content. He notes, for example, that "by God's power ordinary people understand God's free will and his right over all things which are, things which on that account are commonly considered to be contingent. For they say that God has the power of destroying all things and reducing them to nothing. Further, they very often compare God's power with the power of Kings" (*CWS* 1:449). Spinoza immediately notes that he has refuted this; God acts by necessity.

Spinoza, unlike G. W. Leibniz, does not believe this is the best of all possible worlds. Rather, this is the only possible world that could exist. Indeed, his view of the world is pessimistic, with humans subject to forces

---

15. Cf. *CWS* 2:131: "God's will and intellect are one and the same." Cf. *CWS* 2:154. In a footnote Curley, *CWS* 2:131, notes that "since Spinoza's *Ethics* denies both will and intellect to God (E I P31), his argument here may be *ad hominem*."

they have little control over. Spinoza thus articulates a determinist view of the world: "the universal laws of nature, according to which all things happen and are determined, are nothing but the eternal decrees of God, which always involve eternal truth and necessity. Therefore, whether we say that all things happen according to the laws of nature, or that they are ordered according to the decree and guidance of God, we say the same thing" (*CWS* 2:112–13).

In his appendix to part I of his *Ethics*, Spinoza sums up his view of God as follows:

> With these [demonstrations] I have explained God's nature and properties: that he exists necessarily; that he is unique; that he is and acts from the necessity alone of his nature; that (and how) he is the free cause of all things; that all things are in God and so depend on him . . . that without him they can neither be nor be conceived; and finally, that all things have been predetermined by God, not from freedom of the will or absolute good pleasure, but from God's absolute nature, or infinite power. (*CWS* 1:439)

The key to successful human life, according to Spinoza, is the development of adequate ideas. Democratic society, which protects freedom of inquiry is the best political context for such ideas to develop, and Spinoza is concerned to undermine anything that subverts adequate ideas and tolerance. Thus, it is not surprising that his detailed consideration of Scripture and its proper interpretation occurs in his *TTP*. Spinoza was well aware that concepts of reason, religion, and scriptural interpretation have public implications. In *TTP* Spinoza argues, for example, that "since our mind—simply from the fact that it contains God's Nature objectively in itself, and participates in it— has the power to form certain notions which explain the nature of things and teach us how to conduct our lives, we can rightly maintain that the nature of the mind, insofar as it is conceived this way, is the first cause of divine revelation" (*CWS* 2:78).

There is for Spinoza no overarching purpose or telos for the world. Humans are as much a part of Nature as anything else and are subject to the same causal determinism. The human mind is part of God's intellect so that when we speak of the mind perceiving something, we are actually saying that God has a particular idea because he constitutes the essence of the human mind. The highest form of knowledge is an understanding of Nature and its ways, which, for Spinoza, is the same thing as knowledge of God.

Spinoza put aside his work on his *Ethics* in order to write his *TTP*. In a letter to Henry Oldenburg, the corresponding secretary for the Royal Society in England, he explained that "I am now writing a treatise on my views regarding Scripture."[16] Spinoza provides three motivations for his *TTP*: to combat the prejudices of the theologians; to combat the accusation that he is an atheist; and third, to defend the freedom of philosophy.

The *Tractatus Theologico-Politicus*

Spinoza addresses his *TTP* to the "Philosophical reader." His intended audience is, however, contested. Curley suggests his intended readers are the would-be philosophers whose freedom to think is constrained by a prejudice about the authority of Scripture.[17] Strauss observes that "In the *Treatise* Spinoza addresses potential philosophers of a certain kind while the vulgar are listening."[18] As we will see with Kant's *Reason within the Bounds of Mere Religion*, similar questions arise about the extent to which Kant states his views clearly and directly. For both philosophers, the political context held its dangers, and it does appear, as Leo Strauss suggests, that at points Spinoza "pulls his punches," being aware of the potential repercussions of the publication of *TTP*.[19]

What is more disconcerting is the practice of Spinoza, and similarly radically minded philosophers of the day,[20] repeatedly to use the language

16. Epistles 30. Quoted in Nadler, *A Book Forged*, 18.
17. Edwin Curley in *CWS* 2:75.
18. Strauss, *Jewish Philosophy*, 212.
19. Edwin Curley in *CWS* 2:53–56.
20. Cf., e.g., Michiel Wielema, "Adriaan Koerbagh: Biblical Criticism and Enlightenment," in *The Early Enlightenment in the Dutch Republic, 1650–1750*, ed. Wiep Van Bunge (Leiden: Brill, 2003), 61–80, 66, who comments about Adriaan Koerbagh, a member of Spinoza's circle, in this respect. Cf. also Adriaan Koerbagh, *A Light Shining in Dark Places, To Illuminate the Main Questions of Theology and Religion*, trans. and ed. Michiel Wielema, Brill's Texts and Sources in Intellectual History 12 (Leiden: Brill, 2011). Another member of Spinoza's circle was Lodewijk Meyer, who published his *Philosophia S. Scripturae Interpres* in 1666. Meyer argues that true philosophy—in his case Cartesianism—is the infallible norm for interpreting Scripture. Intriguingly, about a century later a Latin edition of Meyer's work was published with extensive notes by one of the major figures in the history of historical criticism, namely Johannes Salomo Semler (Israel, *Radical Enlightenment*, 200). On the in-

of faith and theology, but to mean something completely different from its common meaning. This is particularly important when we bear in mind that the *TTP* was published before the *Ethics*, whereas, in fact, the philosophy of the latter is the lens through which Spinoza approaches the issues dealt with in the *TTP*. Spinoza regularly uses the language of divine action but in fact denies that God has either intellect or will. For example, Spinoza refers to "his [God's] eternal decrees" (*CWS* 2:76). This suggests a view of God as a personal agent, and Curley observes that on Spinoza's part this "reflects a willingness to express his thought in a way he knows may mislead some readers into thinking that he is closer to the tradition than he really is."[21] Similarly, Spinoza speaks of God endowing some of the prophets with more grace, and, when it comes to Moses, he asserts that God used a true voice to address him. When reading the *TTP*, one needs to be alert to this phenomenon, and to avoid mistaking orthodox language for orthodox views.

A poignant example of this is Spinoza's repeated emphasis in the *TTP* that we must rely on Scripture alone in our interpretation of it. Again and again we find statements like this: "But whatever can be said about these matters must be sought only from Scripture" (*CWS* 2:78). This has the appearance of the Reformed doctrine of *sola Scriptura*, and lends support to Strauss's comment that Spinoza "regards his criticism of religion as an immanent critique,"[22] but works to obscure the fact that throughout the *TTP*, the truth of Scripture is being analyzed through the philosophical lens of Spinoza's metaphysics so that he means something quite different to the Reformers.

Religion and Superstition

In Spinoza's view, as long as life is going along just fine, humans manifest little need for religion. It is when life becomes difficult that they start to seek religious explanations, and, in this way, superstition arises. For Spinoza, all humans are by nature subject to superstition, and this logic, found among the pagans, has continued among Jews and Christians. Central to superstition is human imagination, by which humans project onto the world

---

fluence of Semler in NT studies see J. C. O'Neill, *The Bible's Authority: A Portrait Gallery of Thinkers from Lessing to Bultmann* (Edinburgh: T&T Clark, 1991), 40–41.

21. Edwin Curley in *CWS* 2:77.

22. Strauss, "On the Bible Science of Spinoza," 175.

explanations of the nature of things, explanations such as goodness, badness, order, confusion, warmth, cold, beauty, deformity, and so on; and from the belief that they are free agents, humans develop the concepts of praise and blame, sin and merit. Spinoza notes that there are humans mad enough to think that God himself takes pleasure in harmony. Spinoza regards liberation from such superstition as central to his project. Nadler notes that "if there is one theme that runs throughout *all* of Spinoza's writings, it is the liberation from bondage, whether psychological, political, or religious. . . . His goal is a tolerant democratic society of individuals whose deeds are guided by the true (moral) religion."[23]

When it comes to Jews and Christians, much of this superstition is validated by Scripture, with most taking the view that Scripture is "everywhere true and divine" (*CWS* 2:71). Scripture, viewed in this way, forms a major obstacle to Spinoza's project and a veritable endless source of prejudices, and thus Spinoza notes, "I resolved earnestly to examine Scripture afresh, with an unprejudiced and free spirit, to affirm nothing about it, and to admit nothing as its teaching, which it did not clearly teach me." Curley observes that the "project, then, is fundamentally an extension of Cartesian method into an area where Descartes himself had not dared to tread" (*CWS* 2:71n27). Spinoza tells us that he will pursue this question by investigating the nature of prophecy, why the Hebrews were called God's chosen people, and whether or not what he calls universal religion teaches anything other than what the natural light of reason teaches. Central themes in Spinoza's discussion are thus prophecy, miracles, the nature of law, leading on to a discussion of how to interpret Scripture, and then finally on to the nature of a healthy polis. An important conclusion of his is declared in the preface: "I was fully persuaded that Scripture leaves reason absolutely free, and that it has nothing in common with Philosophy, but that each rests on its own foundation" (*CWS* 2:72).

Prophecy, Law, Miracles, and Historical Narrative

Traditionally God's revelation to and through the HB/OT prophets, his giving of the Law, and accompanying miracles, would all be seen as types of divine action. The HB/OT prophets are well known for their words, "Thus says the LORD," indicating revelation for the people from God. Prophecy,

23. Nadler, *A Book Forged*, 32.

according to Spinoza, is the certain knowledge revealed by God to humans (*CWS* 2:76). Spinoza immediately moves on to note that, according to this definition, natural knowledge can therefore also be called prophecy,[24] since it depends upon and is knowledge of God's nature and decrees: "we can call natural knowledge divine with as much right as anything else, since God's nature, insofar as we participate in it, and his decrees, as it were, dictate it to us" (*CWS* 2:77). In terms of its certainty and source, natural knowledge is in no way inferior to prophetic knowledge.

Spinoza argues that in the HB/OT prophecy always involves words and/or images and is thus related to the imaginations of the prophets. God used a true voice to address Moses; the voice Samuel heard was imaginary; God created some voice by which he revealed the Decalogue; and so on. Except for Christ no one received God's revelations without the aid of the imagination, that is, through words and/or images. The arguments Moses uses in the Pentateuch are "not taken from the storehouse of reason, but are only ways of speaking he used to express God's decrees and imagine them more effectively" (*CWS* 2:242). The prophets do not have exceptional knowledge but vivid imaginations and perhaps exceptional virtue. They are generally thought to be inspired by the Spirit of God, but Spinoza takes this to refer to their virtue or piety. The masses were ignorant of the true causes of prophecy and thus it is related to the Spirit of God. The certainty of the prophets was only moral; indeed, their revelations varied according to their temperaments, their dispositions, and their opinions. Because God accommodated his revelation in these ways, we are only bound by the *moral* telos of the prophets, namely to do justice and practice loving-kindness.

Furthermore, neither prophecy nor divine law was unique to Israel but present among other nations. Here one needs to bear in mind that by God's guidance, Spinoza understands "the fixed and immutable order of nature, *or* the connection of natural things" (*CWS* 2:112). He understands God's election of Israel in relation to the universal determinism in nature. From Paul's letter to the Romans we learn that the law was revealed to everyone without exception so that Israel is not unique in this respect either. Thus, "God did not choose the Hebrews to eternity, but only on the same condition on which he previously chose the Canaanites" (*CWS* 2:123).

Central to Judaism and Christianity is a list of authoritative books, the canon of Scripture, containing God's Word to his people. From his examination of prophecy, Spinoza argues that God's revealed Word is not a canon of

24. Note the similarity to Maimonides.

books but the simple revelation of the divine mind to the prophets, and the content of this revelation is nothing other than to obey God wholeheartedly by practicing justice and loving-kindness. For Spinoza, revealed knowledge has no object other than obedience and is completely distinct from natural knowledge: "Revealed knowledge has nothing in common with natural knowledge, but each is in charge of its own domain, without any conflict with the other . . . neither ought to be the handmaid of the other" (*CWS* 2:73). For Spinoza, "our supreme good must consist in the perfection of the intellect" (*CWS* 2:128). The man who is most perfect loves the intellectual knowledge of God above all else.

Because divine law is universal, it does not require faith in *historical narratives*. Divine action is particular in Scripture and rendered through historical narratives. However, for Spinoza "faith in historical narratives, no matter how certain that faith may be, cannot give us any knowledge of God. So it also cannot give us the love of God. For love of God arises from knowledge of him, and knowledge of God must be drawn from common notions certain and known through themselves. So it is far from true that faith in historical narratives is necessary for us to attain our supreme good" (*CWS* 2:129–30). Such narratives retain value in relation to civil life since it is helpful to know a people's customs and character. Natural divine law needs no ceremonies, which are introduced merely in order to accommodate ordinary people, whom Scripture teaches by experience and by historical narrative because their mentality is such that they are unable to perceive things clearly and distinctly. Even here, we do not need the multitude of historical narratives we find in Scripture but only the main ones. For Spinoza "faith in historical narratives, whatever in the end those narratives may be, does not pertain to the divine law and does not render men more blessed in itself, and does not have any utility except in relation to teaching. It is only in this respect that some narratives can be better than others" (*CWS* 2:150).

Just as Spinoza reduces the biblical concepts of prophecy, law, election, and revelation to the dimensions of his philosophy, so too he does with miracles. He relates narratives of miracles in much the same way he does religion to superstition. People call events they do not understand miracles. In fact, miracles are impossible: "if anything were to happen in nature contrary to its universal laws, it would also necessarily be contrary to the divine decree, intellect and nature" (*CWS* 2:154). From this perspective, rather than encouraging faith, miracles should make us doubt God's existence. Neither God's existence nor his Providence can be known from miracles. Indeed, "a

Baruch Spinoza and the Problematizing of Divine Action

miracle—whether [defined as] contrary to nature or above nature—is just an absurdity" (*CWS* 2:159).

Spinoza asserts that we need to know the opinions of those who narrated miraculous events: "For many things are related in Scripture as real, and were even believed to be real, which were, nevertheless, only representations and imaginary things, e.g., that God (the supreme being) descended from heaven (see Exodus 19:18 and Deuteronomy 5:19); and that Mt. Sinai was smoking because God had descended upon it" (*CWS* 2:165). We only know God from perceptions of the pure intellect.

How to Read and Interpret Scripture

Spinoza sees the work of the theologians and the culture of his day as awash with eisegesis when it comes to the Bible. Therefore, we must attend to the true method for interpreting Scripture. For Spinoza, it is the same method we use for nature; we need to establish the history of Scripture and infer from it the mind of Scripture's authors. Here again he emphasizes his principle of *sola Scriptura*: "Therefore, all knowledge of Scripture must be sought only from Scripture itself" (*CWS* 2:172).

By the history of Scripture Spinoza means the nature of the language of Scripture: an index of what it teaches on particular subjects, and its authorship, readership, reception, transmission, and canonization. He is aware that for the most part we do not know much of this so that in a great many places we simply do not know what Scripture means or we are just guessing. For Spinoza, however, the divinity of Scripture is located only in its moral teaching so that these problems are far from debilitating. It is quite enough to grasp Scripture's moral teachings. As with the other sciences, Spinoza's method requires no light beyond the natural light of reason.

Spinoza's discussion of the inconsistencies and errors in the HB/OT narratives is extensive. He, for example, argues against the view that Moses was the author of the Pentateuch or that it is substantially Mosaic. He was not the first to do this but does so far more openly than Ibn Ezra and more comprehensively than contemporary scholars such as Thomas Hobbes[25] and Isaac de la Peyrère. In Spinoza's view, the historical books from Genesis to Kings manifest a basic unity that shows that they were all written by one

25. On Hobbes and the Bible see Hahn and Wicker, *Politicizing the Bible*, 285–338.

99

historian. The most likely candidate is Ezra. The one simple theme of the whole is obedience to the Law. Ezra somewhat randomly assembled collections available to him, and in the final composition there are many errors. Spinoza thinks that there was no canon of the HB/OT before the time of the Maccabees and that the selection of the books to be included was made by the Pharisees.

We do not know why, but Spinoza does not subject the NT to the same critical scrutiny as the HB/OT. Perhaps he simply knew the HB/OT better. He compares the Apostles and HB/OT prophecy and asserts that the Apostles wrote their Epistles only according to their own light, and, once again, it is their moral lessons that are divine. Christians view the Christ event as unprecedented, a radical explosion of good news. For Spinoza, the teaching of the NT merely reflects the universal law so that it is *only new* to those unfamiliar with the universal moral law (*CWS* 2:253). Indeed, the NT contains many things we can now do without: "Scripture is properly called the word of God only in relation to religion, *or* in relation to the universal divine law."

Faith, Philosophy, Theology, and Religious Freedom

When it comes to religious beliefs, Spinoza thinks that each person must be free to judge for oneself; after all, what matters is not beliefs but obedience. True religion is judged by works alone. Even with such a strong emphasis on morality, Spinoza's view of faith is always intellectual. In the HB/OT the heart is often taken to be the center of a person's entire life, encompassing affections and reason, but Spinoza equates the heart with the mind. "What is called sacred and divine is what is destined for the practice of piety and religion," and "nothing is sacred or profane or improper in itself, outside the mind, but only in relation to the mind" (*CWS* 2:250). Furthermore, a thing is sacred only as long as we use it for piety and morality. If we stop the thing itself ceases to be sacred.

Spinoza articulates his own version of *claritas Scripturae*: the central themes of Scripture cannot be missed, namely love of God and neighbor. The same can be said of the teachings that follow from this: God exists; he provides for all; he is all-powerful; in relation to his decree things go well with the pious but badly with the wicked; our salvation depends only on his grace. Chapter 13's heading encapsulates Spinoza's view of the Bible: "That Scripture teaches only the simplest matters, that it aims only at obedience, and teaches nothing about the divine Nature, except what we can imitate by a certain manner of living" (*CWS* 2:257). Faith is "thinking such things about God that if you had no knowledge of them, obedience to God would be destroyed, whereas if you are obedient to God, you necessarily have these thoughts" (*CWS* 2:266).

Spinoza articulates the doctrines of universal faith as follows (*CWS* 2:268–69):

1. God exists.
2. He is unique.
3. He is omnipresent.
4. He has the supreme right and dominion over all things.[26]
5. Worship of him consists in justice and loving-kindness.
6. Everyone who obeys God in this way is saved.
7. God pardons the sins of those who repent.

Spinoza is adamant that there is no relationships between faith/theology and philosophy. Clerics and theologians delight in speaking of the mysteries of faith, which yield knowledge unavailable to reason, thereby substituting revelation for the natural light of reason as our appropriate guide in life. For Spinoza, Scripture should not be the handmaid of reason, nor reason the handmaid of theology.

Spinoza rejects the approaches of both Maimonides, who submits Scripture to reason, and that of R. Judah Alfakhar, who submits reason to Scripture:

> I can find no words to express my amazement that people want to make reason, [God's] greatest gift, a divine light, subordinate to dead letters—which men's wicked conduct could have corrupted—that it should be thought no crime to speak unworthily against the mind, the true original text of God's word, and to maintain that it is corrupt, blind, and lost, but that it should be considered the greatest crime to think such things about the letter, the image of God's word. (*CWS* 2:275)[27]

26. Under this point, Spinoza (*CWS* 2:269) asserts that God "acts only according to his absolute good pleasure and special grace." Once again, the language leads one to think he affirms God as a personal agent, which he does not.

27. Levinson, *"The Right Chorale,"* 13, discerns here a positive and insightful move by Spinoza.

For Spinoza, theology and philosophy are entirely separate domains of knowledge and "each can maintain control of its own domain with the utmost harmony" (*CWS* 2:275). The domain of reason is truth and wisdom; that of theology is obedience and piety. Theology may determine the doctrines of faith *only* insofar as is sufficient for obedience. How they are to be understood is left to reason and philosophy! In terms of truths from theology that reason cannot learn by itself, Spinoza finds this only the case in relation to the truth that men are saved by obedience. Spinoza is dismissive of the doctrine of the internal testimony of the Spirit, maintaining that really the Holy Spirit is nothing but a satisfaction that arises in the mind from good actions. "God's affirmations and denials always involve eternal necessity *or* truth" (*CWS* 2:131).

Spinoza's Reading of the Sinai Event

Spinoza is recognized for having gone beyond Ibn Ezra and his contemporary biblical critics in the depth of his analysis of the HB/OT and its contradictions and errors. In this section, we will take a closer look at his reading of the exodus/Sinai event.

Strauss notes that the *TTP* is full of contradictions, and this is true also of Spinoza's treatment of Moses and Sinai. Whereas, with the prophets, Spinoza thinks that their revelation came indirectly by visions and dreams, with Moses he acknowledges that God spoke directly to him. He refers to Exod 25:22 where YHWH says to Moses, "There I will meet you, and from above the mercy-seat, from between the two cherubim that are on the ark of the covenant, I will deliver to you all my commands for the Israelites" (NRSV), and comments that "this indeed shows that God used a true voice, since Moses used to find God there, available to speak to him, whenever he wanted to" (*CWS* 2:79). Like Maimonides, Spinoza here seems to accept that while God himself does not speak because he cannot, he creates a voice that speaks for him. Spinoza states that it was through a true voice that God revealed his laws for the Israelites to Moses. Indeed, he comments that in the HB/OT this was "the only true voice" (*CWS* 2:79).

When it comes to the Decalogue, Spinoza notes that some—Maimonides would be an example—think that the Israelites did not hear God's voice but only a noise. The two versions of the Decalogue (Exod 20; Deut 5) suggest to Spinoza that the words contain only the meaning and not God's actual voice, but from Deut 5:4 Spinoza argues that God truly created a voice by which he himself revealed the Decalogue (*CWS* 2:80–81). However, he notes that the Decalogue is only a law for the Israelites (*CWS* 2:132). So far, so good. It would appear that Spinoza does believe, with Maimonides, that through creating a voice God does indeed speak to Moses and to the Israelites.

However, for Spinoza revelation by words or visions relates to human *imagination* rather than the direct mental grasp of truth, which Spinoza privileges epistemologically. Having acknowledged that God creates a voice, Spinoza moves on to say that this does not solve the problem of revelation since it is difficult to see how some created thing (the voice), which is dependent on God in the same way as any other thing, could articulate the essence of God. In this way, what Spinoza appears to give with one hand, he withdraws with the other. God's speaking to Moses is reduced to human imagination, in which Spinoza has little confidence. It is only with Christ that God communicates directly: "So, if Moses spoke with God face to face, as a man usually does with a companion (i.e., by means of their two bodies), Christ, indeed, communicated with God mind to mind" (*CWS* 2:85).

Spinoza explores Moses's doctrine of God. Moses views God as a being who exists, who has always existed, and who will always exist. In terms of the nature of God, Moses knows nothing except that God is compassionate, kind, and jealous. He is unique and cannot be expressed by any image or seen.[28] He is singularly powerful. God brought this visible world into order from chaos[29] and put seeds in nature. He chose the Hebrew nation and their land but left the other nations to other gods. He dwells in the heavens. Moses did not clearly perceive that God was omniscient. Spinoza deduces this from the fact that God told him that the Israelites would obey him, but he did not believe God (Exod 3:18; 4:1). Thus, God was revealed to him as indifferent and unaware of future human actions.

Again, Spinoza is confusing. One might be led to think that Moses learned all this from his encounter with YHWH. However, for Spinoza, this is the kind of view of God Moses *already held,* and Moses's revelations are accommodated to his views! "If we attend now to Moses' revelations, we find that they were accommodated to those opinions. For because he believed that God's nature admits of all the conditions we have mentioned, compas-

---

28. But see *CWS* 2:106, where Spinoza argues from Exod 33 that Moses thought God was visible.

29. Spinoza thus reads Gen 1 as denying *creatio ex nihilo.* God creates out of preexisting chaos.

sion, kindness, etc., God was revealed to him according to this opinion and under these attributes" (*CWS* 2:105–6).

As we will see when we come to our analysis of the Sinai narrative, a central motif is that of ascent and descent. YHWH descends on the mountain and Moses ascends and descends. Spinoza relates this to the imagination of Moses. It is because Moses thought that God lived in the heavens above that God is depicted as descending on Mt. Sinai. For Spinoza, "This would not have been necessary at all, if he could with equal ease imagine God to be everywhere" (*CWS* 2:106). By implication, Spinoza is saying that Moses did not really know God, which would come through his mind rather than through encounter with YHWH, or true blessedness. This is also true of Israel. When the HB/OT describes Israel's election, her closeness to God and that God has made himself known only to them among the nations, "it speaks only according to the power of understanding of people who, as we have shown . . . and as Moses himself witnesses (Deuteronomy 9:6–7), did not know true blessedness" (*CWS* 2:111).

And so too it goes with the exodus and the formation of Israel into God's covenant people. Spinoza depicts the slaves released from Egypt as radically free. They were free to form themselves into whatever group they wanted to be. They could enact whatever laws they wished, and they could occupy whatever land they chose and form whatever sort of state they saw as most desirable. However, they were weak and unsophisticated, and, in order to survive, sovereignty had to remain in one leader, namely Moses. It was only in order to secure the cohesion of the liberated slaves into a nation that Moses "introduced" religion among them. "That's why Moses, by divine power and command, introduced religion into the Republic, so that people would do their duty not so much from fear as from devotion" (*CWS* 2:147).[30] Moses, according to Spinoza, perceived by "revelation" how Israel could best be united in a certain part of the world (*CWS* 2:132). Whatever Spinoza means by "revelation" in this context, he asserts that Moses perceived the commands not as eternal laws but as precepts and institutions for Israel: "That's why he imagined God as a ruler, a lawgiver, a king, as compassionate, just, etc., when all these things are attributes only of human nature, and ought to be removed entirely from the divine nature" (*CWS* 2:133). Spinoza's dismissal of the ceremonial law of the HB/OT is in line with Moses's introduction of religion among the Israelites as

30. Note the contradiction in this sentence. It was by "divine power and command" that Moses "introduced" religion among the Israelites.

mere expediency. Such laws were introduced by Moses only to procure the subjugation of the Israelites.

We noted above Spinoza's tendency to use orthodox language, but then to fill it with very different content. His treatment of Moses and Sinai is a good example of this. We know from his *Ethics* that Spinoza does not believe that God speaks or acts in history, and this lurks behind his apparent resorting to affirming that God created a voice, spoke face to face with Moses, gave laws for the Israelites as his chosen people, and so on. The orthodox language serves merely to obscure the radicality of Spinoza's views. Historical revelation is reduced to human imagination, which cannot, from Spinoza's perspective, be trusted when it comes to ascertaining truth. Revelation is said to be "accommodated" to such imagination, but Spinoza never clarifies how this is so and by whom. In fact, Spinoza argues that the historical narratives of the exodus and Sinai are merely projections of the imagination with the political goal in mind of securing the unity of the Israelites as a society.

Spinoza and Modern Biblical Interpretation

Nadler argues that "More than anyone else, Spinoza, with his willingness to go wherever the textual and historical evidence led, regardless of religious ramifications, ushered in modern biblical source scholarship."[31] Strauss notes that "Spinoza's Bible science is first of all a fact in the history of the sciences. Spinoza has the undisputed merit of having established Bible science as a science 'free of presuppositions.'"[32] While it is true that Spinoza is a major figure in the emergence of modern historical criticism of the Bible, portraying him heroically as willing to go wherever the evidence leads perpetuates a myth that has accompanied historical criticism throughout far too much of its history, namely, that historical criticism of the Bible is simply the objective, neutral analysis of the Bible.

Although Spinoza maintains that "Scripture leaves reason absolutely free" (*CWS* 2:72) and argues that reason should not be submitted to Scripture, nor vice versa, in practice his philosophy determines the understanding of scriptural ideas, as we saw again and again above. By the help or guidance of God, for example, Spinoza understands the fixed order of nature and, since no one can do anything except by this order, "it follows that no one

---

31. Nadler, *A Book Forged*, 107.
32. Strauss, "On the Bible Science of Spinoza," 173.

chooses any manner of living for himself, or does anything, except by the special calling of God, who has chosen him before others for this work, or this manner of living" (*CWS* 2:113).

Spinoza's hermeneutic is an important early opponent of the orthodox model that privileged religious or doctrinal truth. In practice, he reverses this relationship, making the meaning of Scripture accountable to the bar of critical reason. Far from Spinoza being willing to go wherever the evidence leads him, when it comes to Scripture the content is funneled through the grid of his philosophy and the results are entirely predictable. One simply could not come to Spinoza's conclusions about the exodus-Sinai event without firstly buying into his philosophical presuppositions. Popkin asserts that "the combination of La Peyrère's Biblical criticism and Spinoza's naturalistic metaphysic eliminated the supernatural dimension and transformed religious history into an effect of human fear and superstition."[33] Hahn and Wiker note of Spinoza's equation of God with Nature that "this identity of human mathematical reason and being meant that reason is indeed the Word of God, rather than Scripture or Christ himself."[34] They rightly note that in the following centuries of critical, biblical scholarship, the philosophies informing critical scholarship change, from Spinoza, to Locke, to Hegel, to Marx, to Heidegger, and so on. However, "the authority of exegesis will reside, not in the political sovereign, but in the enlightened philosophy that informs exegesis."[35] They conclude rightly that, "as strange as it may sound to professional biblical scholars in academia, the fundamental issue deciding the caliber of Spinoza's biblical hermeneutics (and hence what he has bequeathed to his progeny as one of the fathers of modern biblical criticism) is the accuracy of Spinoza's account of reason and nature."[36]

Although a rationalist and a pantheistic[37] monist, Spinoza's historical emphasis anticipates many elements of the historical critical method of bib-

33. Richard Popkin, "Spinoza and La Peyrère," in *Spinoza: New Perspectives*, ed. Robert Shahan and J. I. Biro (Norman, OK: University of Oklahoma Press, 1978), 177–95, 190.

34. Hahn and Wicker, *Politicizing the Bible*, 350.

35. Hahn and Wicker, *Politicizing the Bible*, 390.

36. Hahn and Wicker, *Politicizing the Bible*, 392.

37. The word "pantheism" only came into substantive use in the early eighteenth century. See Benjamin Lazier, *God Interrupted: Heresy and the Imagination between the World Wars* (Princeton and Oxford: Princeton University Press, 2008), 73–74. It was coined by the Dutch theologian J. de la Faye in debate with John Toland. It came into its own at the end of the eighteenth century in the debates about Spinoza's philosophy.

lical interpretation that would develop in nineteenth-century Germany.[38] Already at the end of the seventeenth century Spinoza is stressing the need to re-evaluate traditional authors of biblical books and their contexts of origin. For example, he rejects Mosaic authorship of the Pentateuch and argues that Ezra is the author of the larger narrative of the history of the Jews from their beginning down to the destruction of Jerusalem.[39] Levinson says of Spinoza's identification of contradictions and of post-Mosaic elements in the Pentateuch that, "for this reason, Spinoza's biblical analysis in the first fifteen chapters of the *Theologico-Political Tractatus* is correctly understood to be crucial for the later, more systematic elaboration of the historical-critical method."[40] Spinoza insists that these types of historical questions are crucial for correct understanding of the HB/OT. In the nineteenth century, historical criticism took off in Germany in particular, and by the early twentieth century was dominant throughout Europe and America. If Spinoza's work marked an important starting point it was soon left behind as detailed work on the Bible emerged. As we will see below, the same cannot be said of his philosophical and theological legacy. Thus, we should not expect to, and do not, find detailed engagement with Spinoza among historical critics of the Bible.[41] It must also be noted that Julius Wellhausen, the major figure in the development of historical criticism of the HB/OT, argued that such biblical criticism is never preceded by philosophy, but only followed by it.[42] This view, which remains deeply entrenched among biblical scholars to this

38. See J. S. Preus, "A Hidden Opponent in Spinoza's Tractatus," *HTR* 88/3 (1995): 361–88, for a useful analysis of the difference between Meyer's philosophical hermeneutic and Spinoza's historical one. Preus comments that "Spinoza's definitive substitution of history for philosophy as the categorial matrix for biblical interpretation makes the *Treatise* paradigmatic in the sense of an exemplary work that systematically formulates a new historical, critical, and comparative approach to the Bible" (367).

39. At an elementary level, Spinoza in this way anticipates debates such as that over the Deuteronomistic History.

40. Levinson, *"The Right Chorale,"* 12.

41. Note, however, Levinson's positive engagement with Spinoza (in *"The Right Chorale,"* 4, 11–15), whom he finds helpful in responding to Sternberg's *The Poetics of Biblical Narrative*. Levinson writes, "I found myself returning to Spinoza as a model for breaking free of the methodological dualism" of Sternberg (4).

42. Craig G. Bartholomew, "Philosophy, Theology and the Crisis in Biblical Interpretation," in *Renewing Biblical Interpretation*, ed. Craig G. Bartholomew, Colin Greene, and Karl Möller (Grand Rapids: Zondervan, 2000), 1–39.

day, erased from view the powerful philosophical currents shaping historical criticism, as we have seen with Spinoza.

Wellhausen refers to Spinoza four times in his hugely influential *Prolegomena to the History of Israel*. Early on he notes that since the days of Peyrère and Spinoza, scholars have acknowledged the complex character of the Pentateuch, thereby situating his work in this tradition.[43] Wellhausen moves on to discuss the source criticism of the Pentateuch, and in his discussion of J he refers to the anachronistic statements that already drew the attention of Ibn Ezra and Spinoza (Gen 12:6; 36:31; Num 12:6–7; Deut 24:10).

Remarkably, Wellhausen concludes his *Prolegomena* with a long and extremely disturbing quote from Spinoza's *TTP*. Wellhausen quotes a passage that comes toward the end of chapter 3 of *TTP* on "The Chosen People."[44] Having argued in this chapter that there is nothing special or distinctive about Israel's election, Spinoza reflects on the fact that the Jews have survived for so many years, scattered among the nations and without a state of their own. Spinoza finds this survival nothing extraordinary and notes that "after they separated themselves so from all the nations that they have drawn the hatred of all men against themselves, not only by having external customs contrary to the customs of the other nations, but also by the sign of circumcision, which they maintain most scrupulously. Moreover, experience has already taught that the hatred of the Nations has done much to preserve them" (*CWS* 2:124). The final two sentences in Wellhausen's *Prolegomena* follow his extended quote from Spinoza: "The persistency of the race may of course prove a harder thing to overcome than Spinoza has supposed; but nevertheless he will be found to have spoken truly in declaring that the so-called emancipation of the Jews must inevitably lead to the extinction of Judaism wherever the process is extended beyond the political to the social sphere. For the accomplishment of this centuries may be required."[45] In the light of anti-Semitism and the terrible form it took in the twentieth century it is simply impossible to read such statements and still maintain that Spinoza's—and Wellhausen's—approaches are neutral and scientific.

43. Julius Wellhausen, *Prolegomena to the History of Israel*, Cambridge Library Collection (Cambridge: Cambridge University Press, 2013), 6.

44. Wellhausen, *Prolegomena to the History of Israel*, 548, quotes from Spinoza, *CWS* 2:124: "It's true also . . . to eternity." Wellhausen refers to this extended quote as from chapter 4 of *TTP*, but it comes from the end of chapter 3.

45. Wellhausen, *Prolegomena*, 548.

Spinoza in Philosophy and Theology

To Spinoza's credit, it is refreshing to note that he was well aware that a critical issue in the debate over the interpretation of Scripture is that of the relationship between faith and reason, theology and philosophy. It is rare to find biblical scholars addressing this issue nowadays, but it is a foundational issue that shapes the direction any biblical hermeneutic takes.

The history of the reception of Spinoza's work is complex. Spinoza experienced a renaissance at the start of the nineteenth century, and then another spectacular revival between the two World Wars, among Jews, Christians, and secularists.[46] Amidst this renaissance, the Jewish philosopher Leo Strauss sided with Barth and Rosenzweig against Spinoza, but returned to him on several occasions and came to defend a view of nature as autonomous. Strauss's relationship with Spinoza is complex. In his 1924 essay, he defends Spinoza against the attacks on him made by the Jewish philosopher Herman Cohen.[47] Julius Guttman, a dedicated follower of Cohen and academic director of the Akademie für die Wissenschaft des Judentums, offered Strauss a fellowship to pursue his research on Spinoza further. A result is Strauss's 1926 essay, "On the Bible Science of Spinoza and His Precursors."[48]

Contra Cohen, Strauss argues that Spinoza did not turn against Judaism but "against revealed religion in all its forms" (173). Strauss maintains that Spinoza established historical critical biblical studies as a discipline free of presuppositions. For Strauss the deeper significance of Spinoza's achievement in this respect is that the Bible is now approached as a literary document like any other and must be studied scientifically like any other. "Therefore, the constitution of Bible science is preceded by the justification of its presupposition, that is, the critique of the opposite presupposition made by revealed religion and the critique of revealed religion in general. . . . It is an important moment in the universal movement called the Enlightenment's critique of religion" (174).

Strauss argues that Spinoza's *TTP* is firstly a critique of Maimonides, and secondly a critique of Calvinist orthodoxy. In relation to the first, Strauss argues that "Spinoza's critique of the possibility of revelation follows from the proposition that in God intellect and will are one and the same. This presupposition is equivalent to a denial of creation, of the giving of the Law,

46. The theme of Lazier, *God Interrupted*.
47. Strauss, *The Early Writings*, 140–72.
48. Strauss, *The Early Writings*, 173–200. Hereafter, page references to this work are given in parentheses in the text.

and of miracles" (176). Maimonides seeks to bring theory and Scripture together; Spinoza opens the gap between them. Both, however, believe in the supremacy of theory, but Spinoza such that divine and human freedom are denied. Maimonides presupposes Scripture to be true. For Spinoza it should not be presupposed to be true.

For Strauss, the question for Maimonides and for Spinoza is "what an *interest* in revelation really means" (180) if theory is the highest good. According to Strauss, "it can be shown to be typical of the theory that arises in the context of revealed religion that it calls into question the legitimacy in principle of unaided human thought, while it also attempts to secure its own theory, determined even in its contents by the tradition of revealed religion, against the unbelieving theory of the philosophers" (181). Strauss maintains that the heart of the opposition between Spinoza and revealed religion can be located in the antithesis of belief in the sufficiency of human thought and belief in its insufficiency. "All objective arguments against the doctrines of revealed religion presuppose the conviction that human thought, following its own directives, is competent and qualified to judge revelation" (182).

In his later work on Spinoza, Strauss argues that God's revealing himself is known not just through tradition but through present experience (146).[49] Strauss points out that Spinoza has not defeated a moderate approach to biblical criticism—nowadays commonplace—which rests on the irrefutable premise that God may exist. If this is conceded, then miracles and revelations are indeed possible. For Strauss, genuine refutation of orthodox belief in revelation would require showing that our world and life are perfectly intelligible without the assumption of a mysterious God. Such a proof would need to demonstrate the success of "the philosophical system." It would need to show that humankind is theoretically and practically the master of the world and of this life. "Spinoza's *Ethics* attempts to be the system, but it does not succeed" (170). To concede that revelation is possible means granting that philosophy is not necessarily, or evidently, the right way of life. "Hence the antagonism between Spinoza and Judaism, between unbelief and belief, is ultimately not theoretical, but moral" (171).

Spinoza discerns many contradictions in the Bible, but, as Strauss points out "Spinoza, who regarded the Bible as a book rich in contradictions, has indicated this view in a book that itself abounds in contradictions" (206). An example of this is Spinoza's refutation and assumption of the unity of the Bible.

---

49. In this he is akin to William P. Alston, *Perceiving God: The Epistemology of Religious Experience* (Ithaca, NY: Cornell University Press, 1991).

In an engagement with Simon Dubnow's *World History of the Jewish People,* in which Dubnow seeks to secularize the history of the Jews and to exclude all theological doctrines, Strauss acknowledges the challenges that any notion of verbal inspiration encounters, but asserts that, "still, the central difficulty remains that Scripture speaks unequivocally, adamantly, and compellingly of God's agency: God loves, chooses, rewards, punishes, he is Ruler of the world, also, and especially of nature" (133). When it encounters this, science reduces God's agency to psychology so that God becomes an object of study.

It is intriguing that a scholar of Strauss's stature returned again and again to his engagement with Spinoza. Lazier observes of this interwar period that the "crisis in relations among men, it turns out, had much to do with the innovations in the way Europeans thought about God."[50] Lazier notes that a renewed theological appropriation of Spinoza had to wait for Schleiermacher, who praised Spinoza:

Respectfully offer up with me a lock of hair to the manes of the holy rejected Spinoza! The high world spirit permeated him, the infinite was his beginning and end, the universe his only and eternal love; in holy innocence and deep humility he was reflected in the eternal world and saw how he too was its most lovable mirror; he was full of religion and full of holy spirit; for this reason, he also stands there alone and un-equaled, master in his art but elevated above the profane guild, without disciples and without rights of citizenship.[51]

However, the influence of Spinoza on Schleiermacher is by no means as clear-cut as this suggests. Schleiermacher did wrestle with Spinoza's thought throughout much of his adult life but there are no references to Spinoza's writings in his *Reden,* and no mention of Spinoza in his *Glaubenslehre.* In her *The Living God: Schleiermacher's Theological Appropriation of Spinoza,* Julia Lamm examines the relationship in detail and concludes that Schleiermacher is not a pantheist, and that while he is influenced by Spinoza this influence comes in a post-Kantian way.[52]

50. Lazier, *God Interrupted,* 5.

51. Friedrich Schleiermacher, *On Religion: Speeches to its Cultured Despisers,* trans. and ed. Richard Crouter, Cambridge Texts in the History of Philosophy (Cambridge: Cambridge University Press, 1988, 1996), 24.

52. Julia A. Lamm, *The Living God: Schleiermacher's Theological Appropriation of Spinoza* (University Park: Pennsylvania State University Press, 1996).

Lenn Goodman is one of the major Jewish philosophers of our day.[53] In a major essay on Spinoza and Jewish philosophy, Goodman takes a diametrically opposed position to that of Strauss: "I will state boldly that if Jewish philosophers, speaking as such, hope once again to face the great questions of cosmology and metaphysics, ethical, social and political philosophy, epistemology and philosophy of mind, they will find no more powerful ally—and no more penetrating and demanding interlocutor—than Spinoza."[54] We cannot here engage with Goodman's essay in detail. However, it does provide a rigorous foil through which to articulate the central questions for an adequate philosophy and theology of divine action. Goodman starts off with a list of the many key areas in philosophy that Spinoza addresses in his *Ethics* and declares that "what I aim to show is that the core theses of Spinoza's *Ethics* address the central conundrums of Western philosophy with a rigor whose yield is a system of ideas deeply consonant with the core themes of Mosaic thinking and highly fruitful for future philosophical work that weighs the strengths of that tradition."[55]

Goodman affirms Spinoza's commitment to the natural light: "monism on the upper storeys opens out onto (and rests upon) a naturalistic scientific enterprise and an integrated ethical program."[56] Likewise, Goodman affirms Spinoza's doctrine of substance. It fits well with the Mosaic perspective with its concern to see all of creation as unified within God, and it avoids the dangers of idealism. Goodman concurs with Spinoza's privileging of theory since the most complete elaboration of the idea of monotheism will assume a normative as opposed to a narrative form.

When it comes to divine action, Goodman acknowledges that "Spinoza's God does not perform miracles, answer prayers by intervening from above, or single us out for arbitrary blessings. So it will be natural to identify that God with the God of the philosophers and not what is often called the God of faith. But faith, despite the burdens placed on it, is not a way of knowing but an attitude of hope, expectation, trust, accommodation. It

---

53. I have been privileged to get to know Lenn in our times together as Senior Fellows of the Herzl Institute in Jerusalem.

54. Lenn E. Goodman, "What Does Spinoza's Ethics Contribute to Jewish Philosophy?," in *Jewish Themes in Spinoza's Philosophy*, ed. Heidi M. Ravven and Lenn E. Goodman (Albany: State University of New York Press, 2002), 20. The book is dedicated to lovers of Spinoza everywhere!

55. Goodman, "Spinoza's Ethics," 21.

56. Goodman, "Spinoza's Ethics," 24.

cannot vindicate the reality of a personal God."[57] For Goodman, the biblical claims about *God acting in history* need to be situated within a Spinozean concept of God as the "All-inclusive," who built into the creation the plan that Israel would be elected, that the Torah would be inspired, and that the laws would be practiced. With Spinoza, Goodman affirms that reason shows us that our supreme goal is intellectual. It is the search for a life guided by reason and directed toward the intellectual love of God. Such goals are best pursued in community.

Goodman's reading of Spinoza enables us to articulate key questions for our project. He refers to Mosaic themes and the Mosaic orbit and argues that these are compatible with Spinoza's philosophy. As we will see in the next chapter, in a similar way Wilhelm de Wette and John Rogerson argue that Christian faith implies certain philosophical views. There may be an inevitable circularity to these issues, but we need to ask, As a whole are these indeed the sort of philosophical views implicit in the Torah? At a surface level it would appear, with Strauss, that they are certainly not, but this is surely an area for investigation.

More specifically, is it true that the Torah commits us to monism in our view of God that biblically and logically leads us to a naturalistic view of the scientific enterprise and to an integrated ethics, akin to that of Spinoza? Does Torah lead us to Spinoza's view of reason? Is the love of God supremely intellectual? Is historical revelation adequately accounted for by saying it was built into the plan of creation so that Spinoza's determinism remains intact? Is the retention of a First Cause sufficient compensation for letting go of the doctrine of creation?

Conclusion

As a father of modern biblical criticism, Spinoza's philosophy reveals clearly the extent to which his reading of the Bible was shaped again and again by his philosophical, theological, and political commitments, and thus clearly shows us that Barr and others are quite wrong when they assert that historical criticism is relatively unaffected by philosophy. Similarly, our examination of Spinoza demonstrates that we cannot with Barton bracket off theology from biblical criticism when strong views of God are already present. We cannot simply separate off Spinoza's biblical conclusions as though

57. Goodman, "Spinoza's Ethics," 31.

they are unrelated to his philosophy and his view of God, but will need, instead, to begin by assessing his philosophy and theology and where we stand in relation to it, *before* assessing the genuine insights in his approach to Scripture. This is not to assert that his biblical conclusions are all wrong, but it is to insist that they are of a piece with his broader hermeneutic and cannot simply be extracted as neutral facts.

CHAPTER 6

Immanuel Kant and the Problematizing
of Divine Action

For the final purpose of even the reading of these holy books, or the investigation of their content, is to make better human beings; whereas their historical element, which contributes nothing to this end, is something in itself quite indifferent, and one can do with it what one wills.— (Historical faith is "dead, being alone,"[1] i.e. of itself, considered as a declaration, contains nothing, nor does it lead to anything that would have a moral value for us.)

—Immanuel Kant[2]

In Kant's universal-human philosophy of religion, all historical or quasi-historical elements are omitted . . . Above all, one basic element is omitted: the covenant between a God and his people, that is, the exceptional relationship between Yahweh and Israel.

—Otfried Höffe[3]

In modern theology by the time of Albrecht Ritschl (1822–89)—himself deeply influenced by Kant—and his followers, Immanuel Kant (1724–1804) was already widely viewed as *the* Protestant philosopher because of his work on ethics and his critique of metaphysics. Kant has influenced modern theology in myriad ways, a subject explored by many writers.[4] For example, the leading

1. The reference is to James 2:17.
2. *RWBMR*, 119. For similar statements see Kant, *TCTF*, 242.
3. Otfried Höffe, "Holy Scripture within the Boundaries of Mere Reason: Kant's Reflections," in *Kant's Religion within the Boundaries of Mere Reason*, ed. Gordon Michalson (Cambridge: Cambridge University Press, 2014), 24.
4. Helmut Thielicke, *Modern Faith and Thought*, trans. Geoffrey W. Bromiley

Ritschlian theologian, Wilhelm Herrmann (1846–1922)[5] taught both Barth and Bultmann so that, as Thielicke notes, "we can understand the two dominant schools of our own century only against the background of Ritschlian thought and in reaction to this background."[6] Liberal theology and the cultural Protestantism so evident at the beginning of the twentieth century, and regularly recurring up to and including our own day, goes back significantly to Ritschl.

Kant and Sinai

In Chapter 2 we noted the ways in which Sommer connects Rosenzweig's view of Scripture with Kant, as part of his case for arguing that God did not speak at Sinai. In this chapter our concern is with Kant's view of divine agency and its implications for biblical interpretation, and in particular for special divine action (SDA) and the Sinai narrative. In terms of our project it is notable, as per the quote above, that Kant would single out for attention the idea of a covenant between a God and a people—Sinai—as of no value when it comes to pure, that is, rational, religion. In part 3 of his *Religion*

(Grand Rapids: Eerdmans, 1990), 324–61; Karl Barth, *Protestant Theology in the Nineteenth Century*, trans. Brian Cozens and John Bowden (Grand Rapids: Eerdmans, 2002), 252–98; Bruce L. McCormack, *Karl Barth's Critically Realistic Dialectical Theology: Its Genesis and Development, 1909–1936* (Oxford: Clarendon, 1996); D. Paul La Montaigne, *Barth and Rationality: Critical Realism in Theology* (Eugene, OR: Cascade, 2012), 79–112; Christopher J. Insole, *Kant and the Creation of Freedom: A Theological Problem* (Grand Rapids: Eerdmans, 2016); etc.

5. On Herrmann see Thielicke, *Modern Faith and Thought*, 344–61.

6. Thielicke, *Modern Faith and Thought*, 324. On Ritschl and Kant see Thielicke, *Modern Faith and Thought*, 324–44. Cf. Kenneth Oakes, *Karl Barth on Theology and Philosophy* (Oxford: Oxford University Press, 2012); John Milbank, "The Theological Critique of Philosophy in Hamann and Jacobi," in *Radical Orthodoxy*, ed. John Milbank, Catherine Pickstock, and Graham Ward (London: Routledge, 1999), 21–37. Milbank says of the depth behind things that "there are only two possible attitudes to this depth: for the first, like Kant, we distinguish what is clear from what is hidden: but then the depth is an abyss, and what appears, as only apparent, will equally induce vertigo. This is why critical philosophy, the attitude of pure reason itself, is also the stance of nihilism. The twist added by postmodernism is simply that appearances themselves cannot be made clearly present, but are in ceaseless flux. The second possibility is that we trust the depth, and appearance as the gift of depth, and history as the restoration of the loss of this depth in Christ" (32).

within the Bounds of Mere Reason, in which he discusses the idea of a moral commonwealth, and in which he connects his ideal moral community with that of the kingdom of God and of the church, Kant roundly rejects any possibility of identifying the start of such a universal moral community with the Israel of the HB/OT. Such a beginning can only be located in the Christian church. For Kant, "the *Jewish* faith stands in absolutely no essential connection, i.e. in no unity of concepts, with the ecclesiastical faith whose history we want to consider, even though it preceded it and provided the physical occasion for the founding of this church (Christianity)" (*RWBMR*, 130).[7]

According to Kant, "as originally established" Israel was merely a collection of laws supporting a political state; any moral elements were only later additions and are not part of the essence of Judaism. Israel was meant to be a purely secular state; its status as a theocracy only involved God as a sort of secular ruler with no claims upon the conscience of the individuals. Kant identifies three proofs that the constitution of Israel was never meant to be religious:

1. Its laws and commands deal only with external actions of the sort that any political state could uphold. "For a God who wills only obedience to commands for which absolutely no improvement of moral disposition is required cannot truly be that moral being whose concept we find necessary for a religion" (*RWBMR*, 131–32).
2. The rewards and punishments envisaged by Israel all relate to this world. Israel lacks a sense of the future and of future rewards and punishments that is central to pure religion.
3. Israel excluded all other nations from its community, maintaining that it was a nation specially chosen by God. Thus it lacks the universality essential to pure religion. We should not, according to Kant, place much weight on Israel's monotheism since polytheism tends similarly in this direction and is in fact much closer to monotheism than is often recognized.

For Kant, Christianity is radically different to Judaism; it is a "total abandonment of the Judaism in which it originated, grounded on an entirely new principle" that "effected a total revolution in doctrines of faith" (*RWBMR*, 132). For Kant, the NT language of the kingdom of God assumes its proper

7. For a far more positive Kantian reading of Judaism see Ronald M. Green, *Religious Reason: The Rational and Moral Basis of Religious Belief* (Oxford: Oxford University Press, 1978), 125–58.

symbolic meaning when interpreted through the grid of his doctrine of pure moral religion. His castigation of Israel and the HB/OT is indeed disturbing, as is his rejection of YHWH as a candidate for the moral being pure religion requires, but it should be noted that he similarly rejects the idea of the kingdom of God as related to the kingdom of the Messiah. Indeed, he is quite clear that "a kingdom of God is here represented not according to a particular covenant ([it is] not a messianic kingdom) but according to a *moral* one (available to cognition through mere reason). A messianic kingdom . . . would have to draw its proof from history, and therefore it is divided into the *messianic* kingdom of the *old* and of the *new* covenant" (*RWBMR*, 139).

It is intriguing to note that in making his case Kant appeals to historical inquiry; he refers to Israel "as originally established." His reading of Israel and the HB/OT is such a caricature that one wonders how he came up with such a view. There is a debate among scholars about the extent to which Kant knew contemporary theological literature,[8] but either way, for someone who values reason so highly to dismiss Sinai and to caricature it in such a way is remarkable. Notably, there is no close attention to the text of Exodus, no reference to sources to support his reading, so that one is left with the question of how he could arrive at such a reading.

Whatever Kant might say about "as originally established," his reading of the Sinai event results almost entirely from the philosophical lens he brings to Scripture and decidedly not from an analysis of the text and the evidence. Kant's "performative"[9] reading of the HB/OT might appear to be of little consequence; indeed, I am not aware of it receiving much attention by theologians or philosophers. However, it needs to be taken seriously because of its influence on modern biblical criticism.

One of the fathers of modern biblical criticism, Wilhelm de Wette (1780–1849), before and while he studied at Jena University,[10] was deeply

8. Cf. Josef Bohatec, *Die Religionsphilosophie Kants in der "Religion innerhalb der Grenzen der blossen Vernunft"*: *mit besonderer Berücksichtigung ihrer theologisch-dogmatischen Quellen* (Hildesheim: Georg Olms, 1966).

9. I use "performative" here in accordance with the description of Kant's scriptural hermeneutic in Nicholas Wolterstorff, *Divine Discourse: Philosophical Reflections on the Claim That God Speaks* (Cambridge: Cambridge University Press, 1995), 171–82. Wolterstorff notes of Kant's reading of John 1 that "if one doesn't share Kant's convictions about the moral life, then there won't be much value in reading the Prologue of St. John's Gospel in accord with Kant's suggestions" (180).

10. We know from his library that he possessed most of Kant's works. John

influenced by Kant. "However illustrious his Jena teachers were, the greatest initial impact that was made upon de Wette came from the philosophy of Kant. Indeed, for the remainder of his life, de Wette remained, intellectually, a sort of Kantian, and he spent many years of his life trying to reconcile his intellectual acceptance of Kant with his aesthetic and almost mystical instinct for religion."[11] Kant published *The Conflict of Faculties* the year before de Wette entered Jena. Rogerson notes that, "this then, was something of the view of religion that made an immediate impact on de Wette in Jena in 1799–1800."[12] De Wette spent the rest of his life trying to fit his biblical work into that Kantian paradigm, work that continues to influence biblical criticism to this day. Thus, we can justifiably expect that Kant's approach to Scripture influenced de Wette in this respect, and through de Wette the ongoing tradition of biblical criticism. To understand this, we need to explore key elements of the lens Kant brought to Scripture that facilitated such a disparaging reading of Sinai.

Human Autonomy and Kant's Pure Religion

Once David Hume's philosophy, probably introduced to Kant by the extraordinary Christian philosopher Johann Georg Hamann (1730–88),[13] woke Kant from his so-called dogmatic slumber and alerted him to the threat of skepticism for the Enlightenment project, Kant developed his idealistic philosophy as a major attempt to secure the foundations for Enlightenment thought. Central to Kant's idealistic philosophy is human autonomy, particularly in relation to religion. This is crystal clear in his well-known essay *An Answer to the Question: "What Is Enlightenment?"*

For Kant enlightenment involves the development of the human person from self-imposed immaturity to maturity. Such immaturity is self-imposed if its cause is lack of will and courage rather than a lack of understanding. For Kant, at the heart of the Enlightenment is the exhortation *Sapere aude!* (Dare to be wise / to know / to think for yourself!). The call is for one to

Rogerson, *W. M. L. de Wette, Founder of Modern Biblical Criticism: An Intellectual Biography*, JSOTSup 126 (Sheffield: Sheffield Academic Press, 1992), 22.

11. Rogerson, *W. M. L. de Wette*, 27.
12. Rogerson, *W. M. L. de Wette*, 29.
13. John Betz, *After Enlightenment: Hamann as Post-Secular Visionary* (Oxford: Wiley-Blackwell, 2009), 106–7.

develop one's reason and understanding and to bring *everything* to the test of such autonomy, rather than being guided in one's beliefs and views by other authorities. Freedom is a central theme in Kant's philosophy, and he argues that all that is needed for one to attain maturity of this sort is the freedom to use one's reason publicly in relation to *everything*.

In his stress on human autonomy Kant is particularly concerned with religion: "I have portrayed matters of religion as the focal point of enlightenment, i.e. of man's emergence from his self-incurred immaturity. This is firstly because our rulers have no interest in assuming the role of guardians over their subjects so far as the arts and sciences are concerned, and secondly, because *religious immaturity is the most pernicious and dishonourable variety of all.*"[14] In relation to clerics Kant asserts a strange dualism in this essay. A minister of religion must teach his people the doctrines of his church because he was employed for this purpose. Nevertheless, when he addresses the public as a scholar he is free and should reflect rationally on what he teaches, sharing his doubts and misgivings about any aspects of doctrine with which he has rational problems. Kant discerns no problems of conscience in such a position and asserts that "at all events, nothing opposed to the essence of religion is present in such doctrines."[15] Here we see how Kant marginalizes dogmas and confessions. They are extraneous to the essence of religion. But what precisely is this essence? To understand this, we need to explore the contours of Kant's philosophy and take note, in particular, of where religion makes its presence felt.

The Contours of Kant's Philosophy

At the heart of Kant's thought is the problem of objective knowledge. Kant was deeply influenced by rationalism (Christian Wolff, Leibniz) and empiricism (Hume). However, Hume's empiricism lead to what Penelhum calls Hume's "mitigated scepticism."[16] In this respect Kant famously described Hume as waking him from his dogmatic slumber. Kant saw the danger of Hume's skepticism for the Enlightenment project and believed that it could

14. Immanuel Kant, *An Answer to the Question: "What Is Enlightenment?,"* trans. H. B. Nisbet (London: Penguin, 1970, 1991), 9–10. Emphasis added.

15. Kant, *An Answer to the Question*, 5.

16. Terence Penelhum, *David Hume: An Introduction to His Philosophical System* (West Lafayette, IN: Purdue University Press, 1992).

only be solved by overturning Wolff's and Leibniz's rationalist systems, and by finding a way to reconcile rationalism and empiricism. And thus, in his first *Critique* Kant argues that it is in the synthesis of *reason* and *experience* that genuine, objective knowledge is possible. In developing this argument, Kant articulated his *transcendental critique* of reason, which explores how true knowledge is possible.

Kant makes a fundamental distinction between the *phenomenal*—how things appear to us—and the *noumenal*—things as they are in themselves. Because all our knowledge is a combination of reason and experience, we cannot know the noumenal, things as they are in themselves; this is simply not possible. Against the rationalists, we cannot know reality through reason alone; experience is indispensable. Unlike Hume and the empiricists, for whom the mind was akin to a passive receptacle for sense data, for Kant the mind is like a grid that plays a formative role in knowledge acquisition, and it is here that he focused his attention. The mind plays a substantial, active role in the production of knowledge. The phenomenal world is a world of order, unaffected by miracles, subject to the categories of substance and causality. But it is not the whole of reality. There is also the unknowable noumenal realm.

Unlike Wolff, Kant found the three major arguments for the existence of God—the ontological, cosmological, and the teleological—completely unconvincing, earning him the epithet "der Allzermalmende" (the All-destroyer), although he believed that the teleological argument should always be treated with respect. Metaphysics, that which transcends nature and experience, is unknowable since it belongs to the noumenal realm.

Central to Kant's epistemology is the transcendental deduction and the theory that results, transcendental idealism. Transcendental must be distinguished from empirical argument—the former leads to knowledge not of objects but of how knowledge is possible a priori. For Kant the forms of thought that govern understanding fit with the a priori nature of reality. There is a harmony between the abilities of the knowing subject and that which is known. "The world is as we think it, and we think it as it is."[17] "Almost all the major difficulties in the interpretation of Kant depend upon which of these two propositions is emphasized."[18]

Kant argues that our knowledge requires both sensibility and understanding. These are the two sources of our knowledge. The first involves

---

17. Roger Scruton, *Kant*, Past Masters (Oxford: Oxford University Press, 1982), 23.
18. Scruton, *Kant*, 34.

a faculty of intuition, the second of concepts. Judgment requires both. For Kant the theory of innate ideas is correct; indeed, the premise of self-consciousness is the starting point for Kant's philosophy. Kant identifies the fundamental concept of understanding in twelve categories, examples of which are substance and cause. He distinguishes these from two forms of intuition, space and time, which he calls a priori intuitions. For Kant, these are not categories because concepts are general and allow for a plurality of cases. There is only one time and one space, and every sensation is imprinted with temporal, and sometimes spatial, organization.

Kant stresses the unity of the individual consciousness. "The essence of Kant's 'transcendental' method lies in its egocentricity. All the questions that I can ask I must ask from the standpoint that is mine; therefore they must bear the marks of my perspective, which is the perspective of 'possible experience.'"[19] Each category corresponds to a principle, and principles are rules for the reliable use of the categories. They tell us how to think and how the world must be if it is to be understandable. The principles set out synthetic a priori truths for everyday life and scientific observation, that is, of things that may be the objects of *possible* experience.

The word "possible" alerts us to Kant's stress on the limits of knowledge. As Wood observes, "No thinker ever placed greater emphasis on reason's boundaries than Kant; at the same time, none has ever been bolder in asserting its unqualified title to govern our lives."[20] For Kant, there is a logic of illusion: when employed properly, understanding provides objective knowledge. However, it tempts us with the illusion that we can acquire pure knowledge. Hence the title of his *Critique of Pure Reason*. Such attempts transgress the limits of experience. In this context, Kant develops his distinction between the noumenal and the phenomenal. We simply cannot know the thing-in-itself. Judgment is possible with phenomenal objects alone, and not the noumenal. The latter can be used only negatively to demarcate the limits of experience. This limitation arises since all attempts to embrace the noumenal world in a rational system will ultimately fail because they always end in antinomies or unresolvable contradictions. The idea of a First Cause in cosmology is an example of such an illusion. For Kant, all the arguments for the existence of God reduce to the ontological: existence is regarded as

19. Scruton, *Kant*, 47.
20. Allen W. Wood, "Rational Theology, Moral Faith, and Religion," in *The Cambridge Companion to Kant*, ed. Paul Guyer (Cambridge: Cambridge University Press, 1992), 414.

belonging to the concept of God. However, argues Kant, existence is not a predicate. The idea of a First Cause or God is not, however, without value. It can function usefully as a regulative principle when one acts as if it were true: "the ideal of a supreme being is nothing but a regulative principle of reason, which directs us to look upon all connection in the world as if it originated from an all-sufficient and necessary cause."[21]

If Kant stresses the limitations of reason, he also stresses its autonomy. Rationalism is simply far too ambitious, and he compares it to the building of the Tower of Babel.[22] However, the desire for autonomy is quite right. What is needed is a more modest plan. "Kant represents attempts to ground practices of reason as a matter of proceeding with the 'materials' and 'labor power' that our daily practice of defective reasoning has made available to us, and rebuilding these in ways that reduce dangers of collapse or paralysis in thought or action."[23]

Kant proposes that we conceive of reason as a discipline that rejects external authorities and is reflexive, involving self-discipline and is lawlike.[24] Reason's character of rejecting external authority is especially significant for the relationship between reason and faith/religion. Autonomy is a basic characteristic of reason: "reason is indeed the basis of enlightenment, but enlightenment is no more than autonomy in thinking and acting—that is, of thought and action that are lawful yet assume no lawgiver."[25]

Kant's Pure Religion

Kant grew up in a pietist home and attended a pietist school.[26] At school, he developed an abhorrence of piety with its potential for hypocrisy among his fellow students. As a professor, Kant avoided attending any religious services. The influence of pietism remained with him, however, throughout his life. Pietism stressed individualism, the practical side of religion, and was

---

21. Scruton, *Kant*, 69.

22. Onora O'Neill, "Vindicating Reason," in Guyer, ed., *The Cambridge Companion to Kant*, 289–90.

23. O'Neill, "Vindicating Reason," 291–92.

24. See O'Neill, "Vindicating Reason," for a useful discussion of Kant's mature view of reason.

25. O'Neill, "Vindicating Reason," 299.

26. For the major sources for Kant on religion see *RRT*.

wary of the arid dogmatism of the churches. All three elements are clearly present in Kant's philosophy of religion. Another key element in his philosophy of religion was German deism, which appealed to reason and the intellect. Its roots are found in Leibniz, Wolff, and English deism. John Tolland, for example, lived for a time in Germany,[27] and by 1753 English deism was clearly established in Germany. Wolff, whom we know Kant followed for a time, was a dogmatic rationalist. Kant attended the pietist Schultz's lectures in dogmatics late in his studies, and it was the last time he spent for many years on theology.[28]

Religion is made subservient to morality in Kant's scheme, which defines religion as "the cognition of all duties as divine commands."[29] Kant avoided religious ceremonies and regarded creeds as an imposition upon our inner freedom of thought. Morality leads to religion and we can be justified practically in holding religious propositions, but religious beliefs are necessary only insofar as they support our sense of morality. Religious tutelage is rejected by Kant and, as Scruton puts it, "Kant's writings on religion exhibit one of the first attempts at the systematic demystification of theology."[30] Worship of God becomes veneration of morality, and faith is translated into the certainty of practical reason, the use of reason to determine how to act. "The object of esteem is not the Supreme Being, but the supreme attribute

27. John Tolland, *Christianity Not Mysterious: Or, a Treatise Showing That There Is Nothing in the Gospel Contrary to Reason nor Above it: And No Christian Doctrine Can Properly Be Called a Mystery* (London, 1702).

28. Theodore M. Greene, "The Historical Context and Religious Significance of Kant's Religion," in Immanuel Kant, *Religion within the Bounds of Reason Alone*, trans. Theodore M. Greene and Hoyt H. Hudson (New York: Harper and Row, 1960), xxx.

29. See Wood, "Rational Theology, Moral Faith, and Religion," 406–8. The understanding of Kant's view of religion has recently been provocatively reengaged; see Chris L. Firestone and Stephen R. Palmquist, eds., *Kant and the New Philosophy of Religion* (Bloomington: Indiana University Press, 2006); Chris L. Firestone and Nathan Jacobs, *In Defense of Kant's Religion* (Bloomington: Indiana University Press, 2008); Chris L. Firestone and Nathan Jacobs, *Kant and the Question of Theology* (Cambridge: Cambridge University Press, 2017). Even if Firestone and Jacobs are right, as Wolterstorff suggests in his preface, and Kant's *RWBMR* can be read holistically and literally thereby yielding a far more positive view of religion than has normally been concluded, it remains true, as Firestone and Jacobs (*In Defense*, 6) acknowledge, that "defending the internal coherence of *Religion* from an expository vantage point and commending its desirability for Christianity are two entirely different matters."

30. Scruton, *Kant*, 78.

of rationality."[31] In this way Kant's philosophy embodies the transition from providence to progress.[32]

Richard Kroner has argued that the ethical and religious views of Kant are a better source for accessing his *Weltanschauung* (worldview) than focusing on his epistemology.[33] It is in his *Critique of Practical Reason* that Kant develops his ethics and, according to Kroner, "the whole Kantian Weltanschauung centers, not around the will in general, but around the morally good will or around the individual will which subjects itself to the moral law. Kant, moreover, does not regard this moral will as the hidden core, the substance of the world; he absolutely renounces the task of building up a scientific philosophy of the supersensible world out of the facts of moral life. He merely states that moral life points to the supersensible world."[34]

At the heart of Kant's worldview Kroner discerns ethical voluntarism. The moral will, unlike the faculty of understanding, aims at duty, not truth. One's moral experience involves the immediate intuition of the value and importance of morality. The moral law differs from the laws of nature in that it defines what *ought* to be, and not what is:

- The moral law is dictated to each individual by *one's own moral reason*. "Thus man, as a moral agent, is autonomous and his reason is self-legislative. Man is under no absolute obligation to obey the laws of another, not even the laws of God because they are God's laws. Man's own conscience is the highest moral tribunal."[35]
- The moral law is necessarily universally binding upon all rational beings, finite *and infinite*.
- The moral law can only be known a priori and cannot be derived from experience.

At the heart of the moral law is a commitment to impartial justice and a commitment to treat each person as an end in him- or herself. Those who

31. Scruton, *Kant*, 78.
32. See David Lyon, *Postmodernity*, Concepts in the Social Sciences (Buckingham: Open University Press, 1994), 5, for the description of modernity as a move from providence to progress.
33. Richard Kroner, *Kant's Weltanschauung* (Chicago: University of Chicago Press, 1956), 1.
34. Kroner, *Kant's Weltanschauung*, 7.
35. Greene, "The Historical Context," liii.

follow this law constitute the citizens of a kingdom of ends. This intuition of the moral law is as inexplicable as one's capacity for sensuous experience. The prime condition for the moral law to function is freedom. However, and here Kant ran into a problem, the phenomenal world is determined and not free. He therefore argued that part of man's nature must belong to the noumenal world. The *Summum Bonum* of morality is virtue and happiness, and Kant is moved to postulate the existence of God in order to equate virtue and happiness and the idea of a future life so that one can attain perfect virtue and receive its reward. "The existence of God can be established only by practical reason and the only God we can know is a moral God."[36] God thus remains, in Kant's argument, a *deux ex machina* introduced to resolve our moral problems. "Sense-experience is the sole source of 'knowledge,' and since we can have no such experience of the God of theism, we can make no dogmatic assertions as to His existence."[37]

In his *Critique of Practical Reason* Kant argues that morality is objective and thus rational. He starts with the concept of freedom: "ought implies can." Our freedom, as noted above, does not belongs to the realm of nature but to the transcendental realm to which categories such as causality do not apply. We know the practical self only by the exercise of our freedom. Morality results not in judgments but in imperatives. Kant distinguishes between hypothetical and categorical imperatives. Hypothetical imperatives are conditional—for example, if you want to be accepted, then be still!—but their conditionality means that they can never be objective because they are personal and not universal. Categorical imperatives are universal and unconditional. There is only one principle for the categorical imperative: When deciding how to act, one will be constrained by reason to "act only on that maxim which I can at the same time will as a universal law."[38]

The autonomy of the will is at the heart of Kant's ethics: "This feeling of human independence is most clearly revealed in the idea of autonomy, in the idea that not God but we ourselves, in so far as we embody pure practical reason, are the legislators of the moral law. We submit to the law not on God's behalf but for our own sake. It is our true will that must be done."[39] As Kroner observes, there is a tension in Kant's thought between his ethical motive and a religious one. Faith in a supersensible unity is a result of Kant's

36. Greene, "The Historical Context," lxii.
37. Greene, "The Historical Context," xlviii.
38. Scruton, *Kant*, 85 (paraphrased).
39. Scruton, *Kant*, 36.

system. He argues that it is morally necessary to believe in God, and yet he tends to absolutize the moral law that *we* generate.

Kant, Religion, and Historical Revelation

Kant addressed the issue of religion and theology on several occasions. His most well-known work on religion is *Religion within the Bounds of Mere Reason* (1793). In recent years, *RWBMR* has received sustained and innovative attention, with renewed attempts to argue for its coherence and greater compatibility with Christian faith. It was published during a time when Kant needed to be careful about what he wrote and said publicly about religion, and there is some debate about the extent to which it is tailored with this political context in mind.[40] For our purposes a more relevant work is his *The Conflict of the Faculties* (1798), published when he was no longer under critical scrutiny by the censors, and which specifically addresses the conflict between theology and philosophy. *TCTF* brings into one volume three essays written by Kant in 1794, 1795, and 1796, all after the publication of *RWBMR*; and it thus provides a good lens through which to read *RWBMR* and, perhaps, a more objective assessment of Kant's view of religion.

TCTF deals with the potential conflict between the different departments or faculties of the university and the faculty of philosophy. In *TCTF* Kant pays particular attention to the conflict between philosophy and the "higher" faculty of theology. The major faculties of the German university of this time were theology, medicine, law, and philosophy. Kant identifies the higher faculties—theology, medicine, law—as those esteemed to have most value for government. However, he argues that it is essential to have a faculty independent of government commands that is free to evaluate everything by reason and that concerns itself solely with truth and is free to speak out publicly in this regard. This, for Kant, is philosophy.

For Kant, the "biblical theologian" develops his teaching from Scripture and not from reason. Indeed, he should keep philosophy a safe distance from his work (*RRT*, 251–52). The biblical theologian demonstrates God's

---

40. Greene, "The Historical Context," lxxiii, denies this. Kant's *RWBMR* was written for scholars for whom he felt no need to take care not to undermine their beliefs, in comparison with his lectures to immature students. Cf. Kant, "The End of All Things," 241, who argues similarly that *RWBMR* is a book for scholars and not the general public.

existence on the basis that he has spoken in Scripture. Arguing for this historically is, however, a matter for history, and history as a discipline belongs to philosophy. Indeed, for Kant, the issue of the divine origin of Scripture should not be raised at all in public discourse because it is a matter for scholars to investigate. Biblical theologians should interpret the Bible according to its literal sense and have no authority to impose a nonliteral moral interpretation on it. This, we will see below, is the sole right of the philosopher.

Of course, there is much in Scripture that is historical, but the biblical theologian is not qualified to assess the validity of such material. This is the domain of the philosopher. For Kant, no matter how central an element in Christian faith may be, if it is historical then its origin must be critically investigated by philosophy (*RRT*, 259). Indeed, investigation by philosophy may demonstrate that a doctrine or teaching turns out to be merely aesthetic, based only on a feeling, and philosophy is free to and must scrutinize such a case with "cold reason" (*RRT*, 260).[41]

And here Kant simply brings the lens of his philosophy of pure religion to bear. For Kant the historical aspects of Scripture are merely the husks, the vehicle for moral faith. "On the other hand, what we have cause to believe on historical grounds (where '*ought*' does not hold at all)—that is, revelation as contingent tenets of faith—it regards as nonessential" (*RRT*, 242).

Kant distinguishes on this basis between true religion and paganism: "Religion is the kind of faith that locates the essence of all divine worship in the human being's morality; paganism is the kind that does not" (*RRT*, 272). The historical dimensions of faith are thus nonessential, and religion that makes them essential is a form of paganism! "But it is a superstition to hold that historical belief is a duty and essential to salvation" (*RRT*, 285). For Kant, "faith in a mere historical proposition is, in itself, dead" (*RRT*, 286). Kant defines superstition as "the tendency to put greater trust in what is supposed to be non-natural than in what can be experienced by the laws of nature, whether in physical or moral matters. The question can therefore be raised: whether biblical faith (as empirical belief) or morality (as pure rational and religious belief) should serve as the teacher's guide?" (*RRT*, 285).

It is helpful to see what this means for Kant in terms of the historical

---

41. Greene, "The Historical Context," notes of the Enlightenment that "the movement took on an austere and barren coldness, which was welcomed in the beginning as is the first breath of mountain air after the suffocating heat of the plains; in time, however, it chilled men through and drove them back to a new appreciation of the sunnier and warmer sides of human life" (ix).

aspects of Scripture. Above we saw its implications for Kant's interpretation of the Sinai event. Another example is Pentecost (Acts 2), the birth of the church. Kant argues that the first disciples were confronted with the fact that the promises of the Abrahamic covenant and their hope that Jesus would deliver Israel were destroyed by Jesus's death. When they were gathered at Pentecost, one of their company "hit upon the happy idea, in keeping with the subtle Jewish art of exegesis, that pagans (Greeks and Romans) could also be regarded as admitted into this covenant" as children of faith.

> It is no wonder that this discovery which, in a great gathering of people, opened so immense a prospect, was received with the greatest rejoicing *as if it had been* the direct working of the Holy Spirit, and was considered a miracle and recorded as such in the biblical (apostolic) history. But religion does not require us to believe this as a fact, or obtrude this belief on natural human reason. Consequently, if a church commands us to believe such a dogma, as necessary for salvation, and we obey out of fear, our belief is superstition. (*RRT*, 285; emphasis added)

Another example is Jesus saying to people, "Your sins are forgiven." For Kant, such a statement as a revelation from God would be supersensible, and therefore impossible. Paul's statement that if Christ has not risen our faith is in vain, is well known. For Kant, such a statement is simply untrue. Kant believes in an afterlife but is not very sympathetic to the resurrection of body and soul. Who, he asks, would want to drag around his body for all eternity? "So the apostle's conclusion: 'If Christ had not risen' (if his body had not come to life), 'neither would we rise again' . . . is not valid" (*RRT*, 264). What Paul may have meant, Kant thinks, is that his belief in the afterlife suggested by reason moved him to historical belief in a public event. Much the same can be said for Kant's perspective on the stories of the resurrection and the ascension.

It will be obvious from the above just how radical and destructive Kant's approach is to any kind of traditional Judaism or Christianity. This destructiveness extends to many of the basic elements in Christian faith. For Kant, the doctrine of the Trinity has no practical value and true religion is all about practical morality. The same goes for the doctrine of the incarnation, and, as we noted above, the resurrection and the ascension. Kant simply shrugs off the implications of his approach: "But when we are dealing with religion, where the faith instilled by reason with regard to the practical is sufficient to itself, why should we get entangled in all these learned investigations and disputes because of a historical narrative that should always be left in its proper place (among matters that are indifferent)?" (*RRT*, 266).

Kant's approach to Scripture is shaped by his lens of rational religion and practical morality. He distinguishes between the *biblical* theologian and a *rational* theologian. The former is an expert on Scripture and grounded in the faith of the church whereas the latter is grounded in reason in relation to religion. The faith of rational religion does not require revelation since it "is based on inner laws that can be developed from every human being's own reason" (*RRT*, 262). Religion is thus not the aggregate of teachings viewed as divine revelation, but the aggregate of our duties seen as divine commands. True religion is the same as morality. Kant's rational religion of morality and of categorical imperatives may resort to the idea of God—which is itself derived from morality—to influence people's wills in the right direction, but it can never be grounded in God's revelation of himself; that would be irrational (*RRT*, 262). "To claim that we *feel* as such the immediate influence of God is self-contradictory, because the idea of God lies only in reason" (*RRT*, 279).

According to pure religion the only thing that really matters is morality, that is, deeds. For Kant, faith understood as assent to historical testimony is simply no part of true religion. Church faith changes over time and thus is open to gradual purification until it agrees with religious faith. When it comes to faith and morality human autonomy is essential for Kant. Action must be understood as emerging from the person's own use of one's moral power: "freedom in thinking signifies the subjection of reason to no laws except *those which it gives itself*; and its opposite is the maxim of a lawless use of reason (in order, as genius supposes, to see further than one can under the limitation of laws). The natural consequence is that if reason will not subject itself to the laws it gives itself, it has to bow under the yoke of laws given by another" (*RRT*, 16). The logical consequence, which is a truly remarkable position, is that, for Kant, the only way we can find eternal life in Scripture is by putting it there ourselves!

If we are after truth how then should we interpret Scripture? Kant is happy to step up to the plate and instruct us in this respect. Taken literally, Scripture appears to support the centrality of historical revelation, but we should read it differently to make it fit with pure religion: "whereas dogma requires historical scholarship, reason alone is sufficient for religious faith" (*RRT*, 269). The historical vehicle or husk of religion in Scripture must be peeled away to foreground the moral dimension that comports with rational religion:

But the Scriptures contain more than what is itself required for eternal life; part of their content is a matter of historical belief, and while this can indeed be useful to religious faith as its mere sensible vehicle (for certain people and certain eras), it is not an essential part of religious faith. Now the faculty of biblical theologians insists on this historical content as divine revelation as strongly as if belief in it belonged to religion. The philosophy faculty, however, opposes the theological faculty regarding this confusion, and what divine revelation contains that is true of religion proper. (*RRT*, 263)

If we make the error of including "Judaism in these tenets of faith, they can well make us moan."

For Kant, when conflict arises about the interpretation of Scripture, which is inevitable given his approach, the solution is simple: philosophy decides. Indeed, insofar as we are after truth when it comes to biblical interpretation, the principles of interpretation must be philosophical. Reason has the right to interpret the text in accordance with its own principles. According to Kant this is always what has happened in the history of the church, even when such interpretation is clearly contrary to authorial intent.

Not surprisingly, the way to interpret Scripture is to read it *morally*. Philosophy must be on the lookout for such a reading and even *impose it on the text*. For Kant, when it comes to the Bible "the mark of its divinity . . . is its harmony with what reason pronounces worthy of God" (*RRT*, 270). Only history could prove historical revelation to be true and "history is not entitled to pass itself off as divine revelation. And so for religious faith, which is directed solely to the morality of conduct, to deeds, acceptance of historical—even biblical—teachings has in itself no positive or negative moral value and comes under the heading of adraphoral" (*RRT*, 271). Jesus's injunction to "arise and walk" is not a miracle but comes to the man through his own reason. Only a moral interpretation of the Bible is authentic—only through the concepts of our reason can we recognize a teaching as divine.

The authenticity of the Bible is better established by the moral effect in the hearts of humans than by critical examination of its teachings and stories. The Bible receives its credentials not from its authors but "from the pure spring of universal rational religion dwelling in every ordinary human being" (*RRT*, 284). Even if God were to speak, we could never know it was God: "For if God should really speak to a human being, the latter could still never *know* that it was God speaking. It is quite impossible for a human being to apprehend the infinite by his senses, distinguish it from sensible beings, and *be acquainted with* it as such" (*RRT*, 283). It is, however, possible to falsify any claim that God is speaking. He cannot be speaking if his so-called voice contradicts rational morality.

All of which leaves historical revelation as of no importance. As Kant says, "it matters little that scholars who investigate its origin theoretically and historically and study its historical account critically may find it more or less wanting in proofs from a theoretical point of view.—The divinity of its moral content adequately compensates reason for the humanity of its historical narrative which, like the old parchment that is illegible in places, has to be made intelligible by adjustments and conjectures consistent with the whole" (*RRT*, 285).

Evaluating Kant

As we have seen in earlier chapters, when it comes to Sinai we are dealing with special divine action (SDA), and this Kant rejects outright. It is not hard to see why. The phenomenal world is a world of order, unaffected by miracles, subject to the categories of substance and causality. But it is not the whole of reality. There is also the unknowable noumenal realm. Kant completely separates science and religion by assigning them to distinct realms: science is assigned to the phenomenal realm and religion to the noumenal. Historical knowledge belongs to the phenomenal realm and the possibility of knowledge of God and of interventions by God in this realm is ruled out by Kant's epistemology. True religion, which can be known, is reduced to morality, and as Greene notes, "Kant's absolute insistence upon the reduction of true religion to morality, arising from his distrust of mysticism and a stiff-necked refusal to bow down even before God Himself, rendered him incapable of appreciating true religious devotion. . . . His whole religious theory, then, is anthropocentric, not theocentric . . . his God is certainly . . . related to the world and man in no vital way."[42] If Kant's *RWBMR* is a classic, then, as Greene observes, it is a deistic classic.

As a person Kant may have known more than his philosophy of religion. In his biography of Kant, R. B. Jachmann notes how in his later years he was convinced in his heart of a wise providence and genuinely believed in God's existence. Unlike some of his contemporaries Kant does seek to reconcile his philosophy with Christianity, but Johann Wolfgang von Goethe was on to

42. Greene, "The Historical Context," lxxvi.

something when he remarked in a letter to Herder that Kant "had criminally smeared his philosopher's cloak . . . so that Christians too might yet be enticed to kiss its hem."[43] One cannot escape the fact that human autonomy is the driving force in Kant's philosophy and that his religion is one of rational morality. Intriguingly, although Kant made use of concepts such as the Absolute and the unconditioned, he never equated them with God, whom he thought of as a personal being. But here we run into a moral contradiction for, as Greene notes, "surely, if, on Kant's own principles, it is wrong to use men merely as means to our own ends, we are not entitled to bring God into our scheme of things primarily as a means to our ultimate happiness."[44]

According to Plantinga, Kant's view of reality turns a Christian perspective upside down. From a Christian perspective God's knowledge, and not ours, is creative. The logical end of Kant's view is what Plantinga calls "creative anti-realism."[45] Plantinga finds such creative anti-realism at the heart of postmodernism, which he thinks has its roots in Kant.[46]

Kant's philosophy accounts for human limitations, but his stress on autonomy makes his account of reason irreconcilable with a Christian one. The title of Wolterstorff's *Reason within the Bounds of Religion* captures this well.[47] Gruenler is thus right that "the biblical interpreter who accepts the Kantian dichotomy will confine religious experience to the domain of personal, transcendental faith (which cannot be touched by historical criticism) and confine the historical-critical method to analysis of natural cause and effect without recourse to matters of faith or supernatural revelation."[48]

43. Quoted in Barth, *Protestant Theology*, 178.

44. Greene, "The Historical Context," lxiv.

45. Alvin Plantinga, "Christian Philosophy at the End of the 20th Century," in *Christian Philosophy at the Close of the Twentieth Century*, ed. Sander Griffioen and B. M. Balk (Kampen: Kok, 1995), 29-53, 30-37.

46. Compare this with the suggestion by Christopher Norris, "Criticism," in *Encyclopaedia of Literature and Criticism*, ed. M. Coyle, P. Garside, M. Kelsall, and J. Peck (London: Routledge, 1990), that postmodern indeterminacy has its roots in Christian readings of the OT. For a very different analysis of Kant by a Christian philosopher to that of Plantinga, see Merold Westphal, "Christian Philosophers and the Copernican Revolution," in *Christian Perspectives on Religious Knowledge*, ed. C. S. Evans and M. Westphal (Grand Rapids: Eerdmans, 1993), 161-79.

47. Nicholas Wolterstorff, *Reason within the Bounds of Religion* (Grand Rapids: Eerdmans, 1984).

48. R. G. Gruenler, *Meaning and Understanding: The Philosophical Framework*

The realm of the transcendental ego is the one area of freedom where God can be experienced but only subjectively, so that "encounter with God will be confined to the subjective realm, while the Bible will be subjected to natural-istic criticism according to the rational canons of purely historical research."[49] This shift is clearly evident in Kant's readings of Scripture,[50] and it is confirmed by de Wette and other OT theologians who were indebted to Kant.[51]

Kant and Biblical Criticism: The Case of Wilhelm de Wette

Rogerson lauds de Wette as the "founder of modern biblical criticism."[52] De Wette was, of course, indebted to those who came before him, but Rogerson argues that de Wette's work began a whole new era in critical OT scholarship. De Wette was the first to articulate a view of Israel's history quite different from that implied in the OT on the basis of his critical method.[53] Because of his doctorate on Deuteronomy, which he dated in the seventh century and connected with King Josiah's promulgation of it, de Wette is best known as an OT critic. However, he wrote substantially on the OT, the NT, and Christian theology, and therefore he stands at the origin of biblical criticism as a whole.

De Wette was raised in a Protestant family and studied at the University of Jena, where his professors included Fichte, Schelling, Hegel, and Gries-

---

for Biblical Interpretation, Foundations of Contemporary Interpretation 2 (Grand Rapids: Zondervan, 1991), 38.

49. Gruenler, *Meaning and Understanding,* 40.

50. See, for example, A. Edgar, "Kant's Two Interpretations of Genesis," *Literature and Theology* 6/3 (1992): 280-90.

51. See Rogerson, *W. M. L. de Wette,* 26-32, for the major influence of Kant upon de Wette, a father of OT criticism.

52. Rogerson, *W. M. L. de Wette.* Where to locate the origins of modern biblical criticism is controversial. I think that de Wette is *a* key figure in terms of the radical application of Enlightenment philosophy to the Bible, but the impetus in this direction lies earlier with Spinoza. Resolution of this issue is not crucial for my argument. De Wette is, on all accounts, *a* hugely influential father of modern criticism and bears scrutiny as such.

53. Rogerson, *W. M. L. de Wette,* 28, 29. On de Wette and biblical criticism see also Thomas A. Howard, *Religion and the Rise of Historicism: W. M. L. de Wette, Jacob Burkhardt, and the Theological Origins of Nineteenth-Century Historical Consciousness* (Cambridge: Cambridge University Press, 2000).

bach. However, for de Wette the major challenge to his faith came from Kant. As we noted above, in 1798, the year before de Wette came to Jena, Kant published his *The Conflict of the Faculties*. For the remainder of his life, de Wette remained a Kantian, and he worked to reconcile Kant with his aesthetic, mystical instinct for religion.

Kant's philosophy had major implications for religion and biblical studies. There is no consensus about interpretation of the Bible, but a religion of reason can yield this. Religion is reduced to morality and Christian theology adjusted accordingly. Historical truth is contingent and cannot be revelatory because revelation is disclosed through reason.

De Wette was deeply attracted by Kant's philosophy, but it left him feeling bereft of God and alone in the world. Schelling provided a solution by helping de Wette to critique Kant's over-privileging of philosophy as final umpire in all disciplines. For Schelling, God as the Absolute was primary and reason a part—but only a part—of the Absolute by means of which the individual could discern the Absolute in the particular. Religion contemplates the Absolute as it manifests itself in nature, history, and art. Mythology is therefore to be regarded positively as an attempt to grasp the Absolute. Schelling's understanding of mythology influenced de Wette's reading of the Bible, especially of the OT.

The result was that de Wette looked for an approach that combined the best of Schelling and Kant. It is most likely from Ludwig Tieck and Wilhelm Heinrich Wackenroeder's *Phantasien über die Kunst* that de Wette found an approach that he felt replaced his lost faith with a better one. According to Tieck and Wackenroeder, religion and art are like two mirrors that enable the true spirit of things to be grasped. In his *Eine Idee über das Studium der Theologie*, de Wette thus argues that theology should start with contemplating art. Art brings down from heaven "the divine in earthly form, and bringing it into our view you move the cold and narrow heart to accept feelings that are divine and mediate harmony."[54] From art one can then move on to nature, history, and, finally, theology.

In his dissertation (submitted in 1804) and in his *Aufforderung zum Studium der hebräischen Sprache und Literatur* (1805), de Wette constructed a picture of the history of Israel's religion that differed significantly from that of the HB/OT and that provided the basis for the nineteenth and twentieth centuries' critical scholarship. It is here, for Rogerson, that de Wette's

---

54. Rogerson, *W. M. L. de Wette*, 15. Hereafter, page references to this work are given in parentheses in the text.

THE GOD WHO ACTS IN HISTORY

major contribution is found. But where did de Wette get this picture from? According to Rogerson, he developed it by reading the text unconstrained by theories of the unity of authorship, but also by reading the OT through the lens of a particular view of religion. The *Aufforderung* provides a devastating attack on the historicity of the HB/OT, undergirded by de Wette's view of mythology and religion. De Wette had learned well from Kant that contingent truths of history cannot be revelatory.

Rogerson astutely notes that, "looked at, then, from the perspective of the literary and philosophical world of his day, de Wette was not a rationalizing critic who summarily dismissed the historical value of the Old Testament. It was widely accepted among biblical scholars that the Bible contained myths. De Wette simply applied to their interpretation *a view derived from literary and philosophical interpretation*: that they were to be seen as instances of fantasy-inspired poetry, expressing the ideas of the people" (49; emphasis added). Like Vater, but unlike Eichhorn's Documentary Hypothesis of the Pentateuch, in his *Beiträge* de Wette develops a fragmentary hypothesis of the Pentateuch. His concern is to demonstrate that the Pentateuch is mythical through and through. Narratives with miracles, or with God speaking, are mythical because such accounts contradict the laws of nature and general experience. Thus, the Pentateuchal narratives are generally of minimal value for the historian but of significant value for the theologian as a result of their witness to religion. The Pentateuch "is a product of the religious poetry of the Israelite people, which reflects their spirit [*Geist*], way of thought, love of the nation, philosophy of religion."[55]

The philosopher Jakob Friedrich Fries, de Wette's Heidelberg colleague, helped de Wette bring his philosophy of religion to maturity as de Wette continued to wrestle with the relationship between revelation and reason. De Wette worried that taking reason as the final arbiter of truth replaced God with reason. Fries's distinction between reason (*Vernunft*) and understanding (*Verstand*) came to the rescue. *Verstand* is the way one orders sense perceptions into a whole. *Vernunft* is, by comparison, related to moral and aesthetic experience. "One outcome of this view of things was that de Wette obtained a new way of considering the relation between revelation in historical terms and reason. Revelation in historical terms was no longer to be judged by its correspondence with the empirical understanding of reality; rather, it was to be judged by its correspondence with the understanding of eternal values mediated by reason (*Vernunft*) reflecting upon moral and

55. Quoted by Rogerson, *W. M. L. de Wette*, 55.

aesthetic experience" (78). Through Fries's influence de Wette came to see Christ as "the aesthetic expression of the ideal within the contingency of history" (88).

Evaluating de Wette

Our examination of Kant and de Wette alerts us unequivocally to the philosophical and theological influences on de Wette. But what are we to make of this? At the conclusion of his biography of de Wette Rogerson argues that de Wette's most glaring weakness is his *weddedness to the philosophy of Fries*. If he had been more eclectic or obscure, he might have achieved greater renown! According to Rogerson,

> De Wette was convinced that biblical interpretation and theology were concerned with reality, and that reality could only be understood with the help of philosophy. In this he was surely right. Implicit in Christian belief are claims about the nature of reality, about the sort of world in which we live and about the sort of things human beings are. Although philosophy in a broad sense does not seek to provide answers to these questions, it does offer critiques of attempted answers, it exposes contradictions and tautologies and offers conceptual frameworks for deeper reflection. Those who claim to have no philosophy are simply unaware of their philosophical presuppositions.
>
> In using philosophy so unashamedly in his biblical interpretation, theology and ethics, de Wette was standing in an honourable tradition reaching back through Protestant scholasticism to Aquinas and the church of those centuries that produced the classical creeds of Christian orthodoxy. This was one reason why de Wette rejected such orthodoxy, believing that it was based upon inadequate philosophy. . . . We cannot fault de Wette's sincerity in making his views about the nature of reality affect his biblical interpretation and his theology. (267–68)

Rogerson also comments on de Wette's recurring attention to the relationship of biblical criticism to Christian belief: "Was this any worse than privileging a particular view of the life and significance of Christ because it is held by a believing community? It is probably better, in that de Wette could give reasons for his position, whereas one wants to ask why a believing community thinks about Christ in the way it does" (268).

Rogerson rightly observes how de Wette's aesthetics was tied to an ontology: "It is here, it seems to me, that de Wette demands that we add to our agenda an item long since neglected. What is the status of aesthetic experience in theology and biblical studies? . . . There must be a place for an attempt to integrate biblical studies more closely with an aesthetic-literary exploration of reality" (270).

As Rogerson evaluates de Wette, his own views become visible. Thus we need to reflect on de Wette's *and* Rogerson's evaluation of de Wette.

First, de Wette. Rogerson rightly points out that one of the virtues of de Wette is his honesty and quest for integrity in the sense of integration in his scholarship. There are at least three ways in which de Wette's work is of major significance for our analysis:

1. De Wette was clear that human perspectives or worldviews are unified, and he understood and embodied in his struggles the fact that our view of reason and history and religion, that is, our philosophy, and how we read the Bible are integrally related.

In this respect we have much to learn from de Wette. Nowadays it takes years and years of specialized training to become a biblical scholar. In this respect biblical studies shares in the growing fragmentation of disciplines as we take longer and longer to become experts about less and less. The result is that there is little space for biblical scholars to explore the philosophical and religious subtexts of their research. De Wette's work reminds us that, like it or not, our worldview and our understanding of philosophy and religion will impact the way we read the Bible. To de Wette's credit, he was deeply conscious of such influences.

2. As Jacques Derrida and others recognize, philosophy is like the scaffolding that supports and grounds academic analysis. De Wette got this; he understood the *fundamental role of philosophy* in scholarship. In scholarship there is always an epistemology in operation, always some ontology is assumed, always some understanding of the human person is in view.

Scholars of biblical hermeneutics such as Thiselton have alerted biblical scholars to the fundamental importance of philosophy and philosophical hermeneutics for biblical exegesis.[56] However, as Thiselton observes, biblical scholars are—understandably—often philosophically illiterate and thus

---

56. See, for example, Anthony C. Thiselton's *New Horizons in Hermeneutics* (Grand Rapids: Zondervan, 1992), and Craig G. Bartholomew, "Three Horizons: Hermeneutics from the Other End—An Evaluation of Anthony Thiselton's Hermeneutic Proposals," *EJT* 5 (1996): 121-35.

destined to work within outdated paradigms.[57] In this respect de Wette's work is a healthy reminder of *all* the ingredients involved in biblical exegesis.

3. De Wette came to believe that true philosophy was that in the Kantian/Schelling/Friesian tradition, and he devoted his life to rethinking religion, the Bible, and theology within that framework. Whatever we think of de Wette's Kantianism, his honesty is refreshing, as is his lifelong quest for the integration of his philosophy with his biblical scholarship and his theology.

Inevitably scholars continue to work with philosophies shaping their work. Of course, however, too often they remain ignorant of this scaffolding, with the result that it is hidden from view and their scholarship is given the appearance of neutral, objective analysis. De Wette's openness about his philosophy enables one to examine the total picture that constitutes his work, and this enables the reader to evaluate his work in its totality.

Second, Rogerson. Rogerson concurs with de Wette that we cannot avoid philosophy in biblical studies. Then, however, Rogerson makes some surprising moves. He argues that Christian belief implies certain philosophical views: "Implicit in Christian belief are claims about the nature of reality, about the sort of world in which we live and about the sort of things human beings are."[58] And then, on *this* basis, Rogerson commends de Wette for adopting a *Kantian* framework and positioning religion within it. What, one wonders, has happened to the philosophical views implied by Christian beliefs? Are we to assume that Christian beliefs imply the framework of Kant and then read religion through this lens? Perhaps Rogerson assumes this very thing, as the image of Kant as the "philosopher of Protestantism" reminds us,[59] but then it needs to be argued for.

---

57. In "Communicative Action and Promise in Hermeneutics," in Roger Lundin, Clarence Walhout, and Anthony C. Thiselton, *The Promise of Hermeneutics* (Grand Rapids: Eerdmans, 1999), 137, Thiselton notes that, "curiously, the limits of scientific method to explain all of reality seem to be appreciated more readily in the philosophy of religion than in biblical studies. Views and methods that students in philosophy of religion recognize as 'positivist,' 'reductionist,' or even 'materialist' are often embraced quite uncritically in issues of judgement about, for example, acts of God in biblical narrative. In place of the more rigorous and judicious exploration of these issues in philosophical theology, biblical studies seems too readily to become polarized."

58. Rogerson, *W. M. L. de Wette*, 267.

59. Gordon E. Michalson Jr., *Kant and the Problem of God* (Oxford: Blackwell, 1999), 1.

In this way, de Wette *and* Rogerson focus in an acute way on Kant's legacy in biblical exegesis and theology. As Beiser observes, even in Kant's day the issues of theology and God in relation to Kant's philosophy and theology were fiercely debated.[60] Furthermore, in recent decades Kant's anthropology has been strongly criticized by liberation and feminist theologians and by postliberals, alerting us that "the Cartesian-Kantian model of the self is historically contingent, rather than the indispensable conceptual device for properly framing the issue of faith and transcendence."[61] Personally, I think Michalson is right that Kant's immanentism and human autonomy subvert theism so that Kant, as much as Hegel, should be understood as enabling the developments in European culture associated with the rise of atheism rather than being fit for a mediating theology. Kant is, from this perspective, a central figure on the Luther–Kant–Feuerbach–Marx trajectory, and one of whom, as Buckley argues in his analysis of the origins of atheism, Christian thinkers should be wary.[62] The implications for theology and biblical interpretation are stark:

> The consistent subordination of divine transcendence to the demands of autonomous rationality strongly suggests that Kant's own thought . . . is moving in a non-theistic direction rather than in a direction with obviously constructive possibilities for theology. . . . The religious feature may remain present, but that is not where the real life is, any more than the twitching body of a beheaded reptile indicates real life. As a result, Kant's own example is hardly a comforting model for those committed to holding divine transcendence and a modern sensibility in proper balance. In his case, the balancing act cannot be sustained; his particular way of endorsing modernity is finally too self-aggrandizing.[63]

60. Frederick Beiser, *The Fate of Reason: German Philosophy from Kant to Fichte* (Cambridge, MA: Harvard University Press, 1987).

61. Michalson, *Kant*, 136.

62. See Michael J. Buckley, *At the Origins of Modern Atheism* (New Haven: Yale University Press, 1990), especially 322–33. Buckley rightly notes that "the atheism evolved in the eighteenth century was thus not to be denied by the strategies elaborated in the revolutions of Kant and Schleiermacher: it was only to be transposed into a different key. Argue god as the presupposition or as the corollary of nature; eventually natural philosophy would dispose of god. Argue god as the presupposition or as the corollary of human nature; eventually the denial of god would become an absolute necessity for human existence" (332–33).

63. Michalson, *Kant*, 137.

De Wette is often regarded as the father of modern biblical criticism, and his work is important for biblical studies in its embrace of a Kantian philosophical framework. As we have seen, this has major theological and exegetical implications. Rogerson's assumption of the compatibility of Kant with a Christian perspective alerts us to how powerfully and too often unconsciously Kant continues to influence biblical interpretation. One may— which I do not—argue that Kant is a fruitful mediating figure between faith and modern culture for exegesis, but then this has to be argued for and not assumed. Rogerson rightly foregrounds de Wette's lasting achievement in applying historical criticism to the Bible so as to produce a history radically different to that of the Bible. Nicholson notes the indebtedness of Edouard Reuss, Johann Friedrich Leopold George, Wilhelm Vatke, and Julius Wellhausen to de Wette.[64] What is largely forgotten is de Wette's profound indebtedness to Kant in pushing OT scholarship in this direction in the first place.

Conclusion

Kant argues for a religion of reason and is dismissive of the potential of historical narrative to provide truth. We do not need an empirical example to furnish the idea of a morally well-pleasing person to God; as an archetype this idea is already present in our reason. It is worth pausing to consider the implications of Kant's rational religion. In his *Prolegomena to the History of Israel*, Wellhausen describes de Wette as "the epoch making pioneer of historical criticism in this field."[65] Clearly Kant's view of the Bible and its historical narratives—we can do what we like with them!—is *not* derived from careful study of the narratives but stems from his idealistic philosophy. Here we see modern philosophy's power to frame an approach to Scripture and theology, and clearly it is far from neutral or objective, *unless* one embraces Kant's philosophy. Alvin Plantinga traces postmodernism's "creative idealism" back to Kant, and in much postmodern reading of Scripture it is not hard to see Kant's dictum that we can do what we like with the historical narratives of Scripture coming home to roost, as it were.

---

64. Ernest Nicholson, *The Pentateuch in the Twentieth Century: The Legacy of Julius Wellhausen* (Oxford: Oxford University Press, 1998), 4.

65. Wellhausen, *Prolegomena*, 4.

Inevitably history bounced back on the philosophical agenda of modernity and not least in Hegel's (1770–1831) thought.[66] Right-wing Hegelians in particular sought to argue that Hegel's philosophy was consistent with Lutheran orthodoxy, but clearly his philosophy of *Geist* (spirit) working itself out through history via thesis, antithesis, and synthesis is a far cry from a biblical view of history.[67] Beiser notes that, "although Hegel attempts to reinstate the traditional idea of providence, he also gives it an entirely immanent or this-worldly meaning."[68] God does not exist apart from history. Indeed, he realizes himself only through it, and thus our efforts are necessary for the realization of the divine nature. As Rae notes of Hegel, "in principle, therefore, the truth may be learned without reference to history. In Hegel and Marx, the great modern interpreters of history, we find the modern rejection of the decisiveness of the moment in full cry."[69]

Informed by Kant and modern philosophies of history, historical criticism has furthermore relentlessly questioned the validity of that which lies behind the HB/OT with its overarching narrative. We thus find ourselves in a situation in which many of the concepts of the doctrine(s) of God, such as perfect-being, simplicity, aseity, and so on, are derived from nonbiblical sources, while the possibility of reliable knowledge of God through revelation in history, and thus through the HB/OT, is problematized or dismissed. Sinai, for example, is on all accounts central to the HB/OT but: Did it actually take place? Did God appear, act, and speak there? And does this matter for our doctrine of God? From Kant's perspective it is a waste of time even attending to such questions. In the next chapter we turn to the work of a philosopher-theologian for whom it is precisely through historical narrative that we derive true knowledge of God.

66. For a good introduction to Hegel's view of history see Frederick C. Beiser, *Hegel* (London: Routledge, 2005), 261–81.

67. See Murray A. Rae, "Creation and Promise: Towards a Theology of History," in *"Behind the Text": History and Biblical Interpretation*, ed. Craig Bartholomew et al. (Grand Rapids: Zondervan, 2003), 276–77.

68. Beiser, *Hegel*, 271.

69. Rae, "Creation and Promise," 277.

CHAPTER 7

Colin Gunton, Classical Theism, and Divine Action

> In certain essential respects, Kant's theology is but that of Aquinas
> radicalized. Kant is the fate of the negative theology transposed into a
> mechanistic world.
>
> —Colin Gunton[1]

Colin Gunton (1941–2003) was one of the most significant theologians of
the twentieth century. Following on from the extraordinary contribution of
Karl Barth, the latter half of the twentieth century witnessed a remarkable
resurgence of trinitarian theology, with Gunton as the premier British representative. Gunton's untimely death leaves us bereft of the mature works
that would undoubtedly have emerged were he still alive. Nevertheless, he
bequeathed to us a rich corpus of work, and his students and colleagues have
continued to make available his unfinished work. Gunton taught philosophy
for many years before taking up a position in theology, and his familiarity
with philosophy shows. He is one of those rare contemporary theologians
who produced genuinely constructive works. John Webster says of Gunton
that he "had no ambitions to be a specialist on Barth or any other thinker:
he was primarily a constructive theologian, and though he published a good
deal on theological issues approached 'through the theologians,' his work
as commentator was ancillary to the central enterprise of giving a rational
articulation of the Christian confession."[2]

Gunton's doctorate, published as *Becoming and Being: The Doctrine of
God in Charles Hartshorne and Karl Barth*, was supervised for the first year

---

1. Gunton, *Act and Being*, 53.
2. John Webster, "Gunton and Barth," in *The Theology of Colin Gunton*, ed. Lincoln Harvey (London: T&T Clark, 2010), 18. See this essay on Gunton's use of Barth.

by Robert Jenson. In a review of Gunton's work, Jenson observes in retrospect how fully Gunton's critique of classical theism is already present in his doctoral work.[3] Jenson notes, "When I reread *Becoming and Being* I was taken aback by the way in which abiding determinants of Gunton's thinking were full-blown and decisive already in his dissertation, indeed in its opening pages. The dissertation displays with all possible clarity the parting of Gunton's way from another way, represented or even dominant in the tradition, a way that he then called 'classical theism.'"[4]

Gunton on Classical Theism

Gunton asserts that the agenda for most exploration of the doctrine of God was established in the medieval period, and particularly in the work of Thomas Aquinas. For Gunton, modern philosophy of religion and the critiques of it by philosophers such as Descartes, Spinoza, Hume, and Kant are still carried on against this backdrop.[5] The years since Gunton's death have, if anything, more than confirmed this assessment, as we are witnessing a renaissance of interest in and defense of classical theism under the names of philosophical theology, philosophy of religion, and analytic theology. In a fine collection of essays, *Inquiring After God*, Nicholas Wolterstorff notes that most of his work in this area involves critical engagement with classical theism. He, however, observes that "we would like to hear something positive on these topics; and we would like to see those positive contributions assembled into a comprehensive understanding of God which is an alternative to that found in Aquinas' classic formulation, and indeed, an alternative to that found in all other classic formulations."[6]

In my view Gunton provides much of what Wolterstorff is calling for.[7] Leaning heavily on Karl Barth, he remains constructively engaged with

3. Colin E. Gunton, *Becoming and Being: The Doctrine of God in Charles Hartshorne and Karl Barth* (Oxford: Oxford University Press, 1978).

4. Robert Jenson, "A Decision Tree of Colin Gunton's Thinking," in Harvey, ed., *The Theology of Colin Gunton*, 8.

5. Gunton, *Becoming and Being*, 1.

6. Wolterstorff, *Inquiring After God*, 15. See, however, Wolterstorff's rich work, *The God We Worship*.

7. Cf. also Cremer, *The Christian Doctrine of the Divine Attributes*, an important work upon which Barth draws.

classical theism and affirms virtually all of its concepts while articulating a significantly different framework for understanding the doctrine of God. Significantly, for our purposes, in Gunton's work we find a framework at whose heart is *divine action.*

Gunton identifies three main characteristics of classical theism:

1. Supernaturalism. Classical theism is committed to the negative or apophatic way. The supernatural or God is defined foundationally in opposition to nature. Gunton recognized that we often need to say what God is not, but he rejected any "foundational apophaticism"[8] according to which we start on the road to knowledge of God by negating aspects of nature. The result of such foundational apophaticism is that "any historical action of God will tend to take the form of an isolated intervention which is also a violation of the natural."[9]
2. Timelessness. God is timelessly eternal. "Once again, acute logical difficulties are raised for those, like Christians, who would speak of the historical relations of this God to the world."[10]
3. Hierarchicalism. Classical theism is committed to a hierarchical ordering of reality. Thomas's Five Ways illustrate this, and they also determine the shape of Thomas's doctrine of God. "The universe as a whole is conceived on the analogy of a geometrical theorem, and both meaningful history and Christian theology become impossible."[11]

In his doctorate Gunton lays the blame for the appropriation of Greek metaphysics at the feet of Thomas, but with time he shifted his focus to Augustine as the guilty one, and especially in relation to the doctrine of simplicity. For Gunton the doctrine of the Trinity was at stake here, and especially that of the immanent Trinity. If there can be absolutely no plurality of any sort in God then the doctrine of God as Father, Son, and Holy Spirit is rendered vacuous. For Gunton, Augustine began in the wrong place by seeking to reconcile simplicity with the Trinity, rather than beginning with the revelation of God in the divine economy. The result is that "Augustine tends to call attention away from the concrete historical events in which God is present to the world in the economy of creation

8. Jenson, "A Decision Tree," 9.
9. Gunton, *Becoming and Being*, 2.
10. Gunton, *Becoming and Being*, 3.
11. Gunton, *Becoming and Being*, 5.

and salvation."[12] Gunton follows Barth in making the Trinity the foundation for his reflections upon God. For Barth, "the account of the Trinity in fact takes the place long taken by natural theology."[13] Only the doctrine of the Trinity, for Gunton, could make the space for a creature other than God while God remains intimately engaged with that creature.

There are different types of trinitarian thinking and Gunton discusses that of three: Augustine, the Cappadocian Fathers, and Irenaeus. For Gunton Augustine severs the connection between the economic and the immanent Trinity through his espousal of the doctrine of divine simplicity. Gunton thus reached back in the Christian tradition to find a vein relatively uncontaminated by classical theism. He thought the Cappadocian fathers got far more right than did Augustine. They gave ontological weight to the concepts of "person" and "relations." Nevertheless, they too draw too much from sources apart from the divine economy. Behind them, Gunton found in Irenaeus a theologian who got it nearly all right, the use of whom is clearly on display in Gunton's fine *Christ and Creation*.

For Irenaeus, the divine economy is one history because it is the work of one person, the Father. The Son and the Spirit are the Father's two hands by which he does what he does. Irenaeus's statements about the Son and the Spirit are fairly simple and straightforward. He does not concern himself overly much with the ontological status of the Son and the Spirit, and Gunton thinks that this is how it should always have been. For Gunton, Irenaeus grasps that the function of trinitarian theology is to understand rightly the divine economy of creation, fall, redemption, and consummation. We need to exercise caution in how we develop trinitarian thought beyond Irenaeus, always asking how such developments derive from and illuminate the divine economy.

Divine Attributes

"To speak of God's attributes is to attempt to speak of the kind of god that God is; of the things that characterize him as God; of what makes him to be God, rather than some other being or kind of being."[14] The Trinity identifies

---

12. Colin E. Gunton, *The Promise of Trinitarian Theology*, 2nd ed. (London: T&T Clark, 1997), 48.

13. Gunton, *Becoming and Being*, 186.

14. Gunton, *Act and Being*, 1. Cf. Stephen R. Holmes, "Divine Attributes," in

who God is; his attributes relate to his defining characteristics. For Gunton, the two should never be separated, but we need clarity on how they relate to each other. In Reformation and post-Reformation theology we find something of an often-unhelpful hybrid of scholastic and biblical theology. Charles Hodge, for example, gets to the Trinity only after 250 pages of discussion of the doctrine of God. For Gunton such treatments are symptomatic of theologians too often using the wrong method, developing the wrong content, and in the wrong order.

In relation to the attributes of God, Barth preferred the term "perfections."[15] "From these suggested terms . . . we choose the last [*perfectiones*] because it points at once to the thing itself instead of merely to its formal aspect, and because instead of something general it expresses at once that which is clearly distinctive."[16] Gunton favors this move since it stresses how God has revealed himself to us rather than what we attribute to God. "It is because of his relentless pursuit of this matter that Barth's treatment of the divine perfections is one of the finest accounts of the topic to be found in theological history."[17] Provided we retain the emphasis on God revealing himself, however, Gunton is content to retain the language of divine attributes.

Divine Attributes and the Old Testament

For Gunton there is one feature of such hybrids that must be rejected. Gunton identifies a major weakness in classical theism and in the post-Reformation hybrids in their failure to take the Old Testament sufficiently seriously. "It is when Christian theology becomes dependent on the philosophers' speculations rather than on the equivalent Old Testament polemics against paganism that the troubles begin."[18] Gunton says, for example, of how we treat OT theophanies that the "use of these, it seems to me, is one indication of whether a theology is genuinely incarnational."[19]

Mapping Modern Theology: A Thematic and Historical Introduction, ed. Kelly M. Kapic and Bruce L. McCormack (Grand Rapids: Baker Academic, 2012), 47–65.

15. See Barth, *CD* 2/1, secs. 29–31.
16. Barth, *CD* 2/1, 322.
17. Gunton, *Act and Being*, 9.
18. Gunton, *Act and Being*, 6.
19. Gunton, *The Promise of Trinitarian Theology*, 34.

For Gunton, it is a tragedy, almost a crime, that the OT was pushed aside in favor of Greek philosophy as the basis for our doctrine of God. This is particularly the case when it comes to the divine attributes. Gunton discerns in Clement of Alexandria the reduction of the OT to a place on a par with Greek philosophy, a position Gunton rightly finds comparably in Schleiermacher. Gunton notes with others that the long neglect of the OT has been detrimental to Christian faith, most obviously in the history of anti-Semitism, but more basically in the reduction in our understanding of the immensity of the gospel. For Gunton, "this is no more truly the case than in the treatment of the being of God, that most central of doctrines."[20]

Classical theism starts by developing a view of God that negates or opposes the world and Gunton argues that this has led to a view of God that is vulnerable to the critique that Christianity is Platonism for the masses. Classical theism, as we have seen with Aquinas, works such that Christian faith is grounded in a general philosophy of being. Jenson notes that the Greeks developed their concept of being to prevent any such distinction as the biblical one between Creator and the created.[21] Christian theology, however, must use the concept of "being" to strengthen this distinction. Jenson acknowledges that Thomas does this, but Jenson notes that we urgently need a trinitarian account of this distinction. For Gunton, the danger in Thomas's approach is that the general overwhelms or unhelpfully constrains the particular. Classical theism yields dualisms like creation vs. that which negates the creation: abstract vs. material, immanent vs. transcendent, and so on. By contrast Scripture alerts us to the fundamental distinction as *that between Creator and the created.*

Gunton points out that in the OT we already find a strong polemic against the pagan anthropomorphisms of Israel's surrounding nations, and that theology gets into trouble when it depends on philosophical speculation rather than such OT polemics. As a symptom of there being a problem with classical theism, Gunton points to the fact that prior to the Reformation there was no substantial treatment of God's holiness, a characteristic of God that it could be argued is central to any biblical account of the divine attributes.[22] The OT is also central to any doctrine of the holiness of God.

20. Gunton, *Act and Being*, 4–5.
21. Robert Jenson, *Systematic Theology*, vol. 1: *The Triune God* (Oxford: Oxford University Press, 1997), 212.
22. Cf. Emil Brunner, *Dogmatics*, vol. 1: *The Christian Doctrine of God*, trans. Olive Wyon (Philadelphia: Westminster, 1949), 157–82.

We saw in the previous chapter the centrality of YHWH (Exod 3:13) to Aquinas's theology of God. An incorrect Greek reading of this personal name opens the door to a doctrine of being and negative theology. Gunton acknowledges that while YHWH hides and reveals himself, he does provide us with a name that has to be filled out narratively in future acts of YHWH. "It is surely significant that the biblical texts that take up the reference appeal not to 'being,' but to the name revealed in historical action."[23] Jenson comments similarly,

> "I am the Lord your God, who brought you out of the land of Egypt." The Lord has introduced himself to us, and just so introduced us into the communal life that he is. As God has introduced himself to us, he is hypostatically present to and in our community. As we in this community know each other, we know God. If we may at all speak of a "condition of the possibility" of our knowing God, one located on our side of the relation, this condition is the church. . . . We know God in that the Word of God that is God, that is *homoousios* with the Father, is actual only as conversation with us. If we ask what the divine Word would have been without us, we—again—do not know what we are asking.[24]

YHWH provides a basis for Gunton to affirm God's *aseity*, that God is in and for himself. At the same time, we are not left to determine the meaning of God's aseity philosophically, but firstly through his acts in history, that is in terms of the divine economy as revealed in Scripture. For Gunton the issue of the divine name(s) focuses the issues at stake in classical theism. What is the relationship between the theology of the divine names found in Pseudo-Dionysius and his successors, including Thomas, and the biblical revelation of God as the God of Abraham, Isaac, and Jacob, and as the Father of Jesus Christ? "What, that is to say, is the relation between a metaphysic of being in which God is named by what is essentially a method of philosophical abstraction and the biblical phenomenon of the revealed name?"[25] Schleiermacher shows his hand in identifying three ways to arrive at the attributes of God: removal of limits, negation, and causality, with the third as the most basic. What is omitted is the testimony of Scripture as the primary source.

23. Gunton, *Act and Being*, 11.
24. Jenson, *Systematic Theology*, 1:228.
25. Gunton, *Act and Being*, 12.

Central to Gunton's critique of classical theism is its inadequate *doctrine of creation*, again an area where the witness of the OT is crucial. Dionysius and his followers situate timeless, metaphysical causality over against the temporal and economical depiction of God's action in his world. In this way the spiritual or intellectual is set against the materiality of creation, whereas this is a false dichotomy: the true distinction is between Creator and the created. The material, from this perspective, is as spiritual as the abstract and intellectual.

The resort to *analogy* flows out of these false moves. "Lacking the kind of concept of personal divine action that became possible only in the light of scripture, and in any case associating particular divine action with the anthropomorphic antics of the gods of Greek poetry, the later Greeks took refuge in analogy."[26] Analogy depends upon the neoplatonic doctrine of gradations of being, a view most evident, for Gunton, in Thomas's Fourth Way, which assumes an equation of goodness and being understood hierarchically.

Gunton develops three major critiques of this approach to analogy. First, it operates by projecting from below rather than in response to the particular, historical revelation within time and space that we find in Scripture. This, second, is why the major biblical concepts of holiness and love get overlooked, or, if they are attended to, come after the metaphysical framework that sets the context. Third, for Gunton the worldview undergirding this view of analogy should have been discarded centuries ago and replaced with a doctrine of creation illuminated by the doctrine of the Trinity. Creation, its goodness, and the interaction of God and Christ with the creation embody a critique of the dualism of material–intellectual, sensible–intelligible, which shapes the classical theistic doctrine of the attributes.

For Gunton, *the negative way* commits two sins: first in being overconfident in knowing, in a type of rationalism, which concepts to begin with in talking about God and how to purify them to speak of God; second, in what amounts to a denial of revelation. In a footnote Gunton here again refers to placing the Greek heritage alongside or in place of the OT. For Gunton, beginning with the negative way is at the heart of the problems with classical theism. It should be completely rejected because it privileges ascent out of the creation to a God who is its opposite rather than the Other of creation in relation. Furthermore, we do not need first to ascend from the material to the abstract on the basis of unaided human reason be-

26. Gunton, *Act and Being*, 13–14.

cause the Son of God has tabernacled among us. For Gunton, the negative way thus amounts to a form of unbelief, seeking God first apart from and before the incarnation of the Son of God. The sinful, finite mind cannot attain to the essence of God through its own powers. The same can be said of the doctrine of analogy.[27]

Gunton discerns two rival accounts of language about God. The first is that of the negative way, which begins with the mythical language associated with the Greek gods and negates it. "Because in this idealistic account God is all mind, intellect tends to be played against imagination, concept against metaphor."[28] The second is that of analogy. Gunton recognizes the role of analogy in relation to the divine attributes but rejects the hierarchical metaphysics on which it is based. Intriguingly, Gunton retrieves Duns Scotus, often vilified as a proponent of univocal language about God, noting that the case can be made that Scotus was one who refuted the neoplatonic distortion of theology. Scotus does indeed claim that words are used univocally and not analogically of God and creatures. His concept of univocity is, however, different from that of Aquinas. He does not hold that words are used in exactly the same way but that "that concept [is] univocal which possesses sufficient unity in itself, so that to affirm and deny it of one and the same thing would be a contradiction."[29] I am reminded here of William Alston's defense of partial univocity in language about God.[30] If we take seriously the opening remark of Hebrews that Christ is "the reflection of God's glory and the exact imprint of God's very being," then it follows, according to Gunton, that something like Scotus's view should in fact be the case. A theology of language is at stake here, and Gunton expresses amazement that classical theism has developed without consideration of how the Spirit empowers language to be what is was created for.

Jenson likewise stresses the vital importance of a personal understanding of God. "The Bible's language about God is drastically personal: he changes his mind and reacts to external events, he makes threats and repents of them, he makes promises and tricks us by how he fulfills them. If we understand this language as fundamentally inappropriate, as 'anthropomorphic,' we do

27. Cf. Robert W. Jenson, *The Knowledge of Things Hoped For* (New York: Oxford University Press, 1969), 75–87, and the bibliography there.

28. Gunton, *Act and Being*, 67.

29. Quoted in Gunton, *Act and Being*, 69.

30. William Alston, *Divine Nature and Human Language* (Ithaca, NY: Cornell University Press, 1989).

not know the biblical God."[31] God's speaking to and listening to us is God's faithfulness to himself. God is not God despite changing his mind, despite answering prayer or not; as God he does such things wholeheartedly. Petitionary prayer is, for Jenson, the one decisively appropriate act of creatures in relation to God. Jenson observes that "the one God is a conversation."[32] Language is the possibility of historical being; address and response is its actuality. "If God's being, 'into its furthest depths,' is historical, then precisely such address and response must be the actuality of his being."[33]

Gunton agrees with classical theism that metaphors describing God in terms of created things—rocks, fortresses, lions, and so on—have to be treated as metaphors. The difference emerges in what we make of them theologically. If our language must be purified of reference to material things, then it will be rationalized and all references to the created world will be demythologized. A theology of language should recognize that words are part of God's good creation, and that God has empowered certain humans to use words to speak truthfully about him. Barth notes that the "further we move away from the witness of the Holy Scriptures to the sphere of general conjectures about God, so much the purer, we think, is the air of thought, i.e., so much the less do we need the anthropomorphisms which are found to be particularly suspect. But, if it lets itself be guided by its object, theology ought to try to evade these anthropomorphisms least of all."[34] Insightfully, Barth notes that abstract concepts are just as much anthropomorphic as those developed from concrete, material perception. Gunton also, in true Reformed manner, alerts us to the need to take the effect of the fall of human reason seriously, as well as the influence of redemption on reason. In his *Actuality of the Atonement* Gunton attends to metaphor and religious language.[35] We cannot speak of divine action and being apart from the metaphorical language we find in Scripture, and so we must attend closely to how such language works, moving from there to our articulation of how we should think about God's action today.

Classical theism manifests an excessive reliance on sight, whereas, for Gunton, "we do not see God, but we are given to know his essence, who and

---

31. Jenson, *Systematic Theology*, 1:222.

32. Jenson, *Systematic Theology*, 1:223.

33. Jenson, *Systematic Theology*, 1:223.

34. Barth, *CD* 2/1, 222.

35. Colin Gunton, *Actuality of the Atonement: A Study of Metaphor, Rationality and the Christian Tradition* (London: T&T Clark, 1988).

what he is."[36] Gunton argues that to think of God mainly in terms of intellect, an emphasis we see in Maimonides and Thomas, results in a conception of God at odds with the biblical rendition of God according to which God is mainly known through his particular acts in history. To conceive God primarily in terms of intellect, with priority given to contemplation instead of action, renders the conception antithetical to a concept of God whose being is known primarily through his historical and particular action. This is not to suggest that the biblical God lacks intellect, but rather that his intellectuality is understood in terms of wisdom: that is to say, practical intellect, intellect directed to rather than abstracted from involvement in created being. For Gunton, "an adequate doctrine of creation will affirm that the creator makes a world that is other than he, but not opposed to him—apart from sin, that is. The negative theology runs the risk, if not more, of identifying existence with fallenness."[37]

Classical theism tends to restrict its focus to cosmology rather than attending to the divine economy. Thomas sets up his framework in the Five Ways through a general philosophical analysis with the rest flowing logically. According to Gunton, such an approach is in danger of collapsing into Spinoza's pantheism—"there is not a very great distance from the causal definition of relation in the *Summa Theologiae* to the outright pantheism of Spinoza"[38]—or Kant's idealism. If the negative way is pushed, one ends up with the unknowable God of Kant. "In certain essential respects, Kant's theology is but that of Aquinas radicalized. Kant is the fate of the negative theology transposed into a mechanistic world."[39] To see God as pure intellect risks denigrating the materiality of creation and takes the focus away from the knowledge of God that comes to us through the narratives of God's involvement with Israel climaxing in the incarnation.

Recent decades have witnessed a welcome emphasis in OT studies on the myriad ways in which the OT polemicizes against the worldviews and deities of surrounding nations. Gunton thus rightly points out that it was not only the Greeks who developed critiques of anthropomorphic gods, but also the Israelites, and the latter is very different to the Greek approach grounded in cosmological philosophy. The Israelite version proceeds largely by assertion and not by negation. Gordon Wenham and others have shown

36. Gunton, *Act and Being*, 37.
37. Gunton, *Act and Being*, 47.
38. Gunton, *The Promise of Trinitarian Theology*, 143.
39. Gunton, *Act and Being*, 53.

how this is the case in Gen 1–2, in which the author not only says no to pagan worldviews but also provides a positive, constructive view of God, of his power, sovereignty, creativity, and goodness. Gunton argues that the flood saga in Gen 6–9 can and should be read as an account of God's immutability in Barth's sense of God's constancy. Like Gen 1–2, Gen 6–9 is also directed polemically against alternative, pagan accounts of the flood.

Reversing the Lens

Following Barth, Gunton proposes that we start with revelation and the divine economy, and then ask what the divine attributes look like in this context and how they relate to the traditional concepts of classical theism. "Thus, while the first question concerns the relation of God's act and his being, the second is about his being and, accordingly, the attributes which are revealed in action. If God *is* in his act, then the questions are essentially the same, or different aspects of the same."[40]

In Scripture God is rendered truly to us narratively and credally; in the narratives of his actions and in the creed-like summaries of those actions. Both need to be attended to closely. Neglect of the narratives ignores the historical contexts of God's actions; neglect of the creedal statements risks losing touch with the being of God.

Barth identifies two major characteristics of God: his love and his freedom. For Barth, there are twelve perfections that characterize God; the first six being three perfections of divine love (grace, mercy, and patience) that are dialectically paired with, and whose meaning is therefore controlled by, the perfections of divine freedom (holiness, righteousness, and wisdom). This enables Barth to prioritize what Gunton calls the personal, biblical attributes while still engaging with the metaphysical and philosophical terms like omnipresence, eternity, and simplicity. Barth asserts that "it is dangerous and ultimately fatal to faith in God if God is not the Lord of glory, if it is not guaranteed to us that in spite of the analogical nature of language in which it has all to be expressed God is actually and unreservedly as we encounter Him in his revelation: the Almighty, the Holy, the Just, the Merciful, the Omnipresent, the eternal, not less but infinitely more so than it is in our power to grasp, and not for us only, but in actuality therefore in Himself."[41]

40. Gunton, *Act and Being*, 77.
41. Barth, *CD* 2/1, 325.

For Gunton, Barth's twofold pattern suggests that he may not take adequate account of the role of the Spirit, raising the question of what a more dominant pneumatological approach might mean for the attributes.

A trinitarian starting point means for Gunton that we must confess that *God is knowable*: "Therefore what may seem, in the light of much of the Christian tradition, to be an outrageous claim must be made: that it is part of the Christian claim to truth that human beings are given to know the being of God."[42] God is unknowable only in the sense that we cannot provide a fully rational account of his being. We can agree with Thomas that God is only known by his effects, but *only if his effects include historical revelation.* "Salvation depends on the unflinching affirmation that the God who meets us in the Son and the Spirit is the only God there is."[43] Humans are open to God, not primarily because we have intellect, but because, like God, we too are persons. We should not drive a gulf between the Trinity of the divine economy and a God who lurks behind the divine economy who may be very different to the Trinity. In other language, the immanent and the economic Trinity must be held together, affirming that God is eternally this way.[44] "God's being is a being in relation; without remainder relational."[45]

Gunton begins with two statements in the Johannine literature that provide a way forward. The first is the statement in the Gospel of John (4:24) that "God is Spirit." Classical theism proceeds from this to abstractions about God. It is true that there is a negative element to this statement but there is more to it than that. God, according to Gunton, gives humans a share in this elusive thing called "spirit." God breathes into Adam the *ruah* (spirit) of life. Gunton interprets this to mean that humans are open to God in a way that other creatures are not. "In sum, to have spirit means to be open to God's creative and redemptive Spirit. Spirit is thus a communicable attribute."[46] God being Spirit does not just mean that he is incorporeal but also that he is able to embrace both spirit and matter. As Spirit, God can cross the boundaries between himself and the world even to the point of the Son becoming incarnate.

If patience comes to us as something of a surprising attribute of God, even more so is Jenson's characterization of God as "roomy." God is able

42. Gunton, *Act and Being*, 111.

43. Gunton, *Act and Being*, 93.

44. See the important work by Paul Molnar, *Divine Freedom and the Doctrine of the Immanent Trinity* (London: T&T Clark, 2002).

45. Gunton, *The Promise of Trinitarian Theology*, 143.

46. Gunton, *Act and Being*, 115.

to accommodate other persons in his life without in any way distorting his life. "God, to state it as boldly as possible, is roomy. Indeed, if we were to list divine attributes, roominess would have to come next after jealousy. He can, if he chooses, distinguish himself from others not by excluding them but by including them."[47] God as Trinity can and does make room in himself for other persons, and that room is our created time. Evocatively, Jenson observes that God's act of creation is the opening of that room.

The second statement comes in 1 John 4:8: "God is love." "The important point for us is that John's theology of the economy of love—for it is that with which he is concerned—is grounded in a conception of God's being as love."[48] God's love causes him to send his Son to be a sacrifice for our sins, and here Gunton stresses God's holy love, rather than, with Barth, God's freedom. "In the holiness of God is encompassed a range of concepts which spell out the kind of God with whom we are to do: otherness from the world as its creator, purity as its redeemer and judge, holiness as the consistency between God's being and his action."[49] Holy love leads logically into the further attributes of God's mercy, wrath, grace, covenant-faithfulness. Gunton, following Barth, speaks here also of God's patience.

All of these are what Gunton calls attributes in action, but how do they relate to God's essence? Gunton answers this question by exploring the relationship between the two Johannine statements about God. "God is holy love because he is spirit in a quite definite way."[50] The Spirit perfects the communion of the Trinity, and perfection of particularity is achieved because the persons of the Trinity constitute each other for what they are. Holiness is God's eternal perfection. This provides "an account of God's utter self-sufficiency and his gracious orientation outwards, so that creator and creation are not opposites . . . but two realms which are positively related, and only become opposites by the sin and evil which set themselves in opposition to God's goodness."[51] In this way we arrive at an affirmation of God's aseity; that he has his being entirely in and from himself. Connected with aseity is simplicity. The Trinity is not constituted of separable parts but of persons, who can be distinguished but not separated, and thus constitute a "simple" God. As regards impassibility, we have to take with

---

47. Jenson, *Systematic Theology*, 1:226.
48. Gunton, *Act and Being*, 116.
49. Gunton, *Act and Being*, 117. Cf. Cremer, *The Christian Doctrine*, 20–29.
50. Gunton, *Act and Being*, 119.
51. Gunton, *Act and Being*, 121.

utmost seriousness the suffering of Christ. However, for Gunton we do need to retain the doctrine of immutability to protect our understanding of God's sovereignty, since God is never under the control of emotions or events in the world.

To summarize: "Aseity provides a necessary defence of God's ontological self-sufficiency; simplicity a defence of the indivisibility of his action, immutability of his utter constancy and consistency, impassibility of the indefectibility of his purposes for the perfection of his creation, and omnipotence of the guarantee that what God began in creation he will complete."[52] In terms of God's communicable and incommunicable attributes, Gunton argues that we move from the former to the latter, and that the latter are there for the former.

Conclusion

After being immersed in the Greek philosophy of classical theism, I find Gunton's work like a glass of fresh water on a hot day! In my view Gunton is quite correct that we need to begin with revelation in any attempt to develop a doctrine of God. To think that we can begin with "nature,"[53] unaided human reason and Greek philosophy, and ascend toward God seems to me contrary to Scripture, the fallenness of human beings, and the concomitant danger of creating a God in our image, as well as a manifestation of an unhelpful weddedness to certain types of Greek philosophy. Starting with the divine economy, as we have seen, foregrounds attributes of God that get lost or unnoticed in classical theism. Nevertheless, Barth and Gunton are then able to engage classical theism positively and redefine its traditional concepts with the framework of the divine economy.

Clearly Jewish scholars would not embrace Gunton's trinitarian approach. However, as we have seen in previous chapters, a parallel in the basic paradigm is found in Halevi and Wyschogrod, who begin with revelation while still taking philosophy seriously, and Gunton has helpfully pointed out just how important the HB/OT is for our doctrine of God. The starting point for a doctrine of God is the crucial element for the paradigm at work.

52. Gunton, *Act and Being*, 133.
53. Cf. Jenson's astute comments on "nature" in this respect (*Systematic Theology*, 1:7).

For our purposes, what is crucial is that we get to know God through his acts in his world. Thus, an essential presupposition of the doctrine of God is *divine action*. Clearly, Gunton's type of approach sees no barriers in believing fully in divine action; no problems emerge in relation to God speaking and acting as he does at Sinai. Indeed, this is precisely what we would expect from God.

There is a real sense in which belief in divine action accompanies faith in the living God, and I see no way around this. Nevertheless, we need to move beyond such a confession and explore the different ways in which we might conceive of divine action. This will be the theme of our next chapter.

CHAPTER 8

Models of Divine Action

But for the Bible the whole question of truth hinges upon the fact that it is not something timeless, but something which comes into being, the act of God in space and time.

Because biblical truth is historical, it is also personal. God's revelation of his truth in an historical event in space and time . . . [and] means that he himself, his *person*, is the content of this event.

—Heinz Zahrnt (commenting on Emil Brunner)[1]

In previous chapters we have explored philosophical—and theological—resistance to notions of divine action and have seen that they do not amount to defeaters to belief in divine action. By comparison, we have also explored robust philosophies and theologies of divine action. Naturally, if one embraces the pantheistic monism of Spinoza, for example, then divine action will be a major problem, but there is no need to do so.

The question arises, of course, of how one decides between philosophies and theologies. There is no simple answer to this question since critical engagement will always involve multiple strategies. In my view, such decisions *ultimately* relate back to how one views the world, that is, to one's *worldview*, which has religious roots of one sort or another.[2] One's worldview provides a basic or transcendent means of evaluation that is indispensable in terms of macro critique of different philosophies. Naturally, this must be accom-

1. Heinz Zahrnt, *The Question of God: Protestant Theology in the Twentieth Century*, trans. R. A. Wilson (London: Collins, 1969), 74-75.
2. See Michael W. Goheen and Craig G. Bartholomew, *Living at the Crossroads: An Introduction to Christian Worldview* (Grand Rapids: Baker Academic, 2008).

panied by immanent critique so that one can distinguish genuine insights from distortions in *all* positions.

A lingering sacred cow in scholarship is that while theology may develop from religious commitments philosophy can and should never do so. However, the view that religious beliefs can justifiably be taken as foundational has been creatively developed and honed *philosophically* by Alvin Plantinga, Nicholas Wolterstorff, and others,[3] according to whom belief in God is properly basic and can be rationally appropriated apart from proof. This is not to say that there are not good reasons for belief in God—there are—but that the rationality of such belief does not require such reasons.

For our purposes this is vital because, as noted above, belief in divine action generally accompanies faith in the living God. Such faith is not only noetic but also affective, and results from the belief and experience that God is at work in one's life and in his world, so that it would be impossible to have living faith apart from a belief in divine action. Once again, Plantinga has done fine work on this theme in relation to the internal testimony or instigation of the Holy Spirit bringing a person into a living relationship with God.[4]

Theologically, divine action is normally dealt with under the theme of the providence of God, an indispensable background to any theistic discussion of the concept. We will begin there, and then look at philosophical models for God's activity in the world.[5] After that we will examine scientific objections, before moving on to special divine action (SDA).

Providence and Divine Action

In my view Barth is right to locate providence under the doctrine of creation.[6] God's sustaining, accompanying, and ruling his creation is grounded *in* his act *of* creation. As with belief in creation, belief in providence is *a doctrine of faith*. Ours is not the first age to find providence unbelievable and un-

---

3. Alvin Plantinga and Nicholas Wolterstorff, eds., *Faith and Rationality: Reason and Belief in God* (Notre Dame: University of Notre Dame Press, 1983).

4. See Alvin Plantinga, *Warranted Christian Belief* (Oxford: Oxford University Press, 2000), 241–323.

5. Bruce Ashford and I have dealt with providence in more detail in our *Doctrine of Creation* (Downers Grove, IL: IVP Academic, 2020). This material is drawn from that more detailed treatment.

6. Barth, *CD* 3/3, 3.

palatable, and so it is vital to locate the source of belief in such a doctrine, lest we succumb to "the death of the God of providence," in Ricoeur's provocative words.[7] Although history, when viewed through the lens of providence, undoubtedly provides many evocative and wonderful examples, providence cannot be read off the pages of history. The twentieth century was one of the most brutal in history and, as the Brazilian theologian Leonardo Boff rightly notes, "there is a suffering humanity whose way of the cross has as many stations as that of the Lord when he suffered among us in Palestine."[8] Boff is clear that it is not just humanity but the entire creation that groans amidst these stations of the cross. George Steiner evokes the pathos of history when he writes at the conclusion of his classic, *Real Presences*, "but ours is the long day's journey of the Saturday. Between suffering, aloneness, unutterable waste on the one hand and the dream of liberation, of rebirth on the other."[9]

We *believe* in providence because of God's historical revelation, and not because we are able to trace his workings in history, important as this undoubtedly is. The Jewish philosopher Will Herberg's work is particularly helpful in this respect.[10] He locates the scandal of biblical faith in its deeply historical nature. It deals with historical events in which we find *"faith enacted as history."* Included in this is the fact that biblical faith provides us with a unique view of history.

Herberg identifies three major views of history: first, what I call *paganism*, which identifies reality with nature; second, the *Greek view* in which that which is timelessly eternal and unchanging is located behind nature. Neither of these enables history to come into proper focus. By contrast, biblical faith breaks with both paganism and Greek dualism. Both nature and time are real and part of God's good creation. Humankind is part of nature and yet transcends it as the image of God. "This complex, multidimensional conception makes it possible, for the first time, to understand man as a gen-

---

7. Paul Ricoeur, "Religion, Atheism, and Faith," in Ricoeur, *The Conflict of Interpretations: Essays in Hermeneutics*, ed. Don Ihde (Evanston, IL: Northwestern University Press, 1974), 455.

8. Leonardo Boff, *Passion of Christ, Passion of the World: The Facts, Their Interpretation, and Their Meaning Yesterday and Today*, trans. R. R. Barr, 2nd ed. (Maryknoll, NY: Orbis, 2001), ix.

9. George Steiner, *Real Presences: Is There Anything in What We Say?* (Chicago: University of Chicago Press, 1989), 232.

10. Will Herberg, *Faith Enacted as History: Essays in Biblical Theology*, ed. Bernhard W. Anderson (Philadelphia: Westminster, 1976).

uinely personal and historical being."[11] Humans can realize themselves only in and through history. "It is in and through history that God calls to man; it is in and through history, human action in history, that man responds; and it is in and through history that God judges."[12]

Our partial histories make sense only within a meta-history, and Scripture provides us with this through its *Heilsgeschichte*.

> Underlying and including the partial histories of life, there must be some "total" history, in some way fundamental and comprehensive, some really ultimate history. Such a history, the history which one affirms in a total and ultimate manner, is one's *redemptive history* (*Heilsgeschichte*), for it is the history in terms of which the final meaning of life is established and the self redeemed from the powers of meaninglessness and nonbeing. . . . Whatever history I take to tell me who I "really" am may thus be taken to be my actual faith.[13]

Biblical history is universal and characterized by a threefold pattern: the present is seen as a fall away from the original rightness of creation and headed for restoration as the fulfillment of the kingdom of God. All human history is embraced in its range, but its revelatory center is particular: for Jews, exodus-Sinai; for Christians, the Christ event. Herberg argues that biblical history manifests a double inwardness: first, it involves the interpretation of acts and events through the lens of faith; second, it can only become my redemptive history if I indwell it as the true story of the world.

In the Christ event we find the best and the worst of history: terrible suffering, betrayal, torture, deceit, abandonment, agony, and at the same time supreme love, unutterable compassion, humanity, sacrifice, redemption, glory. At Pentecost, when called upon to explain "What does this mean?" (Acts 2:12), Peter seizes upon Joel 2:28–32 as a hermeneutical key to explain how the Day of the Lord is being inaugurated through the outpouring of the Spirit.[14] He moves from the Joel quote directly to Jesus of Nazareth, "this man, handed over to you according to the definite plan and foreknowledge of God, you crucified and killed by the hands of those outside the law." No attempt is made to downplay the *free actions* of those who precipitated the

---

11. Herberg, *Faith Enacted as History*, 34.
12. Herberg, *Faith Enacted as History*, 35.
13. Herberg, *Faith Enacted as History*, 37.
14. Cf. Bartholomew and Thomas, *The Minor Prophets*.

wrongful accusation and death sentence handed down to Jesus. And yet, precisely in this horror of injustice and agony, in which Peter played his own part of betrayal, he affirms the sovereign action of God working out his plans for his world. The biblical teaching on providence is vast and varied, but, from a Christian perspective this is one of the best places from which to embrace it. Providence is a doctrine of faith in *this* God who was at work in the life, death, and resurrection of his Son.

Barth is thus right to note a christological deficit in the older Reformed doctrine of providence: "unfortunately the connexion between the belief in providence and belief in Christ had not been worked out and demonstrated theologically by the Reformers themselves."[15] It is preeminently at the cross, as the quote from Boff above indicates, that the stations of the cross that litter history and our world *today* are illumined and, without necessarily being explained—indeed, many, many remain shrouded in mystery, cast in what Wendell Berry so evocatively calls "difficult hope."

Providence and Covenant/Kingdom

Through using Joel as the hermeneutical key for Pentecost, Peter unequivocally identifies the outpouring of the Spirit as the inauguration of the Day of the Lord. Pentecost is more than the birth of the church; it is the start of the new creation. In this way Peter interweaves creation, new creation, salvation, and providence intricately together.

This foregrounds a crucial issue, namely the relationship between providence and salvation history. Barth is intensely aware of this issue and notes early on in his treatment of providence that "We have to make at this point a decision of great importance with far-reaching consequence" (*CD* 3/3, 39). Barth notes that the connection between creation and salvation history might "be established only at the end of the two histories and by way of a new creation" (*CD* 3/3, 38). It is not hard to see how a view of providence rooted in creation forces this issue to the surface. Barth rightly rejects the notion of two orders or kingdoms:

> We have not to reckon with a parallelism of the two sequences, but a positive connexion between them. The particular decision of God

15. Barth, *CD* 3/3, 32. Hereafter, references to this work are given in parentheses in the text.

concerning His elect and His government of all things, their love for God and their existence in the totality of things, are obviously not to be regarded apart but in conjunction, in material co-ordination. But if the One who has foreordained them heirs works all things, and if all things work together for good to those who love God, Christians can accept the occurrence of their creaturely history, certainly in faith alone, yet not in a blind faith, but in a faith which is objectively grounded, in a seeing faith, in the faith that there is here not merely a factual but a materially positive and inner connexion, so that even in their creaturely being they are *wholly in the kingdom of Christ and not another kingdom.* (*CD* 3/3, 39–40; emphasis added)

A way to penetrate this issue is to ask, "What is the purpose of creation?" and "What is the purpose of covenant, kingdom, and salvation?" Barth implicitly provides the answer in his framework of creation as the external basis of covenant and covenant as the internal aspect of creation. The covenantal text is Gen 1:1–2:3, and just as covenant is about God's purposes for his creation and then his recovery of those purposes through a people Israel, so too creation sets up God's kingdom. His work in Jesus is about the recovery of his reign over his entire creation, leading it toward the telos he always envisaged for it. "In the covenant of grace it is a matter of the reconciliation of the world with God, of the redemption of man, of the hushing of the sighing of all creation, of the revelation of the glory of God" (*CD* 3/3, 45). Calvin wonderfully describes the creation as *theatrum gloriae Dei*, and, nowhere is the glory of God more clearly seen than in the face of Jesus. As Barth notes, God's faithfulness is not divisible:

It is not first the faithfulness of the One who called Abraham, fulfilled the promise given to him and will finally manifest it in its fulfillment, and then again the faithfulness of the Creator who will not abandon His creature, but give it His support and continually direct its history. But the faithfulness of God is that He gives support and direction to the history of His creature in the fact that in this history He calls Abraham, and rules His people, and gives Himself in His Son, and will finally manifest Himself in this One as the Lord of the whole. The faithfulness of God is that He co-ordinates creaturely occurrence under His lordship with the occurrence of the covenant, grace and salvation, that He subordinates the former to the latter and makes it serve it, that He integrates it with the coming of His kingdom in which the whole of the reality distinct

from Himself has its meaning and historical substance, that He causes
it to co-operate in this happening. (*CD* 3/3, 40–41)

However, just as we must not separate salvation history from providence, neither must we collapse them into each other. It is obviously true
that the focus of most of the Bible is on the *thin line* in history of God's
work with Israel, his way with Jesus, and the birth of the church. Historically
speaking, this is a very narrow focus. However, this thin line never loses sight
of the fact that the God at work in salvation history *is* the creator God, and
his purposes with his people are inseparably connected to his purposes with
his whole creation. As Barth notes, "the goodness and even the perfection
of creation consists in the fact that God has made it serviceable for the rule
of His free and omnipotent grace, for the exercise of the lordship of Jesus
Christ" (*CD* 3/3, 3).

Salvation history occurs *in* history and cannot be understood apart from
it. However, what we learn from salvation history is "that world history in
its totality is the history in which God executes His will of grace must thus
be taken to mean that in its totality it belongs to this special history; that
its lines can have no other starting-point or goal than the one divine will of
grace; that they must converge on this thin line and finally run in its direction" (*CD* 3/3, 36). This is evident in the vocations of Israel, Jesus, and the
church. Israel is called to be a royal priesthood (Exod 19:3–6), Jesus is the
light of the world, and the church is called to be salt and light, to disciple
the nations. All such articulations are embedded in the view that the God
at work in Israel, Jesus, and the church is the creator God and that his purposes with his people, and preeminently in his Son, relate intimately to his
purposes for his entire creation.

Thus, if we want to gain insight into how God works with his world, that
is, into his providence, we need to attend closely to his work with Israel,
Jesus, and the early church, because here we will find reflected his ways with
his world. Take Israel, for example. In the HB/OT God sets up a people in a
land, as his people, in covenant with himself. They have a distinct national,
historical, and geographical identity with God living in their midst so that
now, as one author notes, God has an address on earth! Now, of course, Israel
is historically particular. It is an ANE nation, and its life bears all the marks of
such historicity. But it is intentionally crafted as a paradigm for the nations,
and in its constitution, and in God's journey with Israel, we find myriad clues
to his ways with his world, that is, to his providence and divine action. In our
discussion of providence and the philosophy of history below we will return

to the question of how much we can learn about God's providence through his ways with his people and in Jesus.

In what follows we will discuss God's providence in terms of his sustaining the creation in existence (*preserving*), his active involvement with the creation in its history (*accompanying*), and his sovereignty over the creation (his *ruling*).

Providence as Preservation (*Conservatio*)

In the HB/OT we find ample witness to the fact that God sustains the creation in existence. In Isa 40:12–31, for example, providence is envisioned as a natural, seamless extension of creation. In v. 12, God is the one who "marked off the heavens with a span"; in v. 22 he "stretches out the heavens like a curtain, and spreads them like a tent to live in." Verse 12 speaks of God's initial act of creation whereas v. 22 speaks of his sustaining the creation in existence. Similarly, in v. 26 the author holds creation and preservation closely together. He exhorts us to gaze at the stars and ask, Who created them? God is metaphorically pictured as bringing them out, numbering them, and calling them by name. Verse 26 is preceded by a reference to the fragility of princes and the rulers of the earth before God. As Childs notes, "the only possible rival to God's incomparability—now named 'the Holy One'—lies in the astral powers so widely respected in the ancient Near East. The heavenly bodies move in complete dependency upon God and respond in concert to his sovereign will."[16]

Barth, in our view, is, however, right in refocusing Reformed doctrines of providence along christological lines. Hebrews 1:3 says of Christ that *he* "sustains all things by his powerful word"; presumably "his powerful word" hearkens back to Gen 1 and God's creation by divine fiat. The point then is that not only is creation ushered into existence by God's word, but it is sustained in existence as well by his (Christ's) powerful word. Romans 1–11 concludes Paul's exposition of "the gospel of God" on the note that "for from him and to him and through him are all things. To him be the glory forever. Amen." In the gospel Christ is not only revealed as the one who sustains the universe in existence but also the reason for its being sustained, namely for the glory of God.

16. Brevard S. Childs, *Isaiah: A Commentary* (Louisville: Westminster/John Knox, 2001), 310.

Isaiah 40:22 evocatively pictures God as sitting *above* the circle of the earth! The spatial metaphor "above" alerts us to the fact that God is separate from his creation, and his creation is separate from him. However, the creation's separateness is an utterly contingent and dependent one whereas God's is absolute. God does not need to be sustained in existence whereas creation would cease to exist without being sustained by God. As Berkouwer thus rightly notes, "The confession sees all things as being indebted for their existence to the preserving act of God; let God cease to act and the universe would cease to exist. With this concept of sustenance the confession at once opposes every claimant to absoluteness in this world—gods and idols, and any who would autonomously and sovereignly pretend to a self-sufficient existence."[17] This need is enhanced after the fall in which lethal potentials are released into the creation and history.

Like creation, preservation is a free act of God, but whereas in creation God acts directly, in preservation "there is need of a free but obviously not of a direct or immediate activity on the part of God" (*CD* 3/3, 64). *Preservation* speaks of God holding this separate entity from himself, namely the creation, in existence beside himself and in a temporal sequence in which it can continue to exist. The means by which God does this is mysterious; Barth uses the word "inconceivable" (*CD* 3/3, 67). God is unlimited whereas he sustains creation *as creation* and thus within its creaturely *limits*. For the creature such limits represent genuine freedom *within* the life-giving limits built into the creation and prescribed by God. As Berkouwer notes, "even with a theoretical recognition of the dependency of all creaturely reality, it is possible in practice surreptitiously to make the creature self-existent. At bottom all deifying of the creature is the consequence of substance theories which invest the creature with self-existence. The incomprehensible act of sustaining renders idle all talk of outright independence."[18] God's sustaining rules out any such view of autonomous independence.

Providence as Accompanying (*Concursus*)

The present participle *pherōn* (sustains) in Heb 1:3 can also have meanings such as lead, bear along, carry, or guide. This alerts us to the fact that pres-

---

17. Gerrit C. Berkouwer, *The Providence of God*, Studies in Dogmatics (Grand Rapids: Eerdmans, 1952), 50.

18. Berkouwer, *The Providence of God*, 51.

ervation is not merely a static activity but one in which God *accompanies* his creation in its journey through history. As we will see in the next section, as he accompanies it he also *guides it* to his goal for it. Barth speaks in this respect of the creature's "preservation in activity" (*CD* 3/3, 90). As he sustains his creation in existence God accompanies it, goes with it in its journey through time:

> The activity of the creature takes place in its co-existence with God . . .
> It is therefore accompanied and surrounded by God's own activity. . . .
> The history of the covenant of grace accompanies the act of the creature from first to last. . . . It is accompanied by the divine wisdom and omnipotence in their specific form of fatherliness. . . . Its own activity stands under the controlling sign of the activity of this companion. (*CD* 3/3, 92)

God does not do this as a tyrant, but in his grace he recognizes the *relative* autonomy and *relative* freedom of the creature. "We even dare and indeed have to make the dangerous assertion that He co-operates with the creature, meaning that as He Himself works He allows the creature to work. Just as He Himself is active in His freedom, the creature can also be active in its freedom" (*CD* 3/3, 92). We speak in this respect of God's immanent involvement with his creation.

Now, of course, God does not accompany his creation as any type of companion but as its creator and sustainer. *How* he does this is where the controversy arises. In all its aspects providence is an article of faith but, whereas providence as preservation is "relatively" straightforward, providence as accompanying and ruling is where theologians and philosophers have developed a range of differing and conflicting views. As Bavinck notes, "the difficulty for the mind to maintain both creation and preservation always arises from the fact that by creation God's creatures have received their own unique existence, which is distinct from God's being, and that that existence may and can never even for a moment be viewed as an existence of and by itself, independent from God."[19]

Within the tradition the word for God's working with his creation is *concurrence*, as we will see below. Concurrence traditionally distinguishes between primary and secondary causes as a way of avoiding the dual dan-

---

19. Herman Bavinck, *Reformed Dogmatics*, vol. 2, trans. John Vriend (Grand Rapids: Baker Academic, 2004), 608.

gers of pantheism (Spinoza, Hegel, Schleiermacher, Strauss, Malebranche, etc.) and deism. In pantheism there are no longer any causes and in deism no secondary causes. Bavinck sees this distinction between primary and secondary causes as a major achievement of the Christian tradition since it does justice to secondary causes as real but always and only as subordinate to God as primary cause:

> The constant teaching of the Christian church, nevertheless, has been that the two causes, though they are totally dependent on the primary cause, are at the same time also true and essential causes. It is he who posits it and makes it move into action (*praecursus*) and who further accompanies it in its working and leads it to its effect (*concursus*). . . . Hence, the primary cause and the secondary cause remain distinct. The former does not destroy the latter but on the contrary confers reality on it, and the second exists solely as a result of the first. Neither are the secondary causes merely instruments, organs, inanimate automata, but they are genuine causes with a nature, vitality, spontaneity, manner of working, and law of their own.[20]

Barth is, however, far more cautious than Bavinck in affirming this understanding of *concursus* (*CD* 3/3, 94–107). He notes that Reformed and Lutheran theologians appropriated the language of causality from Aristotle and Aquinas and recognizes the good use to which they put it. According to Barth, formally their view is correct but materially it is not since it missed the relationship between creation and the covenant of grace, between salvation and world history. It thus lacked specifically Christian content, thereby making it vulnerable to distortions. Barth identifies five criteria that must be in place if causality[21] is to be used for providence in this way (*CD* 3/3, 101):

1. The term "cause" must not be regarded as equivalent to a cause that is automatically effective. Bavinck similarly notes that causality in this context must not be understood mechanically.[22]

---

20. Bavinck, *Reformed Dogmatics*, 2:614.

21. The literature on causality is immense. Cf. Phyllis Illari and Federica Russo, *Causality: Philosophical Theory Meets Scientific Practice* (Oxford: Oxford University Press, 2014); Helen Beebee, Christopher Hitchcock, and Peter Menzies, eds., *The Oxford Handbook of Causality* (Oxford: Oxford University Press, 2009).

22. Bavinck, *Reformed Dogmatics*, 2:610.

2. Care must be taken lest it should be thought that in God and the creature we have to do with two "things," which can be examined and analyzed as such.
3. "Cause" is not a master concept to which God and the creature are subject. It could be read as an analogy, but Barth is wary of the danger of ignoring the radical dissimilarity between God and the creature.
4. Causal language should not be used with a view to turning theology into philosophy.
5. *Concursus* must connect the first article of the creed with the second. "His *causare* consists, and consists only, in the fact that He bends their activity to the execution of His own will which is His will of grace, subordinating their operations to the specific operation which constitutes the history of the covenant of grace" (*CD* 3/3, 105).

As for point 4, I do not share Barth's aversion to (Christian) philosophy, although I recognize the danger of uncritically applying philosophical concepts to providence. I recognize with Barth that a human concept of causality cannot simply be applied to God because of his unique otherness and that we need to be wary of a mechanical, reductionistic concept of causality. At its best, however, the tradition is sensitive to these dangers. Bavinck, for example, notes:

> A mechanical connection is only one mode in which a number of things in the world relate to each other. Just as creatures received a nature of their own in the creation and differ among themselves, so there is also difference in the laws in conformity with which they function and in the relation in which they stand to each other.
>
> These laws and relations differ in every sphere: the physical and the psychological, the intellectual and the ethical, the family and society, science and art, the kingdoms of earth and the kingdom of heaven. It is the providence of God that, interlocking with creation, maintains and brings to full development all these distinct natures, forces, and ordinances. In providence God respects and develops—and does not nullify—the things he called into being in creation.[23]

Bavinck here uses the Kuyperian concept of sphere sovereignty[24] to provide a nuanced account of causality. Barth rightly connects providence to God's

23. Bavinck, *Reformed Dogmatics*, 2:610.
24. See Bartholomew, *Contours of the Kuyperian Tradition*.

covenant of grace, but we need to remember that covenant, for Barth, is the internal aspect of creation and thus relates to all that takes place within creation. I conclude that, carefully nuanced, the notion of primary and secondary causality remains a useful heuristic for getting at the mystery of concurrence.

God's accompanying the creation also involves his *preceding* (*praecurrit*) the creature and this raises the issue of God's *foreknowledge*. We have already noted that Acts 2:23 uses the noun "foreknowledge" (*prognōsei*) of Jesus's crucifixion. As with causality God's foreknowledge raises in acute form the question of human freedom. A common solution has been to deny the omniscience of God (Cicero, Marcion), but this is so clearly attested in Scripture that orthodox theologians have sought other ways to resolve this issue. Bavinck neatly divides views along the lines of Origen and Augustine.[25] For Origen (*Homilies on Genesis* 1.14), events "do not happen because they were known, but they were known because they were going to happen." Augustine likewise seeks to maintain both divine foreknowledge and human freedom but argues that if God knows something in advance it is certain to happen as a matter of necessity. Scholasticism in general sided with Augustine, but the Jesuits introduced a different view in Middle Knowledge. In governing creation God made possible many outcomes and knows in advance what he will do, however these possibilities are fulfilled by humans. This theory was advanced by the Molinists and the Congruists and gained wide acceptance among Roman Catholics, and it has been recently defended by Thomas Flint and William Lane Craig.[26]

In my view Scripture supports the stronger Augustinian view, but this must always be held with a sense of the mystery of providence. We return again to Acts 2 and the crucifixion of Jesus. As Hendrikus Berkhof insightfully writes,

> For we derive this certainty from his history with us, in the center of which stands the cross. The cross is the climax of our resistance and hostility toward God and therefore the nadir of God-forsakenness. Here free and guilty man seems to have the final and only say. Yet this God-forsakenness is enclosed by an unfathomable presence of God whereby the God-forsakenness becomes the way leading to a new and

25. Bavinck, *Reformed Dogmatics*, 2:197–203.
26. Thomas Flint, *Divine Providence: The Molinist Account* (Ithaca, NY: Cornell University Press, 1998); William Lane Craig, *The Only Wise God: The Compatibility of Divine Foreknowledge and Human Freedom* (Eugene, OR: Wipf and Stock, 2000).

reconciled communion between him and man. Since this happened we know that even the greatest horrors do not happen apart from God. He does not want them, but they cannot thwart his purpose and must ultimately serve it.[27]

And in terms of God's foreknowledge Acts 2 speaks of God's *"definite plan and foreknowledge,"* indicating that at this moment of supreme rebellion God's will is being executed perfectly.

Providence as Ruling (*Gubernatio*)

In Gen 1 God is portrayed as King par excellence, and it is no different when it comes to providence. God creates the world with a goal, and he rules over it so as to lead it toward its intended goal. He alone rules, and he directs history toward himself. In the HB/OT, covenant, including that of Sinai, is grounded in ANE treaty analogies alive with a sense of the conquering king. In the NT, especially in the Synoptic Gospels, the kingdom of God/heaven is the dominant theme with the Savior-King incarnate in our midst. "Thus in the Old and New Testaments, and in the movement from the one to the other, we see the King of Israel treading always one path" (*CD* 3/3, 181). The eschatology of the NT opens up between the coming of the king and the final consummation of the kingdom.

It is to the thin line of salvation history that we must attend if we wish to know of God's rule. Indeed our view of God as sovereign ruler will depend upon our view of his journey with Israel and his work in Christ. Referring to the particular places and events of salvation history Barth perceptively notes that, "if we cannot apprehend and affirm the idea of the divine world-governance, then quite concretely this means that we stand in a negative relationship to these events which took place at definite periods and in definite places, to this reality, and to this concrete Scripture" (*CD* 3/3, 177). And, as we have noted, God's purposes with Israel and in Christ are always directed toward his purpose for his entire creation.

Barth rightly notes that "we have to look at world events in general outwards from the particular events attested in the Bible, from God's activity in the covenant of grace which He instituted and executed in Israel and in

27. Hendrikus Berkhof, *Christian Faith: An Introduction to the Study of the Faith* (Grand Rapids: Eerdmans, 1979), 218.

the community of Jesus Christ" (*CD* 3/3, 183). In the same passage he rightly stresses that we should not make this history into a private one. Thus, there is in fact no such thing as secular history:

> For the very same reason that we are not allowed to make the history of the covenant a private history, we are also forbidden to make universal history private over against it. If we did . . . we should be denying the public nature and claim of what did occur, and does and will occur, in the history of the covenant and salvation to and from and in Jesus Christ—in the greatest particularity, to be sure, yet not apart from but at the very centre of creaturely occurrence. (*CD* 3/3, 184)

God's reign is a rich concept in relation to creation, as are his dynamic purposes for his creation. Abraham Kuyper was rightly vocal in opposing a shallow conception of providence purely as maintenance. Few doctrines were so superficially handled as providence, in his view. "Imagine," said Kuyper, "that creation were a lifeless metal or granite structure! One can conceive of a granite mountain ridge, or of metal, gold, or silver structures preserved from decay. But then there would be only a dead structure lying in eternal stillness, and Providence would mean only that creation had been preserved in existence."[28] Kuyper insists, like Barth, that God is the fountain of life, and that creation lives. God sustains a world that is constantly changing and developing. Providence is also purposeful. Thus, God's preserving and ruling should not be viewed as two separate activities. One cannot think of God's preserving without bringing the rule of God into the equation.

We noted at the outset of this chapter that one's view of divine action will be shaped by one's view of God and faith in him. Our discussion of providence provides the context for a robust and compelling view of divine action and alerts us to the fact that divine action only makes sense within the context of a network of such beliefs.

Philosophy and Divine Action

Down through the ages theistic philosophers have articulated various accounts of God's action in creation and how this relates to human action, generally assuming that any account of miracles firstly requires God's con-

---

28. Quoted in Berkouwer, *The Providence of God*, 67–68.

tinual involvement in the normal course of events. Our goal in this section is to identify the main views and to see how they relate to our discussion above. The complexity of this issue should not be underestimated. For example, the issue of divine and human action raises the issue of the nature of so-called natural laws, which may appear obvious to us but are, in fact, exceedingly complex. Questions arise such as: Do such laws actually exist? If they do, what exactly are they? How do they relate to God? And to determinism?[29] Plantinga proposes that "natural laws . . . are universal generalizations that enjoy a certain kind of necessity."[30] He relates their necessity to the fact that they cannot be violated by creatures, or, at least human creatures.

Plantinga argues that the most promising ways of thinking about how such laws relate to God are, first, the view that laws of nature relate to the causal powers of the creatures made by God (conservationism and concurrentism); second, the view that natural laws are God's ordinances, part of his means of directing the creation; and third, the view, originating with Del Ratzsch, that such laws are counterfactuals of divine freedom, that is, they indicate how God would treat the creation in various conditions.[31] The second and third fit most closely with occasionalism.

Occasionalism

This view, held by important medieval and some early modern thinkers (Nicolas Malebranche, 1638–1715),[32] argues that it is God alone who causes effects in nature. Natural substances make no causal contribution to any such effect. "The central thesis of occasionalism, a doctrine associated most prominently with certain Cartesian philosophers in the seventeenth century but with its roots in medieval thought, is that all causal efficacy in the uni-

29. Alvin Plantinga, "Law, Cause, and Occasionalism," in *Reason and Faith: Themes from Richard Swinburne*, ed. Michael Bergmann and Jeffrey E. Brower (Oxford: Oxford University Press, 2016), 126–44.

30. Plantinga, "Law, Cause, and Occasionalism," 132.

31. Plantinga, "Law, Cause, and Occasionalism," 127.

32. Nicolas Malebranche's work provides some of the most important and substantial reflections on Occasionalism. Cf. Sukjae Lee, "Occasionalism," *The Stanford Encyclopedia of Philosophy* (Winter 2016 edition), ed. Edward N. Zalta, https://plato.stanford.edu/archives/win2016/entries/occasionalism/.

verse belongs to God."[33] Thus, in the strong version of occasionalism there is no secondary, that is, creaturely, causation in nature.

Intriguingly, this view has its origins among medieval Muslim scholars in the tenth and eleventh centuries motivated by a concern to protect divine action against dangers they saw in Aristotelian and Neoplatonic philosophy, which seemed to them to reduce possible divine intervention to natural causes. Malebranche is the major early modern representative of occasionalism. Leibniz espoused a view known as "preestablished harmony," which accepted that finite substances lack the necessary power to cause changes in other substances, but argued that finite substances are internally active causally in bringing about their own states. "Each creature causally contributes to the occurrence of its own states, and the apparent interaction between distinct substances is due to how the states of distinct substances harmonize with each other."[34]

Plantinga recognizes the problems inherent in strong occasionalism: it subverts the reality of human agency and responsibility and it seem to make God responsible for evil. However, he explores the possibility of a weak occasionalism in which "the only creaturely causation is of the sort involved in my causing my decisions, volitions, and undertakings."[35] For Plantinga, weak occasionalism and secondary causality share similar weaknesses—particularly God causing that which is bad—but the former slightly less so than the latter.

Conservationism: Strong Secondary Causality

Conservationism is, as it were, at the other end of the spectrum of philosophical views of divine action. For conservationism, created entities are genuinely secondary causes and lead to natural effects by themselves, being preserved in existence by God. In comparison with occasionalism God's role is "minimal." As creator he conserves natural substances and their accidents in existence, including their powers. When a substance causes an effect, it alone is the immediate cause of that effect, with God significantly distanced from this immediate effect by his conserving power. Such a view is always

33. Steven Nadler, *Occasionalism: Causation among the Cartesians* (Oxford: Oxford University Press, 2011), 1.

34. Lee, "Occasionalism."

35. Plantinga, "Law, Cause, and Occasionalism," 141.

in danger of heading off in a deist direction and does not fit with God's providence as discussed above.

Concurrentism: Weak Secondary Causality

Concurrentism, which flourished among late medieval scholastics such as Aquinas, and certain philosophers of the early modern period, occupies the median position between occasionalism and mere conservationism. For concurrentism a natural effect is produced immediately by both God and created substances, with the result that the created substance makes a genuine causal contribution to the effect; indeed it determines its specific character, but does so only if God cooperates with it simultaneously. God's action thus goes beyond conservation, making the resulting cooperative action the action of both God and the secondary cause.

Insole argues that Kant's admirable desire to protect human freedom and human action as fully responsible requires an account of divine action such as concurrence to work.[36] Insole acknowledges up front the mystery of concurrence. Theologically it is built on two major pillars: *creatio ex nihilo* and the fact that humans are created free. He wonders aloud, as it were, if we have really understood *creatio ex nihilo*. "God's creating and sustaining of every texture of reality—things, events, actions, thoughts—is as dramatically total and 'from nothing' as God's original action in bringing about something rather than nothing" (118). The other pillar is that human action is free and responsible. If one thinks of these two pillars as the two poles of thinking about divine action, the apparent tension between them can be "solved" in two ways:

1. We can make human freedom subordinate to God's predetermined sovereign will. For Insole occasionalism is guilty of this move.
2. We can make *creatio ex nihilo* subordinate to free, human action so that for humans to really act freely God must withdraw. This "solution" is very much that of Kant who knows of concurrence but overtly rejects it (123–28).

36. Christopher J. Insole, *The Intolerable God: Kant's Theological Journey* (Grand Rapids: Eerdmans, 2016), 111–28. Hereafter, page references to this work are given in parentheses in the text.

Concurrence, by contrast, insists on holding the two pillars inseparably together. Insole quotes David Burrell on Thomas: "God not only causes each thing to be, and thus makes it able to act, but God also acts in its acting by causing it to be the cause that it is" (123).[37] For Thomas, humans act in a genuinely free and responsible way, and can act otherwise, but God acts in this action. Insole argues that a full account of concurrence requires three elements (121):

1. God acts immediately and directly in the action of a creature.
2. Neither God's action nor that of the creature would, by themselves, be sufficient for the action to take place.
3. Apart from this concurrence of action, neither action would exist.

Insole notes the challenges of giving an adequate account of concurrence, mainly because of the unique, one-off relationship of God to creatures. He asserts that concurrence follows on from creation and conservation as a more intense articulation of what is involved in *creatio ex nihilo*.

But how, one might ask, does concurrence save Kant's concern to protect human freedom? Insole asserts that there is a tension at the heart of Kant's doctrine of freedom: although human freedom is vital for human autonomy, it is also potentially destructive of our vocation to become the human beings we ought to be. In response to this tension Insole proposes a metaphor of dancing. We choose to dance but dancing can have rules and the dancer can be led in the dance by another person. "The 'hope of being lead in the dance' involves hoping that our freedom will be led, so that our every movement arises from the true dancer, and every movement is both ours and the other's, but only truly ours—expressive of what we most desire—because it is led by the other, who alone knows how to sway to the music, and how to become the dance" (112).

Above we noted Barth's reservations about concurrence as a philosophical concept. Some of these reservations return at this point. Barth notes that concurrence needs to be connected to God's grace and his representation in salvation history. Insole evocatively refers to the hope that we are being led in the dance of life by the true dancer. However, it seems to me that there is nothing in the purely philosophical doctrine of concurrence that would bring this to the fore since in *every* act, whether obedient or

37. The quote is from David Burrell, *Freedom and Creation in Three Traditions* (Notre Dame, IN: University of Notre Dame Press, 1993), 68–69.

rebellious, God is acting concurrently with the creature. The danger here is to make God responsible for both good and evil actions. Whatever truth there is in concurrence—and we are deep in the territory of mystery here—a further dimension needs to be added, namely that God wishes to be fully and intentionally acting with the creature, whereas, in a fallen and sinful world this is too often not the case.

Undoubtedly causality is one way in which God and humans act, and it will be clear from the above that it is challenging to give an adequate philosophical account of such causality. However, it is important to note that there is far more to divine and human action than causality: God manifests himself, thinks, loves, speaks in a whole variety of speech acts, gives laws, becomes incarnate in his Son, governs the creation and leads it to its destiny, and so on. The biblical representation of God cannot be reduced to causality. God is far more immanently involved in his creation than any of the three models above suggest. We will say more of this in our discussion of SDA below.

Science and Divine Action

The above views were developed in the medieval and early modern periods in the context of the challenge of the revival of Aristotelianism. In modernity, fresh challenges to divine action have appeared largely in relation to science; and, especially in the twentieth century, science has changed in shifts and bounds. A common tendency in modernity has been to see its naturalistic, scientistic worldview as true and superior to theistic worldviews, with the divine element in the latter as *mythical*, and in need of demythologization.

Plantinga refers to Rudolf Bultmann, Langdon Gilkey, and John Macquarrie as examples of theologians who think that modern science rules out divine intervention and, in particular, miracles.[38] For example, in his characterization of myth as embodying supernatural agency, Macquarrie observes that this characteristic is vulnerable to theological and scientific critique. "A more advanced theology protests against the idea that the divine can be objectified, so as to manifest itself in sensible phenomena,"[39] as well

38. Alvin Plantinga, *Where the Conflict Really Lies: Science, Religion and Naturalism* (Oxford: Oxford University Press, 2011), 69–75.

39. John Macquarrie, *God-Talk: An Examination of the Language and Logic of Theology* (London: SCM, 1967), 176.

as against any undermining of human responsibility through a view of divine determinism. Scientifically "we have learned to think of our world as a self-regulating cosmos, so that we look for the explanation of one set of events in terms of events within the same series. We no longer look to supernatural agencies that occasionally supervene to produce special effects."[40] For Macquarrie this conflict is real, and we need to reinterpret such language of divine intervention to refer to an aspect of human being-in-the-world.

For our purposes, it is notable how quickly *naturalism* took hold in modern OT studies. This move gathered momentum through the efforts of the deists and naturalists of the seventeenth and eighteenth centuries. An anonymous manuscript,[41] the so-called *Wolfenbüttel Fragments*, was discovered by Lessing in the Wolfenbüttel Library and published by him in 1774. The *Fragments* not only denies the supernatural in the OT but denigrates Moses, for example, as an evil imposter. Georg L. Bauer in 1820 published *A Hebrew Mythology of Old and New Testaments* in which he sets out the criteria for myth: any narrative that provides a historical account of events, events that are either absolutely or relatively outside of the reach of experience. Events related to the spiritual world fall within this category. Wilhelm de Wette, who we saw in a previous chapter was deeply influenced by Kant, proposes that in order to test the historicity of a narrative we need to investigate the intention of the narrator. If the narrator does not provide a straightforward narration of facts aimed at satisfying the historically curious, but seeks to evoke certain emotions or to teach a religious or philosophical truth, then the narrative has no claim to historicity. For de Wette, we could only try to separate the mythical from the historical in the OT if we had another set of documents to compare the OT with; alas, we do not possess such a set.

Johann Gottfried Eichhorn (1752–1827) concurs with "the Fragmentist" (Reimarus) in refusing to recognize divine intervention, at least in the early narratives of the HB/OT. He argues that the HB/OT shares with all ancient nations the tendency to refer inexplicable occurrences to the deity. We need to translate the language of a bygone age into the language of today. Strauss points out that

> Eichhorn is of the opinion that no objection can be urged against the attempt to resolve all the Mosaic narratives into natural occurrences. . . . Eichhorn agreed with the Naturalists in divesting the biblical narratives

40. Macquarrie, *God-Talk*, 176.
41. The author was Reimarus.

of all their immediate divine contents, but he differed from them in this, that he explained the supernatural lustre that adorns these histories, not as a fictitious colouring imparted with design to deceive, but as a natural and as it were spontaneous illumination reflected from antiquity itself.[42]

For Eichhorn, the fire and smoke on Mount Sinai at the giving of the law came from a fire kindled by Moses so as to evoke the Israelites' imagination. It was accompanied by an accidental thunderstorm at that moment. Moses's shiny face was the natural result of overheating; but Moses himself and the people interpreted this natural phenomenon as contact with the divine. They—unlike us—were ignorant of the true cause.[43]

It is their belief in modern science that makes the above authors think that there is a conflict with theistic belief. Intriguingly, and rightly in my view, Plantinga argues that there is no conflict between Christian belief and modern science, but that there is a conflict between naturalism and modern science. In various publications Plantinga has argued in detail that, "taking naturalism to include materialism with respect to human beings, . . . it is improbable, given naturalism and evolution, that our cognitive faculties are reliable. It is improbable that they provide us with a suitable preponderance of true belief over false."[44]

Thomas Kelly Cheyne, in his *Founders of Old Testament Criticism: Biographical, Descriptive and Critical Studies*, begins his investigation with Eichhorn, whom he describes as "the founder of modern Old Testament criticism."[45] Different scholars are called the founder or father of modern OT criticism; nevertheless, this description of Eichhorn alerts us to just how strongly OT criticism was influenced by naturalism at the outset. Certainly, if naturalism is in conflict with modern science then the criteria scholars like Eichhorn developed for dismissing the supernatural elements in the HB/OT need to be rejected and our approach to the HB/OT carefully rethought.

42. David Friedrich Strauss, *The Life of Jesus Critically Examined*, trans. George Eliot, 4th ed. (London: Swann Sonnenschein and Co., 1902), 48.

43. Referred to by Strauss, *The Life of Jesus*, 48.

44. Plantinga, *Where the Conflict Really Lies*, xiv. On naturalism and mystic experience see William Alston, *Perceiving God: The Epistemology of Religious Experience* (Ithaca, NY: Cornell University Press, 1991), 228–34.

45. Thomas Kelly Cheyne, *Founders of Old Testament Criticism: Biographical, Descriptive and Critical Studies* (London: Methuen and Co., 1893), 13.

Plantinga notes that with recent thinkers like Gilkey, Macquarrie, and most members of what Plantinga dubs the Divine Action Project (DAP), the problem is not so much with creation and conservation, but with *divine intervention*. It is thought that modern science somehow rules out divine intervention, so that SDA becomes the real problem. Modern science, it is argued, shows that God never acts in this way: "The problem, then, as these people see it, is this. Science discovers and endorses natural laws; if God did miracles or acted specifically in the world, he would have to contravene these laws and miraculously intervene; and that is incompatible with science. Religion and science, therefore, are in conflict, which does not bode well for religion."[46] Plantinga asks if this is in fact the case.

In responding to this challenge Plantinga explores what he calls the old picture of science and the new. Under the old picture, he discusses the Newtonian picture and the Laplacean one. Newton envisaged the world as a vast machine evolving or operating according to fixed laws. Newton's famed conservation laws are complete and fixed *in closed or isolated systems*. The latter nuance is crucial, since Newton himself was a convinced Christian and celebrated the fact, for example, that the "most beautiful system of the sun, planets and comets could only proceed from the counsel and dominion of an intelligent and powerful Being."[47] Plantinga says of the Newtonian picture that "there is nothing here to prevent God from miraculously parting the Red Sea, or changing water into wine, or bringing someone back to life, or, for that matter, creating *ex nihilo* a full-grown horse in the middle of Times Square."[48]

It is not the Newtonian picture that is a problem for Christian belief but the Laplacean picture that adds determinism and the causal closure of the physical universe to the Newtonian picture. "It is the Laplacean picture that is incompatible with special divine action, but the Laplacean picture with its causal closure of the physical universe is really a piece of metaphysics unsupported by classical science" (91). Plantinga notes that, in "touting the powers of his calculating demon, Laplace was just *assuming* that God couldn't or wouldn't act specially" (85). As Plantinga points out, it is ironic that theologians were advocating for the Laplacean picture when it is in fact no part of the classical science they supported. Furthermore, the new

46. Plantinga, *Where the Conflict Really Lies*, 75.

47. Newton, *Principia*; quoted in John Lesslie, *Universes* (London: Routledge, 1989), 25.

48. Plantinga, *Where the Conflict Really Lies*, 78–79. Hereafter, page references to this work are given in parentheses in the text.

picture was already upon us when these theologians were anachronistically defending their understanding of the old one.

In terms of the new picture of science, Plantinga refers to relativity theory and quantum mechanics (QM), and focuses on the latter. These are complex issues and in relation to QM Plantinga attends to the characteristic of *indeterminism*. He concludes that in terms of QM "there is no question that special divine action is consistent with science; and even the most stunning miracles are not clearly inconsistent with the laws promulgated by science" (96). In this context, Plantinga discusses the DAP, a series of conferences and publications that began in 1988, associated with specialists such as John Polkinghorne, Nancey Murphy, Philip Clayton, and so on. Most of the members of the DAP agree that an adequate account of divine action in the world needs to be noninterventionist. As Clayton says, "the real problem here, apparently, is that it is very difficult to come up with an idea of divine action in the world in which such action would not constitute 'breaking natural law' or 'breaking physical law.'"[49] Plantinga discerns three major problems members of the DAP find with divine intervention:

1. The problem of evil, namely why God intervenes on some occasions but not on others. As Plantinga notes, God will have a good reason for intervening when he chooses to do so, but why should we be in the position to know when he does and does not?
2. Noninterference by God is thought necessary to provide for genuine human freedom. But, as Plantinga observes, this is God's world, so "interference" is a pejorative word. What is required for responsible human action is sufficient regularity for us to know or make a sensible guess about the consequences of our actions.
3. The theological objection, namely that God simply would not create a world with laws and then occasionally intervene in it contrary to those laws.

Plantinga notes the difficulty of defining "divine intervention." He points out that in terms of QM and its doctrine of collapse, God can cause quantum events without suspending the laws of QM. The warrant for belief in SDA does not, however, come from QM or current science; such beliefs

49. Philip Clayton, *God and Contemporary Science* (Edinburgh: Edinburgh University Press, 1997), 195, 203, 206; quoted in Plantinga, *Where the Conflict Really Lies*, 98.

have their own independent source of warrant, as Plantinga has argued else-where, and current science provides no such defeaters to a belief in SDA. "The sensible religious believer is not obliged to trim her sails to the current scientific breeze on this topic, revising her belief on the topic every time science changes its mind" (121). According to Plantinga, "what we've seen is that there is nothing in science, under either the old or the new picture, that conflicts with or even calls into question special divine action, including miracles" (121–22).

Special Divine Action: Revelation and Experience

Plantinga's conclusion provides an apt segue into a constructive account of the sort of divine action we find at Sinai. Schwöbel rightly notes that theology can only be practiced in the context of the discourses of its time. The danger, of course, is that theology becomes the mirror image of the intellectual fashions of the day. Thus "it is necessary that theologians work not only as fashion designers or retailers of the theological 'trend setters.' They also have to attempt to relate as fashion critics the style preferences of the season to the perennial issues and questions of Christian theology."[50] Schwöbel notes that from the end of World War I until the 1960s theology was dominated by "revelation," whereas in the 1970s onwards a somewhat reactive emphasis on "experience" emerged. He rightly notes that we need a theory that correctly relates revelation and experience; indeed, both are essential to the sort of divine disclosure we find at Sinai. In this final section, following Schwöbel and others, we will set out a constructive account of revelation and experience as central elements in the sort of divine action we witness at Sinai. I agree with Barth, Gunton, and Schwöbel that a Christian account in this respect should be trinitarian, but, for the sake of my Jewish friends and readers, I will lessen the explicit trinitarian emphasis of Schwöbel in order to show that this is a model that Jews can also embrace.

Revelation is inseparably connected with Scripture but far broader. It is an act of divine self-communication through which God communicates himself through created reality as the creator and redeemer of created being. Following Ian T. Ramsey, we can think of revelation as an act of self-

50. Christoph Schwöbel, *God: Action and Revelation* (Kampen: Kok Pharos, 1992), 83.

disclosure,[51] and Eilert Herms has helpfully developed a phenomenology of disclosure events,[52] which Schwöbel uses to articulate a theology of revelation. Schwöbel identifies five central elements in revelation:

1. the author of divine revelation
2. the situation of revelation
3. the content of revelation
4. the recipient of revelation
5. the result of revelation

1. The author of divine revelation: because God is the author of divine revelation, revelation is a species of divine action. Thus, "no other reason can be given for the occurrence of the revelation than God's freedom."[53] It follows from this that we cannot assume God's action to be limited in the way that human actions are constrained. Further, in God's actions there is no conflict between his will and his being so that, according to Schwöbel, we need an analysis of revelation that foregrounds the unity of God's action in the divine economy.

2. The situation of revelation: God discloses himself within the creation with its order, historical structure, and capacity for linguistic interpretation. Within this context revelation is a complex occurrence involving various dimensions, including the witness of those involved.

3. The content of revelation: the disclosure and self-interpretation by God—God discloses who he is—and the narrative interpretation by the witnesses as found in Scripture are all acts of God. "The identity description of personal agents and the self-identification of persons has therefore always a historical (e.g. biographical) structure. In the case of self-identification, this historical structure comprises not only the connection between the intentions of a person and the actions actualizing these intentions but also the communicative representation of this connection for the addressees of this self-identification."[54] Such is the nature of the divine economy that where the hearers become convinced of the truth

51. Ian T. Ramsay, *Models for Divine Activity* (Eugene, OR: Wipf and Stock, 1973).

52. Eilert Herms, *Offenbarung und Glaube: Zur Bildung des christlichen Lebens* (Tübingen: J. C. B. Mohr, 1992).

53. Schwöbel, *God*, 87.

54. Schwöbel, *God*, 91.

claims and their implications for their own lives, created reality as a whole becomes a disclosure situation.

4. *The recipient of revelation*: "Just as the self-disclosure of God has a particular author and content and happens in a particular disclosure situation, so it is also not directed at somebody in general and nobody in particular, but it is addressed to particular persons."[55] Indeed, "the particularity of specific people as recipients of revelation is closely connected to the personal character of God's self-communication."[56] Revelation is thus, to use Gilbert Ryle's formulation, a "success" word.[57] Although the relationship between God and humans in revelation is asymmetrical, reception of God's revelation is required by its hearers for it to "fire successfully" as a "speech" act. Revelation will be concrete but its implications universal because of the character of God. Revelation brings with it human responsibility for how we exercise our freedom and discloses us in all the dimensions of our relationality.

5. *The result of revelation*: Alston notes that the chief advantage of perceiving God is that it makes personal communion with him possible. "The experience of God greatly enlivens one's religious life, it makes an enormous difference to the quality and intensity of one's devotional life, it greatly stimulates one's aspirations to virtue and holiness, and most important, it makes possible the loving communion with God for which we were created" (303). In Schwöbel's language, it makes faith possible. It liberates us from sin and toward liberation and becoming fully human. As Schwöbel points out, faith is no marginal reality but "the fundamental ontological *datum* which defines the perspective from which an ontology can be developed in the reflection of Christian faith."[58] For Schwöbel, such faith excludes any analysis of the God–humanity relationship as one between two self-existing causally interacting substances. The knowledge of faith is the foundation of all forms of knowledge.

Revelation as disclosure involves encounter (cf. Berkovits) and thus *experience*. Schwöbel develops a sophisticated theology of experience in relationship to revelation, and William Alston has left us in his debt with his magisterial *Perceiving God: The Epistemology of Religious Experience*. Alston makes the case for God *presenting* himself to us and argues that experiential

55. Schwöbel, *God*, 92.
56. Schwöbel, *God*, 93.
57. Cf. Alston, *Perceiving God*, 1. Hereafter, page references to this work are given in parentheses in the text.
58. Schwöbel, *God*, 97.

awareness of God contributes to the grounds of religious belief. He refers to beliefs resulting from such presentations of God by God as manifestation beliefs and asserts that people do sometimes perceive God and thus acquire justified beliefs about God: "direct experiential awareness of God is a mode of perception" (5). Alston focuses his work on nonsensory perceptions of God, whereas our concern includes the very sensory revelation of God at Sinai, but Alston acknowledges that "it is not inconceivable that God should appear to us as looking bright or sounding a certain way, even though He does not, in His own nature, possess any sensory qualities. Nor would it necessarily be unfitting or unworthy for Him to do so. It may be that, given our powers and proclivities, this would be the best way for Him to get a certain message across; just as, even if physical substances are not really colored, the system of color appearances enables us to make many useful distinctions between them" (19–20). The precise mechanism of such sensory perception of God need not be available to us; perhaps, says Alston, God doesn't work through natural means but supernaturally brings about the requisite experience: "Why should it not be possible that God should appear to S's experience as good, powerful, or loving without simultaneously displaying to that experience the full riches of His essence, in a way analogous to our grasp of His nature?" (63).

Alston acknowledges the circularity of argument involved in such doxastic experiences and argues that there is no appeal beyond the doxastic practices, firmly established. Alston is strongly realist in his philosophical orientation and argues that such perception can produce true knowledge of and about God. He explores the relationship of nonsensory perception of God to other elements that support belief and emphasizes the importance of claims about God's actions in history being true in a robustly realist sense: "It was important for God's self-revelation, as well as for the divine scheme of salvation, that He actually did these things" (290). He furthermore defends the idea of God speaking: "I have already claimed that the *message* form of revelation involves perceiving God as 'saying' something; and no limits can be put on what God could *tell* a human being, other than limits set by our capacities for understanding" (290).

Schwöbel explores the complex nature of experience and asserts that an interpretive framework is constitutive for experience. Experience is always historically concrete and involves both the constitution of objects and the process in which experience is actualized in the subject so that self-experience is present in all the synthesis of experience. Experience takes place only amidst sociality and rests on the openness of reality. Thus experience "is understood as the determination of reality as an object of experience and certainty by interpreting and organising subjects on the basis of the disclosedness of reality for the signifying acts of self-experiencing subjects of perception and interpretation."[59]

For Schwöbel, revelation is the event of disclosure that is the condition of the possibility of experience, since it discloses the universal truth about God's relationship to humanity and the world. We learn from God's revelation that God is the creator and redeemer of our world; the world is ordered by God in a particular way; humans have their destiny in obedience as the *imago Dei*. The Christ or Sinai event corresponds as particular experience to the structure of experience sketched above: "the specific characteristic of the experience of Christ is therefore that the self-disclosure of God is vindicated as the condition of the possibility of all experience, insofar as the constitution of the certainty of this experience validates its content."[60]

Conclusion

In this chapter we have shown how divine action finds its place against the backdrop of a theology of God's providence, firmly rooted in the doctrine of creation and as an expression of a particular view of God as the living God. Divine action is profoundly mysterious, and we took note of philosophical attempts to account for it. Early historical criticism is awash with naturalism, and many continue to believe that SDA is ruled out by modern science. However, Plantinga shows this not to be the case so that modern science cannot be used as a defeater for SDA.

Against this backdrop we drew on Schwöbel's rich account of the disclosure event that is at the heart of revelation. And so in the concluding chapter we will bring all the insights of our journey thus far to bear on the Sinai event itself.

59. Schwöbel, *God*, 111.
60. Schwöbel, *God*, 117.

CHAPTER 9

Special Divine Action at Sinai?
An Exploration of Exodus 19–24

Old Testament research is an ideational hybrid, a mixing and matching of completely disparate, perhaps mutually exclusive, ways of thinking the world. Perched on the massive superstructures of this peculiar epistemological base the most self-conscious biblical exegete is aptly described by Saul Bellow's poignant depiction of the soul in modernity: "poor bird, not knowing which way to fly."

—Jacques Berlinerblau[1]

Mount Sinai dominates the landscape of biblical law. Its shadow looms so large—and stretches so far—that there are times when it seems to eclipse the subject as a whole.

—Jonathan Burnside[2]

We began this book with a puzzle, namely the tendency of many scholars, both Jews and Christians, to affirm the centrality of Sinai and yet to be unsure as to whether we can affirm its historicity. For many it is *the* generative "event" and yet may be entirely imaginary. It is not therefore surprising that Berlinerblau describes HB/OT research as an "ideational hybrid" akin to a bird not knowing which way to fly!

1. Jacques Berlinerblau, "'Poor Bird, Not Knowing Which Way to Fly': Biblical Scholarship's Marginality, Secular Humanism, and the Laudable Occident," *Biblical Interpretation* 10 (2002): 281. The quote is from Saul Bellow, *Mr. Sammler's Planet* (New York: Penguin, 1969, 1970), 1.
2. Jonathan Burnside, *God, Justice, and Society: Aspects of Law and Legality in the Bible* (Oxford: Oxford University Press, 2011), 45.

188

Much of this book has been an investigation of many of the forces shaping the ideational hybrid of HB/OT-Sinai research, and yet some continue to be ignored. In what is a useful introduction to the historical-critical approach to the Pentateuch, Jean-Louis Ska, in agreement with Sommer, notes that "from a methodological viewpoint, this book seeks to convince its readers that it is impossible today to read the Pentateuch without recourse to the historical-critical method."[3] Ska positions himself with scholars such as Sommer who are seeking to revive the historical-critical reading of the Pentateuch. Intriguingly, and helpfully, Ska begins with literary and holistic approaches to the Pentateuch, before moving on to make his case for historical criticism. Nevertheless, what is telling is that Ska notes in his preface that "the starting point must be 'neutral.'"[4] Ska's overarching methodology is refreshing, taking, as it does, the literary turn in HB/OT interpretation seriously. He includes a chapter on the history of research into the Pentateuch and extends this as far back as the church fathers. Several of the figures we have attended to crop up—for example Spinoza, Eichhorn, de Wette, and Wellhausen.

Apart from the attempt by Sommer, Ska, and others to renew the Documentary Hypothesis approach to the Pentateuch, it should be noted that there are many divergent voices. Already in 1983, in his *At the Mountain of God: Story and Theology in Exodus 32–34*, Moberly concluded that the "problem is that a new comprehensive model or paradigm for Pentateuchal traditions is required."[5] Loewenstamm notes that classical documentary analysis did not attend closely to literature outside the Pentateuch bearing on the early history of Israel.[6] In a very important recent work, Joshua Berman refers to a conference in Jerusalem in 2013 entitled "Convergence and Divergence in Pentateuchal Theory: Bridging the Cultures of Israel, North America and Europe," which was the culmination of a year-long research group composed of eight of the most distinguished scholars in Pentateuchal criticism. The result indicated crisis and gridlock. Berman writes in the context of a new movement in historical critical analysis of the Pentateuch:

3. Jean-Louis Ska, *Introduction to Reading the Pentateuch*, trans. Sr. Pascale Dominique (Winona Lake, IN: Eisenbrauns, 2006), xi.

4. Ska, *Introduction to Reading the Pentateuch*, ix.

5. R. W. L. Moberly, *At the Mountain of God: Story and Theology in Exodus 32–34*, JSOTSup 22 (Sheffield: JSOT Press, 1983), 187.

6. Samuel E. Loewenstamm, *The Evolution of the Exodus Tradition*, trans. Baruch J. Schwartz (Jerusalem: Magnes Press, 1992), 15.

The root of the problem, heretofore, according to this movement, is that scholars have rooted their compositional theories for the growth of the biblical text entirely in their own intuition of what constitutes literary unity. For those of us working in this new movement, the time has come to root compositional theory in the so-called empirical findings of the writings of the ancient Near East. We must canvas and analyze documented examples of compositional growth and editing across a wide field of ancient Near Eastern texts, both within ancient Israel and outside it.[7]

In my view this is undoubtedly correct, and I would refer to this evaluation of the authenticity of the Pentateuchal writings as according to the criterion of similarity. In a future work, I plan to engage fully with Berman's and his colleagues' creative work.

What is notably missing from Ska's approach is hardly any attention at all to the philosophical and theological shaping of historical criticism as it developed. Most of this book has been devoted to demonstrating again and again just how value-laden were the philosophies shaping the work of scholars such as Spinoza, Eichhorn, de Wette, Wellhausen, and so on, but virtually none of this is attended to in Ska's narrative of the progressive development of historical criticism. The result is that the so-called—or assumed—"neutrality" of modern historical criticism remains in place. We cannot and will not ignore Ska's arguments for a historical critical approach to the Pentateuch as we return to Exod 19–24 in this chapter, but it is surprising that the paradigms shaping the emergence of historical criticism can still be ignored.

Questions such as the following insist on being raised: Should we embrace the naturalism of an Eichhorn? Do we affirm the pantheistic monism of a Spinoza and an impersonal view of the deity? Do we, with de Wette, embrace Kant's autonomous, idealist philosophy, which resists any idea of divine action in the world? We have learned from Thomas Kuhn that science always takes place within a paradigm that forms the matrix out of which scholars work.[8] Once a paradigm gains hold the paradigm recedes into the background generating the idea of "normal" sci-

---

7. Joshua A. Berman, *Inconsistency in the Torah: Ancient Literary Convention and the Limits of Source Criticism* (Oxford: Oxford University Press, 2017), 2–3.

8. Thomas S. Kuhn, *The Structure of Scientific Revolutions*, 50th anniversary ed. (Chicago: University of Chicago Press, 2012).

ence, but the paradigm continues to exercise a formative influence. As Ska notes, the historical critical paradigm has been challenged again and again, and one would think that this would cause scholars to investigate *all* the dimensions of its origins and framework closely, but alas, too often this is not the case.

We *all* acknowledge that the data of the Pentateuch are complex. We are all in debt to historical critics for exploring this data with rigor. But we ought to take seriously the underdetermination of theory by the facts, especially as the literary, postmodern, and theological turns in biblical and HB/ OT studies have emerged to raise trenchant questions about the results of historical criticism. By "underdetermination" I mean that a theory about the Pentateuch, such as JEDP, always involves *more* than the data referred to by it, which opens the possibility of alternative and better theories accounting for such data.

Historical critical analyses of the sources of the Pentateuch are inevitably speculative, with "the sources" being reconstructed from the documents we have. The more speculative a reading of the HB/OT becomes, the more influence the paradigm within which it is taking place wields. How then should we proceed? The answer seems to me clear. Let scholars declare and be open about the paradigms within which they are working. Let these competing paradigms come to fruition so that we can compare readings of the Pentateuch from the ground up, as it were, without the pretense of Enlightenment-style neutrality. Let us scrutinize one another's paradigms and the fruit of our interpretive work; only thus might we make real progress. This is one reason why I find Sommer's work on Sinai so helpful. As will be apparent, I disagree with it strongly, but I find his willingness to set out the whole picture very helpful indeed.

It will be obvious to readers that I bring a distinctively theistic paradigm to the task of reading Exod 19–24, as outlined in the previous chapter. This paradigm has been rigorously championed philosophically in recent years by prominent philosophers such as Alvin Plantinga, Nicholas Wolterstorff, and William Alston, to name only a few. Yes, I do believe that God is the living God who speaks and acts in history; the God of Israel and the God who has come to us in Jesus of Nazareth. And, contra to what I perceive as Ska's nature–grace approach, I believe that my quest for the truth about Sinai is enhanced by bringing such beliefs with me into the heart of my scholarship. Does this necessarily make my scholarship less reliable? The answer depends to a significant extent on one's own philosophical and theological commitments. But in my view, Hans-Georg Gadamer is right that it is our very prejudices—in the sense of our pre-judgments—that make progress in knowledge possible.[9] The ensuing dialogue central to the knowing process need not obscure textual resistance to one's reading; indeed, in my view a theistic paradigm should make one *more* sensitive to data that resist a reading and *ever willing* to learn from alternative paradigms.

Our Approach

Contra Berlinerblau, I do not think it a good thing for an HB/OT scholar to be perched on an ideational hybrid, like a bird not knowing which way to fly. *A* test of reliable knowledge is coherence,[10] and, in my view, HB/OT scholars should aim at a coherent reading of the HB/OT from the ground up. In a future work, I plan to map out in far greater detail a coherent approach to the OT from a theistic perspective.[11] There are multiple dimensions to any text, including the OT, but, as several scholars have noted, epistemologically there are three that require especially close attention—namely the literary, the historical or referential, and the kerygmatic or theological.[12] These are deeply interwoven and, of course, do not come to us as separate strands but as part of one text. The philosophical, to which much of this book has been devoted, is more part of the matrix or paradigm within which one interprets, which shapes our understanding of the three strands and their interrelationship, and we will return to it at the end of this chapter. Our approach will be to begin with some comparative comments about notions of divine presence and action in the ANE, and then we will attend to the literary, historical, and theological aspects of Exod 19–24, before revisiting philosophical questions in conclusion.

9. Hans-Georg Gadamer, *Truth and Method*, revised 2nd ed. (London: Bloomsbury, 2004).

10. Cf. Peter Murphy, "Coherentism in Epistemology," *Internet Encyclopedia of Philosophy*, https://www.iep.utm.edu/coherent/#SH1b. Note that I am not arguing for "strong coherentism" but "necessity coherentism." Coherence is a structural condition of warranted belief.

11. Craig G. Bartholomew, Old Testament Origins and the Question of God, a multiple-volume series. For a taster see my "Old Testament Origins and the Question of God," *Bulletin for Biblical Research* 27/2 (2017): 169–84.

12. As represented in the work of, e.g., Meir Sternberg, N. T. Wright, and Andreas Köstenberger.

Divine Presence and Action in the Ancient Near East

The belief in divine action is pervasive across the ANE. So too is the belief in what is called special divine action (SDA).[13] Gwynne defines SDA as "the presupposition that in order to reveal himself, God has acted in specific ways at certain points in human history rather than at others."[14] However, it is here that a potential gulf opens up between Israel and the surrounding nations. One could use any of the ANE nations as a point of comparison with Israel, but I follow the Sinai narrative in making Egypt the focal point of comparison. The name "Egypt" occurs some 546 times in the HB/OT, an indication of its influence on the thought world of Israel.

Jan Assmann and Mark Smith have written about the "translatability" of concepts of the divine in the ANE. It is important to understand what they mean by "translatability." Smith notes that, "perhaps at its most basic, translatability is evident in the *specific equation of individual deities across cultures.*"[15] Assmann asserts the radicality of the "Mosaic distinction,"[16] and Smith, by comparison, argues for some translatability, especially in early Israel.[17] Assmann describes the Mosaic distinction as follows:

> The Mosaic distinction was . . . a radically new distinction which considerably changed the world in which it was drawn. . . . We may call this new type of religion "counter-religion" because it rejects and repudiates everything that went before and what is outside itself as "paganism." It no longer functioned as a means of intercultural translation; on the contrary, it functioned as a means of intercultural estrangement. Whereas polytheism, or rather "cosmotheism," rendered different cultures mutually transparent and compatible, the new counter-religion blocked intercultural translatability. False gods cannot be translated.[18]

13. Paul Gwynne, *Special Divine Action: Key Issues in the Contemporary Debate (1965–1995)*, Tesi Gregoriana Serie Teologia 12 (Rome: Editrice Pontificia Università Gregoriana, 1996).

14. Gwynne, *Special Divine Action*, 8.

15. Mark S. Smith, *God in Translation: Cross-Cultural Recognition of Deities in the Biblical World* (Grand Rapids: Eerdmans, 2008), 50. Emphasis added.

16. Jan Assmann, *Moses the Egyptian: The Memory of Egypt in Western Monotheism* (Cambridge, MA: Harvard University Press, 1997); Assmann, *Of God and Gods: Egypt, Israel, and the Rise of Monotheism* (Madison: University of Wisconsin Press, 2008).

17. Smith, *God in Translation*, ch. 2.

18. Assmann, *Moses the Egyptian*, 3.

Smith attends to particular texts in the HB/OT, which we cannot explore here. For our purposes, an element in his case is one's view of the Sinai event. In his epilogue he notes that "the 'Mosaic distinction' was hardly a constitutive aspect of ancient Israel. Instead, it is at best an eventual outcome of Israel's religious struggles and political conditions."[19] Such a view of the history of Israel's religion rejects the idea that the "Mosaic distinction" was given at Sinai, but rather evolved over a long period of time. If, as I will argue below, Sinai should be understood as an epochal, historical event, then the scales are tipped, as it were, toward Assmann's view as the pervasive and normative one in the HB/OT, even though Assmann himself does not regard Moses and Sinai as historical.

However, the definition of translatability that Assmann and Smith work with is specific, and somewhat angular in my view, and a broader view of translatability would allow one to notice the many common elements in ANE views of the divine with that of Israel, commonalities that allow the Mosaic distinction to come to the fore. Such an approach also allows one to affirm genuine insights in ANE religions without equating ANE deities with YHWH. For example, as we will see below, the theme of YHWH's descent is a significant one in Exod 19–24, and we find a comparable theme in Egyptian "theology."

For ancient Egyptians, the sky was the home of the gods, and thus the theme of descent was central to the cultus. The *ba* of the god alights on his *sekhem*.[20] Assmann uses a variety of terms to evoke this descent: uniting, fraternizing, embracing, installation, indwelling.[21] The gods did not "dwell" on earth; instead they repeatedly installed themselves in their images. Comparably, YHWH descends upon Mt. Sinai.

However, it is at the level of SDA that the gulf opens between the HB/OT and Egyptian religion to allow us to glimpse the Mosaic distinction. In ancient Egypt, daily rituals and festivals constituted the heart of the cultus. The god resided in the temple in two forms: as a cult statue and as a portable processional barque. During a festival, the temple doors were opened, and the god processed outside. This turning to the outside sanctified the world. The god's processional route extended beyond the temple; there would, for example, be a sacred avenue leading to the river and other avenues to other sacred places. Assmann notes that this blurring of inner and outer boundaries constituted a festival. In the history of Egyptian religion oracular deities

19. Smith, *God in Translation*, 324.
20. Jan Assmann, *The Search for God in Ancient Egypt*, trans. David Lorton (Ithaca, NY: Cornell University Press, 2001), 42.
21. Assmann, *The Search for God in Ancient Egypt*, 43.

spoke through moving so that in Egypt oracles related to festivals. The procession of gods actualized the land in its social aspect. Related to this is the fact that no deity was the sole occupant of his or her temple.

Egyptian gods acted and "spoke" so that Assmann discerns divine presence at the heart of Egyptian religion. However, the contrast with divine action as portrayed in the Sinai narrative could not be stronger. At a basic level images of the deity are forbidden in the Decalogue, thereby excluding the Egyptian concept of SDA at festivals. YHWH descends on Mt. Sinai but decidedly not into an image, and he asserts sovereignty over Egypt and the whole earth (19:5; 20:2), an emphasis at the heart of the Mosaic distinction. Clearly, when it comes to SDA, there is something unique in the ANE going on in the Sinai narrative.

Another example would be that of theophany in the HB/OT and the ANE. Sarna notes the commonality between the theophany at Sinai and theophany in the ANE:

> The conventional and stereotypical nature of the language employed here, and the numerous parallels found in ancient Near Eastern religious compositions, prove that a widespread and well-entrenched literary tradition lies behind it. However, the gods in pagan religions inevitably inhere in nature. . . . The upheavals and disturbances are taken literally as aspects of the lives of the gods. In Israelite monotheism, by contrast, God the Creator is wholly independent of His creation and is sovereign over it. The picturesque imagery constitutes, so to speak, the overture that sets the emotional tone for the grand drama that is to follow.[22]

Again, it is the very commonality that allows the distinctiveness to come to the fore. We might call this criterion that of dissimilarity.

In our exploration of SDA at Sinai we will examine Exod 19–24[23] in the following four ways: (1) literary analysis; (2) theological analysis; (3) historical analysis; (4) philosophical analysis.

---

22. Nahum M. Sarna, *Exodus*, The JPS Torah Commentary (Jerusalem: The Jewish Publication Society, 1991), 106.

23. Note that the Sinai narrative includes Exod 19–40; Lev; and Num 1:1–10:10. Indeed, it is only in Num 10:33 that the Israelites set out from Sinai.

Literary Analysis

Historical criticism cut its teeth on the Pentateuch, and Wellhausen's identification of the major sources as JEDP is well known. Such source criticism continues to be the default mode for most Pentateuchal scholars, and we are witnessing a renewed attempt to defend this approach, as with Ska and Sommer. For Wellhausen, law was originally associated with Kadesh,[24] and not Sinai. The revelation at Sinai was inserted into the Pentateuch, thus separating the law traditions in Exod 18 and Num 10:29–14:45. The earliest version of the Sinai tradition was as a theophany and not a promulgation of law. It is Deuteronomy that first combines law, covenant, and narrative, a move that enabled P to make law central to Sinai.

Gerhard von Rad identified two separate cycles of tradition underlying the Sinai narrative: that of the exodus-conquest at Gilgal and that of the law at Sinai and Shechem. In comparison to Wellhausen, von Rad placed law early in Israel's traditions, and this pushed scholars to explore the cultic origins of these separate traditions. W. Beyerlin pointed out the speculative nature of cultic traditions and observed that only the literature itself could be analyzed with any certainty. L. Perlitt sees the emergence of covenant as late in the life of Israel and argues that the theme of covenant in Exod 19–24 is from a Deuteronomistic redactor. More recent redactional studies have identified yet more authors behind 19–24. W. Oswald, for example, discerns four stages of Deuteronomistic redaction.[25]

Childs is always interesting because of his concern to take historical criticism seriously while attending to the final form of the text as we have received it. Following on from von Rad, he identifies the relationship of exodus and Sinai as the major problem.[26] He notes that serious opposition to the separation of the exodus and Sinai traditions came from the Albright school, which rallied around Mendenhall's 1954 essay[27] to establish the historical connection between the two. Childs concludes that, in his "judgment, there has been no final clarification of this extremely complex

---

24. Yehezkel Kaufmann, *The Religion of Israel: From Its Beginnings to the Babylonian Exile*, trans. and abridged by Moshe Greenberg (Chicago: University of Chicago Press, 1960), 232, says of this association with Kadesh, "this theory is groundless."

25. Thomas B. Dozeman, *Exodus*, Eerdmans Critical Commentary (Grand Rapids: Eerdmans, 2009), 423.

26. Childs, *Exodus*, 337.

27. George E. Mendenhall, "Law and Covenant in Israel and in the Ancient Near East," *BA* 17 (1954): 26–46, 49–76.

problem."[28] For Childs, both approaches fail to attend to the present form of the text. Indeed "the history of research has often demonstrated how effectively the study of the prehistory has functioned in obscuring the biblical text through false parallels and mistaken ideas of historical development."[29]

In terms of literary criticism Childs discerns the following tensions in Exod 19–24: Moses is described as ascending and descending without any purpose; the people are portrayed at times as fearful and remaining at a distance but at other times we find warnings against desecration;[30] God is portrayed as both dwelling on the mountain and occasionally descending; the theophany is variously depicted as smoke, fire, as well as clouds and the thunder of a rainstorm. Childs also explores tensions in the portrayal of Moses's office, relating Exod 19–24 to Deut 5:4–5.

Childs helpfully resists the separation of theophany from the giving of the law: "In the theophany Israel begins to experience the nature of her God. In the law she hears the clear expression of God's will which the covenant demanded. A deliberate profile of the 'holy nation' has been sketched with the ten words of the divine will."[31]

As an example of recent literary critical analysis of Exod 19–24, Dozeman observes that "the composition of Exodus 19–24 continues to pose problems for interpreters, giving rise to a variety of literary solutions to account for the present organization of the literature. The identification of sources continues."[32] He says of 19–24:

- It contains literature from different authors and time periods (418).
- God's appearance in a storm (19:16–17) and the meal (24:10–11) may be independent accounts of the theophany (418).
- The Decalogue and the Book of the Covenant are independent law codes now introduced into the revelation of Sinai.
- The combination of theophany and law code has dominated modern analysis of the composition of Exod 19–24. The literary criteria that have been used to discern sources are: different names for God, namely YHWH and Elohim; and the multiple accounts of Moses ascending.

28. Childs, *Exodus*, 338.
29. Childs, *Exodus*, 339.
30. See Jon Levenson, *Sinai and Zion: An Entry into the Jewish Bible* (San Francisco: HarperSanFrancisco, 1985), ch. 1, for an intriguing analysis of this paradox.
31. Childs, *Exodus*, 371.
32. Dozeman, *Exodus*, 424. Hereafter, page references to this work are given in parentheses in the text.

Exodus 19–24 has generally been assigned to J and E, with P related to the construction of the tabernacle (Exod 25–31, 35–40).

- Dozeman in his commentary settles for non-P and P material while noting that non-P includes a wide range of literature.
- The "mountain of God," "Mount Horeb," and "the mountain" may come from different religious traditions (426). Mt. Sinai is the mountain of revelation in P. "The identification of the mountain of Revelation as Mount Sinai . . . is the creation of the P author" (430).

When it comes to detailed source, form, and tradition criticism, the vicissitudes of historical criticism offer little hope for a (constructive) reading of Exod 19–24. When attention to the HB/OT as literature arose in the 1970s, it challenged many of the presuppositions of historical criticism, but before such literary analysis could be fully appropriated the postmodern turn was upon us, with the result that source, tradition, and redactional analysis of Exod 19–24 remain the bread and butter of most scholars. There is a real need for attention to the synchronic shape of Exod 19–24 as literature *before* embarking on speculation about sources.[33] This is particularly important, bearing in mind the view that that when it comes to the history of Israel's emergence, "the composite nature of the texts makes identifying a coherent story difficult."[34] Below we will attend to the macro-structure of Exodus and the centrality of YHWH and creation to its structure and theology, and then to synchronic literary readings of Exod 19–24.

The Literary Structure of Exodus 19–24

Exodus as a Whole

The most obvious division of Exodus relates to *place*: most of 1–18 occurs in (and around) Egypt; 19–40 occurs at Sinai; 1–18 revolve around Moses; 19–40 around Israel. YHWH is central to the entirety.

---

33. Cf. Meir Sternberg, *The Poetics of Biblical Narrative: Ideological Literature and the Drama of Reading* (Bloomington: Indiana University Press, 1987), on the relationship between synchronic and diachronic analysis.

34. Megan Bishop Moore and Brad E. Kelle, *Biblical History and Israel's Past: The Changing Study of the Bible as History* (Grand Rapids: Eerdmans, 2011), 91.

Mark Smith discerns the following overarching structure to Exodus.[35]

EGYPT

A. 1–2	Moses's movements from Egypt to Midian
B. 3–14	Two calls and two confrontations
i. 3:1–6:1	Moses's first call and confrontation with Pharaoh
ii. 6:2–14:31	Moses's second call and YHWH's confrontation with Pharaoh
15:1–21	Victory at the Sea: the conflict between Egypt and the powers of Sinai

SINAI

A.' 15:22–18:27	Israel's move from Egypt to Midian
B.' 19–40	
i.' 19–31	Israel's first covenant with YHWH; the first tablets
ii.' 32–40	Israel's second covenant with YHWH; the second tablets

According to Smith, "the two halves of Exodus dramatize the foundational events of Israel's origin as a pilgrimage in a developed sense, namely as a journey . . . call and commission, and cultic experience of Yahweh."[36] Both Moses (Exod 3) and Israel (Exod 19:1–2) travel to Mt. Sinai. Exodus 15:1–21, which, as per the outline above, Smith sees as the center of Exodus, presents Sinai as the holy sanctuary, reading "the mountain" in 15:17 as referring to Sinai. For Smith, "pilgrimage to Sinai functions as the book's representation of earliest Israel and the pattern to be replicated throughout its history."[37]

Exodus 3 and 6: YHWH

Exodus 3, at Sinai, and Exod 6, are the major passages in Exodus and the HB/OT relating to God's proper name, YHWH. In Exod 3 Moses encounters YHWH in the burnishing bush in the region of Sinai. This encounter parallels

35. Mark S. Smith, *The Pilgrimage Pattern in Exodus* (Sheffield: Sheffield Academic Press, 1997), 190.
36. Smith, *Pilgrimage Pattern*, 264.
37. Smith, *Pilgrimage Pattern*, 264.

Israel's encounter in Exod 19. LaCocque refers to the burning bush narrative in Exod 3 as "an entirely original event within a general context of proclamation followed by popular or individual recognition."[38] Zimmerli speaks of "I am YHWH" as the "formula of self-introduction" (*Selbstvorstellungsformel*), and asserts that "the phrase 'I am Yahweh' carries all the weight and becomes the denominator upon which all else rests . . . everything Yahweh has to announce to his people becomes an amplification of the fundamental statement, 'I am Yahweh.'"[39] There has been endless discussion on how exactly to translate the explanatory phrase in Exod 3:14: *'ehyeh asher 'ehyeh*.

In his fine discussion of YHWH, LaCocque asserts that this phrase is not, contrary to Aquinas and classical theism, a call to ontological abstraction. Indeed, akin to Gunton, he notes that such philosophical speculations about the nature of God need to be rethought "*sub specie historiae*, instead of *sub specie aeternitatis et absoluti*."[40] The name and this "explanatory" phrase must support the affirmation that "I will be with you" (Exod 3:12). As Childs asserts, YHWH makes himself known at certain historical moments and confirms his nature in his redemption of Israel.[41] YHWH evokes exclusivity in his relationship to Israel. The name is both theophanic and performative,[42] revealing the ultimate meaning of the redemptive event of the exodus. Zimmerli pays close attention to the use of this formula of self-introduction in Exodus and concludes, perhaps one-sidedly, that "to know Yahweh does not mean to encounter some part of Yahweh's transcendent being, but rather to recognize his beneficial deed on Israel's behalf."[43]

LaCocque speaks evocatively of the Decalogue as *a legal commentary on YHWH*, and notes that "now we must shift the emphasis to Sinai as an event, even as the symbolic event par excellence. Strikingly, the formula is closely knit with that event, the paradigm of all subsequent events of the *Heilsgeschichte*, meant, according to their accompanying interpretation, to provoke a decision from their audience. . . . Either one rejects the conviction and its

---

38. André LaCocque, "The Revelation of Revelations," in LaCocque and Paul Ricoeur, *Thinking Biblically: Exegetical and Hermeneutical Studies*, trans. David Pellauer (Chicago: University of Chicago Press, 1998), 321.

39. Walther Zimmerli, *I Am Yahweh*, ed. Walter Brueggemann, trans. Douglas W. Stott (Atlanta: John Knox, 1982), 9.

40. LaCocque, "The Revelation of Revelations," 324.

41. Childs, *Exodus*, 88.

42. LaCocque, "The Revelation of Revelations," 316.

43. Zimmerli, *I Am Yahweh*, 44.

evidence, or one recognizes that God is the Lord, Yhwh, the One who is up to his name."[44] Indeed, the recognition of YHWH does not emerge from conceptual and metaphysical reflection but from an encounter with YHWH. The name YHWH is not an invitation to reflect upon the aseity of God: "It does not refer to a divine *causa sui*; on the contrary, it always takes place within very concrete happenings."[45] According to LaCocque, "within Israel's consciousness, the Exodus inaugurates not only its history as a people . . . but also the world's redemption. The exodus from Egypt is toward the promised Land, the microcosm and 'bridge-head' from where the whole of creation has started its transfiguration into the Kingdom of God. The Exodus is thus *the* event par excellence, the 'V-Day' of history, the day when the world is changed into itself by eternity."[46]

To use the language of speech-act theory,[47] the reflections above alert us to the fact that the very name YHWH misfires or is rendered infelicitous as a speech act if YHWH does not in fact act in history and—in our case—at Sinai. Divine action in history is built into the very name of God and its revelation.

We saw in the last chapter how revelation is rooted in creation and there are strong creation motifs in Exodus. Martin Buber and Franz Rosenzweig pointed out the strong parallels between Exod 39–40 and Gen 1–2: Exod 39:43a//Gen 1:31a; Exod 39:32a//Gen 2:1; Exod 40:33b//Gen 2:2a; Exod 39:43b//Gen 2:3a.[48] "While the account of Genesis marks the creation of the world, the creation language of Exodus 39–40 might be viewed as heralding the new creation of Israel's cultic life with its deity."[49] Zevit has argued that the narrative of the plagues presents them as a judgment of a kind of uncreation, being deliberately modeled on Gen 1.[50] Thus, "the major theme of creation clearly links the beginning and end of the book."[51] Furthermore, the creation language in 19–24 fits with the new creation language of 39–40.

44. LaCocque, "The Revelation of Revelations," 320.
45. LaCocque, "The Revelation of Revelations," 322.
46. LaCocque, "The Revelation of Revelations," 326.
47. See Austin, *How to Do Things with Words*, and the many other works in this tradition.
48. Smith, *Pilgrimage Pattern*, 266.
49. Smith, *Pilgrimage Pattern*, 266.
50. Ziony Zevit, "The Priestly Redaction and Interpretation of the Plague Narrative in Exodus," *JQR* 66 (1976): 194–205.
51. Smith, *Pilgrimage Pattern*, 266.

In Exod 24:16 we read that after Moses ascended and the cloud covered Mt. Sinai, "The glory of the LORD settled on Mount Sinai, and the cloud covered it for six days; on the seventh day he called to Moses out of the cloud." YHWH's six days on Mount Sinai symbolizes his work of a new creation— Israel in covenant with himself.[52]

The link between the exodus-Sinai and creation is further strengthened if, with Albright, we take the form *Yahweh* to be causative: "The enigmatic formula in Exod 3:14, which in Hebrew means 'I am what I am,' if transposed into the third person required by the causative *Yahweh*, can only become *Yahweh asher yihweh* (later *yihyeh*), 'He Causes to be what Comes into Existence.'"[53] For Albright, even if this reading is incorrect, "there is ample evidence in the Bible that the Israelites had always regarded Yahweh as Creator of All."[54]

Within Jewish tradition there is widespread recognition of a connection between the *yehi* "let there be" of Gen 1 and the name of God "YHWH." Both are related to the verb "to be," *hayah*.[55] Davies notes in the move from the jussive *yehi* to God blessing in Gen 1 that "the institutionary and cosmological function of the divine jussives gives way to modes of divine speech which establish a *relation* between living creatures and God within that cosmology."[56] Intriguingly, Davies discerns the next stage in this deepening creativity of God's speech in Exod 3 and 6. He notes the possible reading of YHWH as causative and asserts that "whatever its original derivation may be, YHWH as name of God richly resonates with the opening verses of Genesis. . . . Accordingly, God's self-naming to Moses at this point represents a new and fuller realization of the mutuality of language that has been inaugurated in the Genesis accounts."[57] Davies asserts that

This linguistic-creative process of the Old Testament culminates in the conversation, or "speaking with," that takes place on Mount Sinai be-

52. Jeffrey J. Niehaus, *God at Sinai: Covenant and Theophany in the Bible and Ancient Near East*, Studies in OT Biblical Theology (Grand Rapids: Zondervan, 1995), 199.

53. William F. Albright, *From the Stone Age to Christianity: Monotheism and the Historical Process* (New York: Doubleday Anchor, 1957), 261.

54. Albright, *From the Stone Age*, 261.

55. Oliver Davies, *The Creativity of God: World, Eucharist, Reason* (Cambridge: Cambridge University Press, 2004), 82.

56. Davies, *Creativity*, 77-78.

57. Davies, *Creativity*, 79.

tween God and Moses, who is to be God's agent for his intervention for the sake of his people. Divine presence here is not exercised from outside language, by some sovereign and independent agent, but is rather enfolded within language which acquires revelatory functions. Such an active penetration by God into the heart of human history implies a particular structure of revelation, grounded in the mutuality which inheres in language as such. . . . As a God whose speaking is originary and creative of the world, God too must enter the realm of human speaking, acting and knowing. This kenotic, revelatory movement is necessarily a saving moment, for the divine presence of itself redeems and liberates as it enters and shapes the human condition in a deepening creativity.[58]

Davies's theology of divine speech and the connection between the Sinai event and Gen 1 adds, in my view, theological weight to the importance of God actually speaking, of real dialogue between YHWH and Moses, and of Moses and Israel receiving and hearing God's speech.

The intertextual links between Sinai and creation indicate that Egypt is thus portrayed as the place of death, judgment, and uncreation, whereas life and new creation are initiated at Sinai. Egypt is the place of slavery, Sinai of freedom. "The freedom from the Egyptians was made complete only by the Sinai legislation."[59] Smith asserts that "it is a gross understatement to say Sinai occupies a central place in the priestly theology of the Pentateuch. . . . Sinai became the Mount Everest of priestly theology which looms larger than subsequent cultic sites such as Jerusalem. For the priestly tradition Sinai would represent the site of the definitive covenant and model for cultic recollection in the land. In short, this mountain defines life inside and outside the land."[60]

Smith's statement alerts us to an intriguing aspect of Sinai; as strong as the pilgrimage motif may be in Exodus, Sinai was a one-off event, and this was so much the case that it is hard to be sure of the exact location of Mt. Sinai. As Hoffmeier notes, "the location of Mt. Sinai, the mountain of God, has never been identified with certainty."[61] Hoffmeier connects this uncertainty with the ongoing presence of YHWH with his people: once the

---

58. Davies, *Creativity*, 83.
59. Smith, *Pilgrimage Pattern*, 268.
60. Smith, *Pilgrimage Pattern*, 306.
61. James K. Hoffmeier, *Ancient Israel in Sinai: The Evidence for the Authenticity of the Wilderness Tradition* (Oxford: Oxford University Press, 2005), 115.

tabernacle was built and consecrated, it replaced the mountain. The tabernacle embodied a new Mt. Sinai: although Exodus locates Sinai as the place
where the law was given, the new Mt. Sinai of the tabernacle superseded
the old and functioned as the dwelling place of YHWH. There is never any
indication in the HB/OT of Sinai remaining a sacred site to which pilgrimage
is encouraged. The uncertainty of the location of Sinai can be interpreted in
different ways. From my perspective, it points to the revelation of YHWH
and the establishment of the covenant as the crucial and historical event with
the actual location being of less importance.

Clearly, macro-analysis of the structure of Exodus is fertile theologically.
Below we will explore positive work on the possibility of reading Exod 19–24
as a literary unity.

Synchronic Literary Analysis of Exodus 19–24

Repetition characterizes the whole of Exodus. It is most obvious in 25–40
but is also dominant in 1–2; 3:1–7:7; 7:18–15:21; 15:22–18:27; and in 19–24.[62]
In 19–24, "the story builds through repeated trips by Moses to the summit
of the mountain."[63] However, as we would expect from the subject matter
of 19–24, the strong forward movement of 1–18 is replaced by placial sta-
bility—"at the mountain"—with a strong vertical dimension. Indeed, this
verticality accounts for the density of vocabulary related to divine action in
chs. 19 and 24. According to Dozeman, the key for interpreting repetition
in Exod 19–24 is the setting of the mountain, not the development of the
plot or the unfolding chronology of the story. The repeated trips by Moses relate the two worlds of heaven and earth in the setting of the divine
mountain.[64] The result is a narrative that is spatial in form, whose aim is to
address the central theme of *holiness*. A spatial-form narrative is, according
to Dozeman, *like an orange, not a roadway*. Individual scenes are organized
around the center, focusing on the single subject at the core of the story.
The scenes of the story do not progress in one direction but are juxtaposed
to one another, providing a different perspective on the same core event—
the revelation of God on the mountain. The result is a narrative in which

62. Dozeman, *Exodus*, 432–33.
63. Dozeman, *Exodus*, 433.
64. On the sacred mountain in the ANE and Mt. Sinai see Hoffmeier, *Ancient
Israel in Sinai*, ch. 6.

temporal sequence is replaced by a more circular movement around the central core subject.[65]

Overall Dozeman is insightful in this respect, but he unhelpfully plays down the role of Exod 19–24 in the overarching plot. As is typical of narrative, at crucial points the narrative slows down, and 19–24, indeed through to Num 10:10, is just such a point: "Time warps around Mount Sinai."[66] Sarna underlines the importance of 19–24 when he notes that "the idea of a covenant relationship between God and an entire people is unparalleled. Similarly unique is the setting of the covenant in a narrative context."[67] Dozeman's view that the scenes of the narrative are made up of different perspectives juxtaposed stems from his commitment to source-critical (non-P and P) analysis, which the text does not, in my view, support.

Moses's ascending and descending is a central motif in Exod 19–24,[68] but he is not the central character dictating the action; YHWH is the central character, and Moses's and Israel's actions are entirely in response to him. The centrality of YHWH also foregrounds the motif of holiness and the spatial gradations of holiness around Sinai that are entrenched in the tabernacle and later the Temple. Recognition of this helps to discern the narrative movement in 19–24.

Many of the problems with our reading of Exod 19–24 stem from a natural, modern tendency to read forward assuming a chronological sequence. Chirichigno[69] and, more recently Sprinkle, have argued that Hebrew narrative often works very differently, and that synoptic or resumptive repetition solves the problems of an apparently disparate narrative.

Chirichigno acknowledges the creative work done on the poetics of narrative but points out that little work has been done on the poetics of biblical narrative connected with legal material. He argues that this is especially true of Exod 19–24, which is part of the larger Sinai account running from Exod 19 to Num 10. Both Chirichigno and Sprinkle list the typical literary difficulties discerned in Exod 19–24 by historical critics, as discussed above. Ska, for example, asserts that "the Sinai pericope is one of the most complicated

---

65. Dozeman, *Exodus*, 433–34.

66. Burnside, *God, Justice, and Society*, 45.

67. Sarna, *Exodus*, 102.

68. The repeated references to Moses ascending and descending are as follows: 19:3, 7, 8, 14, 20, 21; 24:1, 9, 12, 18; 32:7, 15.

69. Gregory Chirichigno, "The Narrative Structure of Exodus 19–24," *Biblica* 68 (1987): 457–79.

passages in the entire Pentateuch."[70] Chirichigno argues, however, that the "awkward surface structure of the narrative, which results in the non-linear temporal ordering of events, can be explained when one takes into account the sequence structure of the narrative, particularly the use of the literary device called resumptive repetition."[71]

Chirichigno employs structural analysis and *resumptive repetition* to develop his analysis of the literary structure of Exod 19–24. Brichto refers to this latter device as the synoptic/resumptive or the synoptic-conclusive/ resumptive-expansive device.[72] It involves one event being narrated twice. The first narration is normally briefer; the second is a freestanding, independent unity, which may or may not be able to stand alone. "The second treatment seems to go back to the opening point of the first episode and, resuming the theme of that treatment, provide a more detailed account (hence *resumptive-expansive*) of how the bottom line of the first episode (hence *conclusive*) was arrived at."[73] According to Brichto, often the second narration may not just fill out the first but differ so as to provide another version, thus raising the question of how a sophisticated author can retain both versions. In a footnote, Brichto notes that, while this is the stuff of source criticism, "the surface plausibility of charging the two treatments to two different sources (or authors) . . . falls away when one queries the sense of resolving one absurdity at the expense of positing another one: if it is not plausible that one author gives two conflicting versions of an event, why is it plausible that an editor (whose task it is to improve an author's work) should parade his ineptness by attaching two such versions and passing them off as a unitary composition?"[74] Brichto observes that such is the rich range of effects made possible by resumptive repetition that each case must be examined individually. He refers in this respect also to the related "flashback technique" and notes that flashbacks and resumptive repetitions frequently make use of the nominal sentence construction in Hebrew.[75]

---

70. Ska, *Introduction to Reading the Pentateuch*, 213.

71. Chirichigno, "The Narrative Structure," 478–79.

72. Herbert C. Brichto, *Toward a Grammar of Biblical Poetics: Tales of the Prophets* (Oxford: Oxford University Press, 1993), 13–14. Brichto does not discuss Exod 19–24, but he does analyze Exod 32–34 (ch. 4), and his identification of resumptive repetition in that narrative is compelling.

73. Brichto, *Toward a Grammar of Biblical Poetics*, 14.

74. Brichto, *Toward a Grammar of Biblical Poetics*, 260.

75. Brichto, *Toward a Grammar of Biblical Poetics*, 16–17.

Following Todorov,[76] Chirichigno asserts that narrative prose is composed of narrative propositions and sequences. The narrative proposition is the smallest unit of narrative and is made up of agents and predicates. Syntactic function is the term for the relationship between two agents such as Moses–YHWH. Narrative propositions are organized into cycles that provide a sense of completion and are recognized intuitively by the reader. The name for this unit or cycle is *sequence*, with the end of the sequence indicated by a repetition, but an incomplete one, of the opening proposition. A complete sequence consists always and only of five propositions. A text generally consists of several sequences with three possible combinations of sequences: embedding, in which a sequence substitutes for a proposition in the first sequence; linking, in which the sequences are placed one after the other; and alternation or interlacing, which places a proposition of the first sequence after or before one of the second sequence.

In Exodus there are three principal agents, namely YHWH (Y), Moses (M), and the people of Israel (P). The interaction between these three yields five propositions in the following pattern:

Moses ascends the mountain	MA[77]
YHWH addresses Moses	YM
Moses descends from the mountain	MD
Moses addresses the people	MP
The people address Moses	PM

Based on this pattern, Chirichigno identifies three sequences within Exod 19:1–24:8, which he maps out in detail and with reference to the best work on the poetics of the Hebrew Bible. The three are:

1. 19:3–8b
2. 19:8c–20b; 20:18–21
3. 19:20c–25; 24:1–8

The three have parallel structures that are placed one after the other, an example of linking. Strikingly, in (2) and (3) PM is isolated from the main

76. Tzvetan Todorov, *Introduction to Poetics*, Theory and History of Literature 1, trans. Richard Howard (Minneapolis: University of Minnesota Press, 1981).

77. Chirichigno uses MU for Moses goes *up* the mountain, but MA = Moses *ascends* seems to me clearer.

THE GOD WHO ACTS IN HISTORY

sequence distorting the logic and temporal succession. The result is that the two PMs form an additional sequence of their own, an example of embedding, which reiterates and expands upon actions within the initial sequences.

Chirichigno argues that the events in 20:18–21 are contemporaneous with 19:16–20b, an example of resumptive repetition. He suggests that the request for mediation came during the giving of the Decalogue. Exodus 19:16–20b and 20:18–21 present the same event from a different point of view. Exodus 20:18–21 is the point of view of the people, thus marking a change in viewpoint from narrator to character. The "stood at a distance" inclusio in vv. 18 and 21 isolates the request for mediation from the description of the mountain, that is, from the main narrative of the second sequence. Why? Because, not only has the account of the fear of the people been isolated through resumptive repetition but the legal discussions have also been isolated. Exodus 20:18–21 with its emphasis on the fear of the Israelites has been isolated to form the preface to the Decalogue and the covenant code to signal a proper response to the Lord who gives the laws. "Therefore, the entire theophany experience is synoptically recorded in Exod 19, which is mainly told from the perspective of God, and retold and expanded in two resumptive narratives which discuss the fear of the people and the ratification of the covenant, both of which are told from the viewpoint of the people."[78]

Sprinkle does not develop Chirichigno's structural analysis, but he does develop his theory of resumptive repetition. He argues that once we take this technique seriously the chronological problems that plague scholarship evaporate. Exodus 19:16–25 provides a synopsis of the theophany as a whole and all the sections that follow (the Decalogue, 20:1–17; the fear of the people, 20:18–21; and the laws of 20:22–23:33) occur simultaneously with 19:16–25. Exodus 24:1–3a repeats and resumes the end of 19 but with more detail. Only in 24:3b do we move chronologically beyond the theophany as described synoptically in Exod 19.

Exodus 20:18 uses a circumstantial clause with a participle to indicate resumptive repetition, going back to 19:16–19.[79] Exodus 20:21 is thus not an additional—but the same—ascent by Moses mentioned in 19:20. Exodus 24:1–3a is similar to 19:21–25, and this is another case of resumptive repeti-

---

78. Chirichigno, "The Narrative Structure," 477.

79. Joe M. Sprinkle, *"The Book of the Covenant": A Literary Approach*, JSOTSup 174 (Sheffield: Sheffield Academic Press, 1994), 21.

tion.[80] Additional information is added, namely that Moses and Aaron are accompanied by Nadab and Abihu and seventy of the elders. The Decalogue itself is, according to Sprinkle, an act of resumption and must fit somewhere in 19:18–20. Sprinkle notes that it could have been spoken

- before the people's request for mediation;
- contemporaneously with their request;
- after Moses ascended in 19:20 but before Moses descended (19:21);
- such that it overlapped with more than one of the above.

Exodus 19:20 = 20:21, so that the laws of 20:22–23:33 were given to Moses after he ascends but before he descends to warn the people and to fetch Aaron, and so on.

Sprinkle asks why the author would arrange the material in this way, and proposes five reasons:

1. As a technique, it allows for simultaneous action.
2. Nonchronological arrangement isolates particular materials for didactic purposes. The Decalogue is an example.
3. It allows for different points of view to be represented.
4. The juxtaposition of the Decalogue followed by the people's fear (20:18–21) evokes the awesomeness of the law; the people ought to fear and obey.
5. By placing the people's fearful response (20:18–21) between the Decalogue and the Book of the Covenant (20:22–23:33), the author forms a chiastic structure for his narrative of the development of the covenant. In common with material in Exodus–Numbers, Sprinkle notes that we find a pattern of narrative–law–narrative in Exod 19–24. He sets this out chiastically as follows:[81]

> A. Narrative: the covenant offered (19:3–25)
>> B. Laws (general): the Decalogue (20:1–17)
>>> C. Narrative: the people's fear (20:18–21)
>> B'. Laws (specific): the Book of the Covenant (20:22–23:33)
> A'. Narrative: the covenant accepted (24:1–11)

---

80. Sprinkle, *"The Book of the Covenant,"* 22.

81. Joe M. Sprinkle, "Law and Narrative in Exodus 19–24," *JETS* 47/2 (2004): 235–52; *"The Book of the Covenant,"* 27.

Sprinkle interprets this chiasm to mean that the emphasis is on A and A',
namely the establishment of the covenant. B and B' relate the stipulations
to be obeyed for the covenant to work. C draws attention to the operating
principle of the covenant, namely the fear of YHWH.

In the light of his literary analysis of Exod 19–24, Sprinkle summarizes
the narrative as follows:

> In summary, the story line, rearranged chronologically, begins with
> Moses bringing the people to the mountain where the theophany is
> occurring. Moses calls to God and God answers him with a clap of
> thunder, or so it sounds to the people (19.16–19, cf. 20:18), though
> the real message includes at least part of the words of the Decalogue
> (20.1–17). While all this is occurring, the people are overwhelmed with
> terror, falling back away from the mountain and asking Moses to medi-
> ate for them (20.18–19). Moses tries to reassure them, but ultimately as-
> cends the mountain at the call of God alone as their mediator with God
> (19.20, 20.20–21). There he receives the remainder of God's revelation
> for Israel pertaining to the establishment of the covenant (remainder
> of Decalogue and 20.22–23.33). At the end of his stay on the mountain
> Moses is told to descend from the mountain to warn the people and the
> priests again not to approach the mountain, but he is to ascend again up
> the mountain with Aaron and others (19.21–25, 24.1–3b). The warning
> is necessary because sufficient time has passed for the initial terror of
> 20.18–21 to wear off while Moses was alone on the mountain, and be-
> cause Moses would later be returning part way with Aaron and others,
> an act that might embolden some to attempt the ascent on their own.[82]

Sprinkle also assembles evidence for the Decalogue being synoptic and
20:23–23:33 being expansive of the Decalogue.[83] He argues that 20:22–23:33
is not a law code but contains moral comments on some legal and non-
legal precepts. Doubtless there were law codes in existence that were drawn
upon, "but it is doubtful that any law code that the author/editor(s) had at
his disposal would have had the literary characteristics manifested by the
biblical corpus."[84] Sprinkle concludes that his discourse-oriented approach
is generally in no way inferior to source-critical approaches; indeed, most

82. Sprinkle, *"The Book of the Covenant,"* 24.
83. Sprinkle, *"The Book of the Covenant,"* 25–26.
84. Sprinkle, *"The Book of the Covenant,"* 206.

often it is superior. He argues that 20:22–23:33 is well integrated into the Pentateuch, 20–23 being intelligently and intentionally placed in the context of the Sinai narrative. There are substantial links between 20–23 and its surrounding narrative. Exodus 20–23 is an expansion of the Decalogue, and later passages in the Pentateuch draw on these regulations and can be interpreted in harmony with it. They also help in its interpretation. Exodus 20:22–23:33 is thus well structured in relation to its narrative context, and sections in 20:22–23:33 are well structured individually and in relation to each other.

In his review of Sprinkle's *The "Book of the Covenant,"* Davies says of his use of resumptive repetition that "this involves a number of improbable interpretations and serves only to show the lengths to which some writers will go to avoid a source-critical explanation of the text."[85] However, I do not think that Chirichigno's and Sprinkle's work can be dismissed so easily. Brichto, Sprinkle's supervisor, shows persuasively how resumptive repetition functions in Exod 32–34,[86] and there can be no doubt that analysis of the poetics of the Hebrew Bible has challenged the results of source criticism in myriad ways. The crucial question that emerges is the relationship between poetics and exegesis. Todorov helpfully articulates the relationship between interpretation and poetics as follows:

> Interpretation both precedes and follows poetics: the notions of poetics are produced according to the necessities of concrete analysis, which in turn may advance only by using the instruments elaborated by doctrine. Neither of the two activities takes precedence over the other: both are "secondary." This intimate interpenetration, which often makes the work of criticism an incessant oscillation between poetics and interpretation, must not keep us from distinguishing, in the abstract, the goals of one attitude from those of the other.[87]

Doubtless, there is far more work to be done on the literary structure of Exod 19–24. What is clear is that structural analysis and resumptive repetition provide a very different perspective on many of the problems in the text discerned by source critics, and provide *a* persuasive way to read Exod

---

85. G. I. Davies, Review, *VT* 48/2 (1998): 285.
86. Brichto, *Toward a Grammar*, 88–121.
87. Todorov, *Introduction to Poetics*, 7–8.

19–24 as a literary whole. It is notable that Sommer lists neither Sprinkle nor Chirichigno[88] in his bibliography.

The Theology of Sinai: Divine Action

The Sinai narrative, read as a whole, is exceptionally rich theologically. Some readers may wonder why the theology of Exod 19–24 should play a significant role in a discussion of the historicity of Sinai. Previous chapters will have gone a long way to answer this question, but it also needs to be noted that while it is useful to distinguish the historical, literary, and theological dimensions of a text, in practice we encounter them as a rich unity and they interact with each other in all sorts of ways. For example, we saw above how attention to the literary centrality of YHWH in Exodus and how unpacking God's proper name theologically bear on the historicity of Sinai.

Childs is certainly right in his comment that "the history of research has often demonstrated how effectively the study of the prehistory has functioned in obscuring the biblical text through false parallels and mistaken ideas of historical development."[89] Such obscuring is unhelpful, reductive, and needs to be overcome not least through repeated explication of the theological wealth of this narrative. My concern in this section is not to explore all dimensions of the theology of 19–24, let alone 19–40, but to focus particularly on the doctrine of God and divine action as portrayed in this narrative, including the laws.

88. Chirichigno, "The Narrative Structure," 457, refers to M. Greenberg, "The Book of Exodus," *EncJud* 6 (1971): 1056, and J. Licht, *Storytelling in the Bible* (Jerusalem: Magnes Press, 1978), 19; "The Sinai Theophany," in *Studies in the Bible and the Ancient Near East* [Hebrew], ed. Y. Avishur and J. Blau (Jerusalem: Rubinstein, 1978), 251–68, as examples of authors who read Exod 19–24 as a unity, but he points out that they do not explain the literary difficulties foregrounded by source critics. Cf. also Martin R. Hauge, *The Descent from the Mountain: Narrative Patterns in Exodus 19–40*, JSOTSup 323 (Sheffield: Sheffield Academic Press, 2001); Yitzhak Avishur, "The Narrative of the Revelation at Sinai (Ex. 19–24)," in *Studies in Historical Geography and Biblical Historiography*, ed. Gershon Galil and Moshe Weinfeld (Leiden: Brill, 2000), 197–214, who explores chiasm in Exod 19–24.

89. Childs, *Exodus*, 339. The way in which contemporary historical approaches marginalize the Sinai event is evident in the minimal attention paid to it in Moore and Kelle, *Biblical History*; indeed, Sinai is not even listed in the index.

In its narrative context and in 19–24 itself YHWH is clearly portrayed as the deliverer of the Israelites from slavery in Egypt (19:4; 20:2). This speaks of YHWH's *immanent involvement in the creation* and of his sovereignty over the creation. He attends to the cry of the Israelites, raises up Moses as his deliverer, and through the plagues demonstrates his power over the pharaoh, who was regarded as a god in Egypt.[90] The occasional but poignant uses of "Elohim" in 19–24 plus the aside "Indeed, the whole earth is mine," as well as the clear reference to creation in 20:11, point to the fact that YHWH is not just the Israelite god but the sovereign Creator, and thus to the fundamental ontological distinction between the Creator and the created. Indeed, we have seen above how creation motifs are prominent at the beginning and end of Exodus; they are also prominent in 19–24.

Connected with YHWH's immanent involvement in his creation is his nature as *personal*. He says to the Israelites that "I have brought you to myself" (19:4), speaks to Moses and the Israelites as a whole, establishes Israel in a covenant relationship with himself, provides them with instructions (law) that will enable them to flourish as a "good neighborhood,"[91] promises them a land of their own (23:23–33), and in 25–40 oversees the establishment of his residence among them. He describes his relationality in terms of jealousy and steadfast love (20:5–6). All of this connects integrally with the points made above by Davies in terms of the relationships established by God in creation and at Sinai.

Clearly the personal language used of God is *anthropomorphic*. God is portrayed as speaking, bringing, descending, and so on.[92] This brings us onto the contested terrain of the nature of language about God, about which a variety of models have been proposed. Brian Howell, in his *In the Eyes of God: A Metaphorical Approach to Biblical Anthropomorphic Language*, seeks

90. Cf. Henri Frankfort, *Kingship and the Gods: A Study of Ancient Near Eastern Religion as the Integration of Society and Nature* (Chicago: University of Chicago Press, 1948, 1978), who discerns a significant distinction between Egypt and Mesopotamia in this regard. Frankfort notes of both the Egyptian and the Mesopotamian view of kingship that "both, moreover, are thrown in stronger relief by a comparison with the Hebrews, who were familiar with the cultures of Egypt and Mesopotamia and fanatically rejected the highest values recognized by both" (x).

91. Patrick D. Miller, *The Way of the Lord: Essays in Biblical Theology* (Grand Rapids: Eerdmans, 2004), 51–67.

92. During my research I made a list of every action predicated of God in Exod 19–24. For the sake of the length of the book I have not repeated that here. Clearly, however, Exod 19–24 is awash with the language of divine action.

to develop an appropriate metaphorical view of language about God and focuses in particular on God seeing (cf. Gen 1). He explores the variety of contemporary and ancient approaches to language about God and concludes,

> In sum, biblical anthropomorphisms are metaphorical, but not
> strictly derived from the human arena. Because humans are created
> as the image of God, there is an ontological basis for their descriptors
> to refer and refer accurately to God. They describe God in a supernat-
> ural sense of these terms, and yet one in which humans have poten-
> tial to access. Thus, it is misleading to speak of these attributes and
> actions as drawn from the human realm and somewhat naively ap-
> plied to God. Rather, the concepts, originally understood from their
> employment in the human realm, are applied to God metaphorically
> in such a way as to "point" to the divine attribute or action, without
> fully defining it.[93]

Doubtless we could debate the issue of language about God. What is
insightful about Howell's approach is that it recognizes the ontological or
creational basis for such language; it recognizes that such language refers or
points to God's action, it leaves open the precision or conceptual tightness
of such reference, and it affirms the accuracy of such metaphorical language.
Being made in the likeness of God we would expect human language about
God to be anthropomorphic, as we have seen in our discussions of Colin
Gunton, Eleanore Stump, and others. Such language is not smoke without
fire, as it were. It is smoke with fire!

There is much discussion over the extent to which Exod 19–24 asserts
monotheism.[94] In my opinion it is at least implicit, if not explicit, in 19–24. In
terms of Israel and its role as a covenant partner the reality of other gods is
not denied but the first commandment makes it clear that the covenant requires allegiance only to YHWH, with any other gods in the cultus—"before
me" 20:3—being expressly forbidden. The purity of Israel's worship is one
thing, the implied doctrine of God another. YHWH is clearly portrayed as
sovereign over nations other than Israel, specifically Egypt and Canaan and
the surrounding nations (23:23–33). If this is implicit monotheism, then the
aside "the whole earth is mine" and the clear reference to God as Creator

---

93. Brian C. Howell, *In the Eyes of God: A Metaphorical Approach to Biblical
Anthropomorphic Language* (Cambridge: James Clarke and Co., 2014), 103.

94. Cf. Albright, *From the Stone Age*, 257–72.

in the Decalogue seem to me to make monotheism explicit. As we would expect in the Torah, for the people the focus is on "practical monotheism" but this presupposes actual monotheism.

A major theme of Exod 19–24 is the *transcendence and holiness of God*. Cremer notes that "we understand that this attribute of God can only be known where he enacts or reveals it. . . . Thus we understand that, before God's revelation in Christ, Israel alone knew this attribute, for they alone knew the one who dealt with them as such. Israel alone spoke of the holiness of God—as did no one else."[95] The theophany evokes his otherness and character such that his contact with humans is dangerous for them. His otherness is also reinforced in the prohibition of images (20:4–6). We have already noted how spatial distinctions of gradations of holiness are established around the mountain, distinctions with significant parallels in the tabernacle and Temple. Already in 19:6 we read of YHWH's intention for Israel to be a "holy nation" and in the purification for the third day and the reinforcement of the boundaries around the mountain we see YHWH forming his people into a nation fit for the one Isaiah repeatedly refers to as the "Holy One" of Israel. As we noted in Chapter 7, biblically this is a central attribute of God but one neglected by classical theism.

Central to Exod 19–24 is the view of YHWH as *the one who reveals himself* to his people in event *and* word, with both being held inseparably together. Moses brings out the people to "meet Elohim" (19:17); they hear YHWH speaking; and the group who ascend the mountain after the ratification of the covenant "saw the God of Israel. . . . they beheld God, and they ate and drank" (24:10–11). In Chapter 8 we attended to Schwöbel's rich analysis of disclosure events, and his description fits precisely with what we find at Sinai. (1) YHWH is the author of the revelation at Sinai; (2) YHWH discloses himself within the creation at a particular time and place; (3) YHWH's disclosure includes the narrative interpretation by the witnesses themselves of his disclosure; (4) YHWH's disclosure is directed at a particular people, namely the slaves rescued from Egypt; (5) YHWH's disclosure makes personal communion with himself possible. As Vriezen notes, "all Old Testament teaching rests . . . on the certainty of the communion between the Holy God and man, a belief founded on the intercourse between Yahweh and Israel experienced in the history of revelation."[96]

---

95. Cremer, *The Christian Doctrine*, 22.

96. Th. C. Vriezen, *An Outline of Old Testament Theology*, 2nd ed. (Oxford: Basil Blackwell, 1970), 176.

Item (3) needs further comment. We saw in Chapter 1 how Sommer sets up the contrast between a stenographic and a dialogical approach to the Hebrew Bible. In my view this is an unhelpful dichotomy. Revelation includes "narrative interpretation by the witnesses" of YHWH's self-disclosure and this alerts us to the historical and human dimension in the composition of Exod 19–24. Thus, oral testimony handed down over a long period and the use of sources *may* well underlie the Sinai narrative. Especially with the Covenant law code, it is, in my view, likely that such codes were not static but updated in relation to new circumstances as time passed. It is also likely that the Sinai narrative is recorded in such a way as to make memorization and liturgical use as straightforward as possible. All of these human dimensions are possible—indeed likely—while still holding to the fact that the Sinai event and its account have their origins in YHWH's actual revelation of himself at Sinai.

Central to the word element of Sinai is law so that YHWH is portrayed as the *Lawgiver* through Moses. The Sinai covenant has been recognized as having important similarities with Hittite suzerain–vassal treaties of the Late Bronze Age (1450–1200 BCE),[97] an argument for its historicity. The covenant/treaty law is comprehensive in that it relates to all dimensions of the life of Israel, personal and corporate, outer and inner. Familiarity should not detract from the extraordinary nature of the law in Exod 19–24 and elsewhere in the HB/OT. Eichler rightly points out that "for seminal characteristics of biblical notions of law and morality to be more fully appreciated, one must situate them within the cultural milieu of ancient Near Eastern thought."[98]

To date we have discovered no Egyptian law codes. If this results from the view of pharaoh as a god so that no written legal tradition was needed, then the law code in Exod 19–24 is truly remarkable against an Egyptian background, and signifies a radically different approach to law compared with the Egyptian view.[99] However, as Eichler observes, the absence of such

97. Jeremiah Unterman, *Justice for All: How the Jewish Bible Revolutionized Ethics* (Philadelphia: Jewish Publication Society, 2017), 16–19. Cf. Benjamin Uffenheimer, *Early Prophecy in Israel*, trans. David Louvish (Jerusalem: Magnes, 1999), 127–54.

98. Barry L. Eichler, "Law and Morality in Ancient Near Eastern Thought," in *Ethics, Politics, and Democracy: From Primordial Principles to Prospective Practices*, ed. J. V. Ciprut (Cambridge, MA: MIT Press, 2008), 34. See also the excellent chapter on Sinai in Unterman, *Justice for All*, 15–40.

99. Unterman, *Justice for All*, 19. Since writing his book, Unterman was alerted to Eichler, "Law and Morality," and he kindly alerted me to this chapter.

law codes from Egypt may be due to the fact that Egyptians wrote on papyrus, which was subject to decay, whereas Mesopotamians wrote on clay tablets, which, once baked, were virtually indestructible.[100]

Eichler notes the similarities between the ethics of the HB/OT and that of the ANE but argues that biblical ethics is distinct because of its *distinct view of God*:

> The biblical worldview, normally termed monotheistic, is not mere belief in the existence of one God. Rather, it is the idea that the Deity is transcendent and sovereign over all. It differs fundamentally from polytheism in the absolute freedom of the Godhead. Unlike ancient Near Eastern gods, who are born into a primordial realm of natural and supernatural forces, which precede them in time and transcend them in power, the Biblical God is there from the very beginning, and the forces of the cosmos are all-inherent inside him. Thus the biblical Deity acts in total freedom, unrivaled either by the will of other gods or by the cosmic forces of the universe. (43)

In Egypt and Mesopotamia, the cosmic, moral standard for ethics is of an abstract and impersonal nature: neither *kittum* (Mesopotamia) nor *maat* (Egypt) were capable of communicating their will to people. However, "much in contrast to Mesopotamian and Egyptian thought, the Bible conceives of law and morality as the expression of the divine will of an omnipotent—and caring—sole Deity. . . . This biblical conception of law as the revealed will of God stands high and clear, in contrast to the myriad uncertainties and innumerable insecurities associated with the Mesopotamian and Egyptian conceptions of law and morality" (53–54).

Law as an expression of God's covenant with the entire people of Israel, both individual and communal, is unique in the ANE and effectively democratizes the Mesopotamian understanding of a covenant between king and god, so that the Israelites are placed on a par with Mesopotamian and Egyptian kings.

Eichler and Unterman note the many ways in which HB/OT law is distinctive: unlike Mesopotamian law there are no legally sanctioned classes among Israelites; except in cultic matters "there is no evidence of a developed class structure" (45). Only in biblical law do we find the attempt to

100. Eichler, "Law and Morality," 39. Hereafter, page references to this work are given in parentheses in the text.

change the conditions of the poor by prohibiting interest-bearing loans (Exod 22:24); the concern for the stranger or foreigner (*gēr*; Exod 22:20) is also absent from Mesopotamian law collections. There are unique elements in Israel's slavery laws and both minors and women are treated as "persons" before the law. Vicarious punishment is forbidden in Israel and this "material economic valuation of human life contrasts sharply with the Bible's religious valuation of human life as a spiritual entity" (47). Property crimes cannot be escalated to capital crimes. There is little emphasis on the role of the king in Israelite law, unlike in Mesopotamian law in which it is so central. Rather the people, both individually and corporately, are to keep the law and to take responsibility for it.

There are not many motive clauses in the laws of Exod 19–24, but the ones that are present are telling. The law concerning the altar in 20:22-26 is motivated by the fact that the Israelites have "seen for yourselves that I spoke with you from heaven."[101] The treatment of the alien in 20:21 and 23:9 is motivated by Israel's experience as aliens in Egypt. In my view the effectiveness of the illocutionary force of such laws depends on Israel having been slaves in Egypt and on having heard God speak at Sinai.

We noted above LaCocque's comment that the Decalogue is a commentary on "YHWH." N. T. Wright, in his creative *The Lord and His Prayer*, turns the telescope around, as it were, to see what the Lord's Prayer teaches us about *the Lord of the prayer*. The same approach can be applied to *YHWH and his Decalogue*. This succinct text is prefaced by the statement that "God (Elohim) spoke all these words." As throughout the HB/OT God is clearly portrayed as *speaking*, confirmed by the use of the first person in 20:2, 5, and the second-person singular imperatives throughout. In vv. 7, 11, and 12 we find, by comparison, third-person references to YHWH. This does not subvert the statement that "God spoke all these words." Benno Jacob says of v. 7, "henceforth the statements speak *of God in the third person*, but we would involve ourselves in great difficulties if we assumed that someone other than Moses spoke after this."[102] Jacob cites Num 14:21 and 2 Sam 12:9 as examples of cases in which YHWH refers to himself in the third person. Indeed, 2 Sam 12:9, "Why have

---

101. Note the interesting juxtaposition of "seen" and "spoke." Cf. 20:18, which literally reads, "And all the people seeing the voice . . ." On this issue cf. Oswald Bayer, *A Contemporary in Dissent: Johann Georg Hamann as a Radical Enlightener*, trans. Roy A. Harrisville and Mark C. Mattes (Grand Rapids: Eerdmans, 2012), 75.

102. Benno Jacob, *The Second Book of the Bible: Exodus*, trans. Walter Jacob (Hoboken, NJ: Ktav, 1992), 557.

you despised the word of the LORD, to do what is evil in his sight?," is followed in v. 10 by the statement "for you have despised *me*." Clearly the Decalogue presents us with the living God who speaks to his people.

Exodus 20:2 starts with the self-identification formula "I am YHWH" and then in parallel expands on his proper name in terms of YHWH's action to rescue the Israelites from Egypt and slavery. This confirms our comments above about YHWH's name being revealed in and through his actions. The whole Decalogue hangs on this action of YHWH on behalf of a slave people. SDA is clearly enunciated here, and the speech acts involved in the Decalogue and the laws that follow would be vacuous if YHWH had, indeed, *not* acted to rescue his people from slavery in Egypt. A strong argument for the historicity of exodus-Sinai is that Israel remembers its history as one originating *in slavery*. No other nation in the ANE develops such a national history beginning in shame and oppression. How is this possible? Again, it all turns on the character of YHWH. Exodus 20:2 links us back into the exodus narratives and to the character of YHWH who heard the cry of his people amidst oppression and slavery (3:7). Exodus 3:7 identifies three actions of YHWH: I have seen;[103] I have heard; I know. Following from this YHWH intervenes in history to rescue his people and to bring them to himself. It borders on the ridiculous to ask if it *matters* whether YHWH actually did this. The "honest historian" may conclude that there is no evidence for the exodus and that it never happened, but then that same historian must follow through on the theological consequences of such a view. It cannot be denied that in 20:2, YHWH himself is represented as making the weight and authority of what follows dependent upon his having acted by rescuing the Israelites from slavery in Egypt. To work in the reverse direction, if we take the theological claims of the Decalogue seriously, we should be exceedingly cautious of concluding that the exodus never happened or that we can know virtually nothing about it. YHWH's SDA in the exodus-Sinai event cannot simply be bracketed out as though of no consequence.

The portrayal of YHWH in the Decalogue is intensely personal. YHWH's response to the excruciating pain of slavery and oppression is

---

103. On the language of YHWH seeing cf. Howell, *In the Eyes of God*. From Dan 5:23 we learn that God's seeing is an activity that makes him distinctive from other gods: "You have praised the gods of silver and gold, of bronze, iron, wood, and stone, *which do not see or hear or know*; but the God in whose power is your very breath [cf. Gen 2], and to whom belong all your ways, you have not honoured." Seeing, hearing, and knowing are here predicated of the living God.

to rescue the Israelites and to set them free. He is a God of *hesed*, of faithfulness in relationship (20:6). He seeks to be loved and obeyed (20:6). He enters into covenant relationship with the rescued slaves as "your [singular] God" (20:2). Indeed, the use of the second-person singular throughout the Decalogue is noteworthy, addressing, as it does every*one* who makes up the community of Israel.

But YHWH, although personal, is by no means an equal partner on the same level as the Israelites. This is obvious from the language of his intervention in history, but also from his self-descriptions as *'el qana'*, a jealous God (20:5). YHWH is completely *intolerant* of rivals, determined to punish those who reject/hate him (*le-son'ay*, 20:5). Here we encounter YHWH's *attribute of holiness*. He is other than, or separate from, us in two ways; first, as God, and second, as without sin and intolerant of sin. His otherness as God does not prevent him for a moment from entering into relationship with us, as Gen 1–3 makes clear. As creatures in the *imago Dei* we are made for relationship with God; but as sinners we are endangered by God's proximity. Hence the liturgical shape of the Sinai event, ensuring that appropriate boundaries are in place.

YHWH is God; as such he is radically different from the creation that is his handiwork. His name or character is thus special or, as Jesus might say, hallowed, and abuse of it for manipulative purposes is forbidden. The name Elohim (20:1, 2, 5, 7, 10, 12; cf. Gen 1:1–2:3), his acting in Egypt, and the explicit reference to creation in v. 11, all speak of YHWH as Creator. As he himself says in 19:5, "Indeed, the whole earth is mine." His being Creator is present more indirectly in v. 4, in which idols in the form of things in heaven, on the earth, and in the seas are forbidden. Idolatry always absolutizes some aspect of the good creation, venerating the created as the Creator. Jacob notes of this threefold description that "we should more appropriately see it as a reflection of the threefold *environment of all creatures*."[104]

YHWH is portrayed by the Decalogue as transcendent and immanently involved in his creation. His life and way of acting is the model for human, indeed all created life, as is most evident in the sabbath commandment (20:8–11). He rests and so should we, our animals, and the alien resident in our towns. God has ordered time in a particular way and all should benefit from following this order. He is faithful in relationship, as noted above, and so should we be, especially in the one-flesh relationship of marriage (20:14) and in family life (20:12), but also in how we relate to our neighbors (20:13,

104. Jacob, *Exodus*, 548.

15, 16, 17). The ethics of the second half of the Decalogue flow directly from the character of YHWH, and thus tell us a great deal about him. They are designed to (re)make us in his image, so that, although the *imago Dei* is not mentioned, it is implicit throughout. YHWH is generous, giving the gift of the land (20:12) to rescued slaves, making sure the resident alien and animals receive good treatment, and so should we be.

All this is clearly present in the Sinai narrative and there is far more. In terms of SDA, God is undoubtedly portrayed as the central character and as a God of action. As we have seen with Maimonides, Halevi, Spinoza, Kant, Barth, and Gunton, what we make of this historical narrative and its central character will significantly be informed by our view of God.

History and Sinai

We have already surveyed historical critical approaches to Exod 19–24 above, and clearly they have radical implications for any notion of the historicity of the Sinai narrative. In the early and mid-twentieth century, the approach to the historicity of the HB/OT shifted to the maximilist one of the Albright school. John Bright was a central member of the "Albright school,"[105] which identified the need for and encouraged him to write his well-known *A History of Israel*. Bright argues, for example, that:

- Moses was, as the HB/OT portrays him, the great founder of Israel's faith: "The events of exodus and Sinai require a great personality behind them. And a faith as unique as Israel's demands a founder as surely as does Christianity—or Islam, for that matter. To deny that role to Moses would force us to posit another person of the same name."[106]
- Similarly, we are driven to assume that the covenant league, like Yahwism, reaches back to Sinai. Bright dates the exodus to the thirteenth century and says of the mixed group that left Egypt, "this group, led by Moses, made its way to Sinai where in solemn covenant it formed itself as the people of Yahweh."[107]

105. Burke O. Long, *Planting and Reaping Albright: Politics, Ideology, and Interpreting the Bible* (University Park: Pennsylvania State University Press, 1997).

106. John Bright, *A History of Israel*, 3rd ed. (Louisville: Westminster John Knox, 1959, 1972, 1980), 127.

107. Bright, *A History of Israel*, 140.

- Covenant law was central to Israel's life from the outset.
- An approach like Bright's has been defended more recently by Provan, Long, and Longman in their *A Biblical History of Israel*,[108] and by Hoffmeier[109] and others. However, such views form a minority against the backdrop of the radical views of the history of Israel that have dominated recent decades, works by scholars such as Van Seters, Davies, Whitelaw, and Lemche. Moore and Kelle conclude their overview of scholarship on Israel's emergence by noting that, "in academic study of the HB/OT . . . a variety of historical and nonhistorical interpretations of the stories about Israel's emergence exists."[110] It is easy, in the light of current ferment, to be agnostic about Sinai in terms of its historicity. However, before we move too quickly in that direction, several points should be noted:

1. Mark Day points out that the idea of *historical narrative* was rejected for much of the twentieth century by historians and philosophers of history.[111] However, through the work of philosophers such as Paul Ricoeur it has made a significant comeback. Alter describes biblical narrative as "fictionalized history" but makes the important point that it is "peculiar, and culturally significant, that among ancient peoples only Israel should have chosen to cast its sacred national traditions in prose."[112] Ricoeur and Meir Sternberg have pointed out that the poetics of narrative prose are common to both fiction and historical narrative, with *intent* being the crucial distinction between the two. Thus, the clearly crafted, literary and theological nature of the Sinai narrative does not for a moment mean that it is unhistorical. As Bruce Halpern observes, "whether a text is history, then, depends on what its author meant to do."[113] In relation to Exod 19–24 the question then becomes, What was the intent of the author(s)? Meir Sternberg has tenaciously defended the intent of

108. Iain Provan, V. Philips Long, and Tremper Longman III, *A Biblical History of Israel* (Louisville: Westminster/John Knox, 2003).

109. Hoffmeier, *Ancient Israel in Sinai*; Hoffmeier, *Israel in Egypt: The Evidence for the Authenticity of the Exodus Tradition* (Oxford: Oxford University Press, 1996).

110. Moore and Kelle, *Biblical History*, 141.

111. Mark Day, *The Philosophy of History* (London: Continuum, 2008), 167.

112. Alter, *The Art of Biblical Narrative*, 25.

113. Bruce Halpern, *The First Historians: The Hebrew Bible and History* (San Francisco: Harper and Row, 1988), 8.

the HB/OT narrative writers to write history and he relates this to their monotheism.[114] He asserts that,

> Were the narrative written or read as fiction, then God would turn from the lord of history into a creature of the imagination, with the most disastrous results. The shape of time, the rationale of monotheism, the foundations of conduct, the national sense of identity, the very right to the land of Israel and the hope of deliverance to come: all hang in the generic balance. Hence the Bible's determination to sanctify and compel literal belief in the past. It claims not just the status of history but, as Eric Auerbach rightly maintains, of *the* history—the one and only truth that, like God himself, brooks no rival.[115]

In grappling with Sternberg's account, Levinson reaches for Spinoza to account for the dualisms he discerns in Sternberg's account.[116] As per our earlier discussion of Spinoza, I do not find this a helpful move. Levinson argues that Sternberg's account becomes to an extent a "secular narrative theology."[117] Here, I suspect, he rightly pinpoints an element of Sternberg's analysis, but, from my perspective, an appropriate response is not to reach for Spinoza but to explore the contours of a *theistic* narrative theology in relation to the HB/OT, which would agree with Sternberg in most ways. Levinson rightly flags the need to extend literary analysis to the law codes of the HB/OT, a complex task we cannot attend to here.[118]

2. The *coherence* of a narrative account is *an* important element in taking it seriously as historical narrative. In this respect, we should not underestimate the impact of historical criticism in undermining the possibility of the historicity of Sinai. Historical criticism works with a strong sense of the incoherence of the Sinai narrative as it stands but, alas, without attending closely to its literary form. However, as we have shown above, the Sinai narrative does—at least potentially—cohere as a narrative, and this is important in assessing its historicity. Day insists that a historical account is larger than the sum of its parts: "without a view of the whole one could not make

---

114. Sternberg, *The Poetics of Biblical Narrative*, 23–35.

115. Sternberg, *The Poetics of Biblical Narrative*, 32.

116. Levinson, *"The Right Chorale,"* 4, 7–39.

117. Levinson, *"The Right Chorale,"* 25.

118. Note that I plan to attend to this issue in my future series Old Testament Origins and the Question of God.

sense of an account being objective (or not), and misleading (or not)."[119]
He writes, "part and whole are connected both *semantically*, and in *rational historical debate*."[120]

This is not to deny that sources and oral traditions underlie Exod 19–24 or that many other factors need to be taken into consideration, such as editing and updating, but it is to emphasize that we first need to read the narrative closely as we have received it before speculating about underlying sources to which we have no access.

3. It is, alas, not uncommon nowadays to find the polytheism of the ANE being lauded as an example of the sort of religious toleration we need in contrast to the intolerance of what Assmann calls the "Mosaic distinction." A major need of our day is to take a fresh and deep look at the precise nature of ANE polytheism and to determine if such a revival would be in our best interests. I think not! Similarly, there is a tendency to play down the unique contributions of Israel and the HB/OT.

In exploring the latter issue, we should not make the mistake of denigrating Israel's similarities with its ANE context as unhistorical. As with Jesus research, we should not privilege the criterion of *dissimilarity* at the expense of *similarity*. We would expect Israel to have much in common with the ANE, and indeed it does. And some of these elements support the historicity of Sinai. Hoffmeier has shown that there are strong Egyptian elements in the early chapters of Exodus. Similarly, the way in which the Sinai covenant is modeled on suzerain–vassal ANE treaties, and especially Hittite ones, lends credence to its authenticity. As Sarna observes, "the Israelite covenant concept of the forging of a formal, legal, binding relationship between God and a people is so extraordinary that to have been intelligible, it would have had to be expressed in terms of its contemporary, universally recognized, legal instruments. By the very nature of the situation, such a relationship between God and Israel would find its closest analogy in the suzerain–vassal treaties."[121] However, as Sarna points out, "we do not mean to suggest, however, that the biblical *b'rit* is a slavish imitation of contemporary Near Eastern norms. On the contrary, it displays an originality and independence that transforms it into a wholly new creation, the innovative nature of which can only be adequately appreciated against the background of the classical model."[122]

119. Day, *The Philosophy of History*, 195.
120. Day, *The Philosophy of History*, 198. Emphasis original.
121. Sarna, *Exploring Exodus*, Kindle locations 2999–3002.
122. Sarna, *Exploring Exodus*, Kindle locations 3009–11.

In terms of the revolutionary adaptation of this ANE treaty pattern, Sarna discerns firstly the expansion of the treaty concept so that God and a people become parties to it, for which he finds no parallel in history. Second, unlike other treaties the Sinai covenant is positioned in a narrative from which it takes its meaning and profoundly influences the subsequent storyline.

Read against its ANE context, Exod 19–24 is clearly ANE but also provides us with a host of unique insights:

- monotheism, or what Assmann refers to as the "Mosaic distinction";
- the portrayal of YHWH as Creator-Redeemer;
- the idea of a covenant between God and an entire people;
- the setting of a covenant in a narrative context;
- the preoccupation of the treaty-like covenant with internal, social affairs;
- the concern with both the individual[123] and society; René Girard, for example, has argued that the tenth commandment is unique in its constraint of desire, the gateway to the four heinous acts preceding it;[124]
- the nature of the Decalogue as a self-enforcing document.

As we would expect, many of the legal provisions have close parallels with the ANE and yet there are also significant differences, as noted above. In the ANE, furthermore, the king was the source of law, whereas in Exod 19–24 it is YHWH and neither Moses nor the nonexistent king. All the imagery of kingship associated with the treaty parallel is accrued to YHWH.

In terms of historicity, a crucial question is how we account for this radical difference and innovation in Israel situated firmly in the context of the ANE. In his fascinating book *The Invention of Hebrew*, Sanders maintains that the Hebrew Bible speaks and communicates in a distinctive way: "no other Near Eastern texts talk like the Bible does; virtually all other literature was by and for scribes, courts, and kings. . . . How and when did the Bible's way of communicating become possible, and what were its politics?"[125] He asserts that "the Bible is the first text to address people as a public."[126] I find

123. The Decalogue is for all the Israelites and yet addresses them in the second-person singular.

124. René Girard, *I See Satan Fall Like Lightning* (Maryknoll, NY: Orbis, 2001).

125. Seth L. Sanders, *The Invention of Hebrew* (Urbana, IL: University of Illinois Press, 2009), xi.

126. Sanders, *Invention*, 1.

it hard not to wonder if such distinctives do not in fact emerge from the Sinai event. One cannot escape the possibility that the Sinai event took place and that it is YHWH who accounts for the novelty of the Sinai covenant.

4. In drawing this section to a conclusion, I raise two larger issues that bear on historicity. Most textbooks refer to Herodotus as the father of historiography and there can be not doubt about the significance of his contribution. However, the Jewish philosopher Will Herberg argues, in common with Frankfort et al. in their *Intellectual Adventure of Ancient Man*, that the unique worldview of Israel in the HB/OT, and that of the NT, allows history to come into focus for proper attention for the first time so that "Moses" rather than Herodotus is the father of history. If this is the case, then clearly it would bear on our reading of the Sinai narrative and incline us toward a positive approach to its historicity.

5. Herberg argues, furthermore, that the biblical view of history possesses a double inwardness.[127] First, it is an interpretation through the lens of faith of events and happenings that, from another perspective, might be read in an entirely different way. Second, it can only become redemptive for me if I *appropriate it as my personal history*. "Faith is responding to the call of God that comes to us from out of the midst of redemptive history."[128]

For all the value of his work, Halpern sets believing reading against historical reading: "Worshippers do not read the Bible with an intrinsic interest in human events. . . . Confessional reading levels historical differences."[129] Herberg's approach, and here I think too of the work of philosophers like Alvin Plantinga and Nicholas Wolterstorff, suggests precisely the opposite, namely that biblical faith increases one's interest in the historicity of the Bible and orients one toward history in a particular way.

I cannot conceive of any way in which historical evidence could be used to "prove" the historicity of the Sinai narrative in the modern scientific sense. What needs to be borne in mind as we weigh the evidence is *the nature of historical proof* or demonstration. Events from the past cannot be put under the microscope and subjected to repeated experiments. Nor is history or history writing simply about what happened, which is far too broad a definition. Historians are dependent on testimony from the past, which they evaluate carefully as they construct a narrative of the event under consideration.

---

127. Herberg, *Faith Enacted as History*, 40–42.
128. Herberg, *Faith Enacted as History*, 41.
129. Halpern, *First Historians*, 4.

Sinai is clearly portrayed in liturgical, sanctuary-like ways, and Smith may well be right about the centrality of the motif of pilgrimage in Exodus. However, the poetics of the Sinai narrative—its nature as literature and its theological dimension—does not discount it as reliable historically. As many have recognized, such elements are not by any means exclusive to nonhistorical literature. Authorial intent becomes the key to distinguish historical from nonhistorical literature, and it will be clear from the above that, in my view, the author intended to narrate what took place.

There are other elements that confirm this view. Jewish scholars evocatively refer to the need for every generation to be brought before Sinai. Nevertheless, it is remarkable that Israel never turned Sinai into a pilgrimage site. Sinai, for Israel, was a *one-off event*, looking forward to life in the land, which makes it likely that something definitive happened once and for all at Sinai. Furthermore, we can seek to show that the narrative is coherent, and we have examined views of the Sinai narrative as coherent against the alleged incoherence of the narrative. We *can* seek to show that it fits with what we know about ancient Egypt and attend to Hittite analogies, and so on, as others have done in great detail.

What makes an evaluation of the historicity of the Sinai event different from most historical interpretation is the centrality of YHWH. The result is that much will depend on the matrix or paradigm within which we read the Sinai narrative. If God does not exist or cannot speak, then clearly it is not historical or very minimally so. Following Herberg, how one conceives of faith and its relationship to history will, thus, deeply influence one's assessment of the historicity of Sinai.

Philosophy Once Again

Herberg's approach backs us into philosophical issues related to the Sinai narrative, for if literary, historical, and theological analyses do not present barriers to taking the Sinai narrative seriously as history, philosophical issues might well do so. In this book we have shown that simply not to be the case, unless one assumes—against Scripture—that God cannot speak and act in history. Once we take seriously the biblical witness to the fact that God certainly can and does speak and act in history, we approach the Sinai event in a very different way to that of, for example, Sommer and Ska. Contra Sommer, there is no reason why Moses's experience at Sinai could not have been verbal and audial. Indeed, this is just what we would expect of God as portrayed in Scripture.

Such has been Spinoza's, Kant's, and other modern philosophers' influence that Jewish and Christian philosophers, theologians, and exegetes have struggled to come to grips with that influence in relation to their own traditions. Utterly central to the philosophy of Spinoza, and especially of Kant, is the doctrine of human autonomy, about which Leo Strauss rightly comments that "the Bible rejects the principle of autonomous knowledge and everything that goes with it."[130] Clearly if one works within such philosophical traditions one will interpret the Sinai narrative in ways that preclude thick notions of God acting and speaking. However, in my view, such philosophical traditions themselves need to be explored in critical dialogue with the biblical traditions. I think here of passages like the following:

Exod 4:11: "Then YHWH said to him [Moses], 'Who gives speech to mortals? Who makes them mute or deaf, seeing or blind? Is it not I, YHWH?'"

Ps 94:9: "He who planted the ear, does he not hear? He who formed the eye, does he not see?"

What both these verses have in common is a strong doctrine of *creation* and a confirmation of Gunton's point that the basic division in a Christian view of the world is that between the created and the uncreated God. If YHWH is the Creator God, and if he created humans as speaking, hearing, and seeing beings, then it is hard to see the—philosophical or theological—problem with God speaking to, listening to, and seeing his people. Of course, if we resist seeing this world as God's creation, then we will see it as something else, develop our basic frameworks from there, and then try and relate them to Exod 19–24. Essentially, we will find ourselves trying to connect one worldview with another, forgetting that worldviews are, by their nature, antithetical.

Far from YHWH's speaking and acting being somehow shameful philosophically, it is a wonderful example of his *condescension* to human creatures. Jean-Yves Lacoste, in his phenomenology of liturgy,[131] points out that our human embeddedness in place has its roots in our flesh. Part of the glory of being a human creature is that we are *not* omnipresent but "confined"

130. Strauss, *Jewish Philosophy*, 374.
131. Jean-Yves Lacoste, *Experience and the Absolute: Disputed Questions on the Humanity of Man*, trans. Mark Raftery-Skehan (New York: Fordham University Press, 2004).

to particular places.[132] Liturgy is thus inherently local and particular, just like Sinai, and it is God's glory in his extravagant condescension to disclose himself to us in particular, local contexts.

But liturgy also contains the possibility of being liberated from the false immanence of the local and the particular, just as at Sinai. Lacoste discusses two immanent approaches to history: history as being-in-the-world and a dialectical approach whereby we make history. He argues that "liturgy represents, on the one hand, a symbolic exodus out of phenomenological historiality, but also a certain, more real exodus from 'dialectical' historiality, on the other."[133] Liturgy is a work of overdetermination through which we are enabled to contemplate the world as a totality: "the man who finds complete repose in God escapes the world's rule over him, and participates in God's lordly reign over the universe."[134]

In Luke's narrative of Jesus's transfiguration, Jesus uses the word "exodus" to describe his work in discussion with Moses and Elijah. It turns out that his "exodus" is far bigger than Peter's imagination, who suggests building huts for Jesus, Moses, and Elijah to remain on the Mount of Transfiguration. LaCocque rightly notes the eschatological dimension of the Sinai event. If all the earth belongs to YHWH (Exod 19:5), then something much bigger is going on at Sinai than God's covenant with Israel. Instead, real as is God's election of Israel, YHWH's dominion over the whole creation is already in view. When Jesus speaks of his coming exodus, he has in view nothing less than the liberation of the entire creation from sin and evil. It turns out, I suggest, that the exodus-Sinai events are too often far bigger than our scholarly imaginations, which need themselves to be turned inside out by Sinai, a revolution that would itself lead us to fresh, and, in my view, thick *historical* readings of the Sinai event. These would open out into the typological and figural interpretations discussed by Ephraim Radner in his recent *Time and Word*,[135] but only because God did indeed act decisively at Sinai. Our confidence that God will act in the present and decisively in the future is dependent on the fact that he has already acted in the past, not least in the events of exodus-Sinai.

---

132. See Craig G. Bartholomew, *Where Mortals Dwell: A Christian View of Place for Today* (Grand Rapids: Baker Academic, 2011).

133. Lacoste, *Experience and the Absolute*, 50.

134. Lacoste, *Experience and the Absolute*, 26.

135. Ephraim Radner, *Time and Word: Figural Readings of the Christian Scriptures* (Grand Rapids: Eerdmans, 2016).

SUMMARY

I imagine that for many readers this has been an unusual and uncommon journey, and so we will review it in this epilogue. The *theme* of this book is divine action in history, and it emerges from a *puzzle*. Jewish authors in particular, but also Christians, assert the fundamental importance of the Sinai event as foundational and generative for Israel and the HB/OT. At the same time many are reluctant to affirm the historicity of this "event." This is the puzzle: How can an event that is so formative, so foundational, and so generative have no basis in divine action in history and perhaps turn out to be an imaginary projection onto the past by later Israelites?

Using Benjamin Sommer's creative work as a foil for our exploration, it soon became apparent that there are many different and complex threads that make up the cord of any reading of the Sinai event and its historicity: the legacy of historical criticism and the alleged inconsistencies in the Sinai narrative; philosophy; theology; one's view of God; one's view of history; one's view of how faith relates to academic work—and so on.

Sommer leans on Maimonides to argue that God cannot speak and therefore does not speak at Sinai. This led us to take a close look at Maimonides to see how he arrives at this view and just how compelling it is. Maimonides arrives at this view through appropriating Greek and medieval philosophical views of God and then reading the HB through the lens of such views so that one would only need to follow Maimonides if one finds *such* views compelling, and one would need to make the case for accepting them.

To show that there are very different alternatives available in the Jewish tradition, we attended to Halevi, who privileges historical, sensory revelation and affirms the historicity of Sinai. The juxtaposition of Maimonides and Halevi enables us to see how profoundly philosophy can affect one's reading of Sinai and pushes one's view of God to front and center. If one thinks that we arrive at a true view of God through philosophy apart from revelation, then one might well go the route of Maimonides. But, if one thinks that we can only know God through his revelation of himself, then Halevi's route becomes far more likely.

However, Maimonides's perfect-being theology is only one among various versions of this approach. We live amidst a revival of interest in Aquinas's classical theism or perfect-being theology, and so we attended to his approach as a Christian parallel to Maimonides, to see how it fits with the view of God we find in the Sinai narrative. Aquinas's theology and philosophy are bent much more toward the biblical portrayal of God than that of Maimonides, but we found potential trouble in his dependence on unaided reason and philosophy to arrive at a view of God that is then perfected by grace.

Sommer refers to Spinoza as one of the founders of historical criticism and draws on Kant for his view of HB/OT law. Spinoza and Kant sit between the medieval era and our own, and both have been hugely influential on modernity and on philosophy and biblical interpretation. Through our examination of them we saw that their denigration of historical revelation, and of Sinai in particular, stems from their very particular philosophical and theological commitments: Spinoza's pantheistic monism and Kant's idealism and doctrine of human autonomy. Thus, one would need to follow their approach to Sinai only if one appropriated their philosophical and theological positions, which I do not. However, were a biblical scholar to do so, then he or she would need to provide arguments for such approaches to the world, knowledge, and God.

As a Christian parallel to Halevi we then turned to Colin Gunton's work as an example of a very different approach to God and divine action compared to that of perfect-being theology, whether that of Maimonides or Aquinas. For Gunton, our knowledge of God emerges from God's revelation in history grounded in the fundamental ontological distinction between God as Creator and the creation. Such a distinction makes "traffic" between the uncreated God and humans—not least through language—highly likely and removes many of the potential barriers erected under the influence of Greek and modern philosophy. In the light of this fundamental distinction and Gunton's work, we explored a theology and philosophy of divine action rooted in providence and articulated the key elements in a disclosure event of revelation.

In the final chapter we homed in on the Sinai event through an examination of the intertwined elements of literature, theology, and history. We explored often ignored synchronic readings of Exod 19–24, argued that the rich theology of YHWH and Sinai carries with it a commitment to its historicity, and examined some of the nuances in affirming—as I do—the historicity of Sinai.

Doubtless many readers will be struck by—if not overwhelmed by—the many aspects informing one's reading of Sinai. This is intentional because I think it reflects the reality on the ground, as it were. No less a scholar than Meir Sternberg has commented that biblical studies takes place at the intersection of the humanities, and I hope this book demonstrates that point. If I have correctly identified many of the strands constituting the cord of one's reading of Sinai, then this book will have gone a long way toward achieving its goal. This also means that a great deal of work remains to be done to take this discussion forward.

Doing this research, I have been struck again and again by the way in which the issue of God keeps emerging and refuses to go away, whether one is attending to Sommer, de Wette, Maimonides, Halevi, Aquinas, Spinoza, Kant, Barr, Barton, Barth, Gunton, and so on. Alas, a legacy of modernity is that this is the one subject that is often taboo in scholarship and academic biblical interpretation. In my view it is a taboo that needs to be broken, and in my future series, Old Testament Origins and the Question of God, I hope to explore what HB/OT study looks like when the God who comes to us in Scripture is taken seriously.

BIBLIOGRAPHY

Abraham, William J. *Analytic Theology: A Bibliography*. Dallas, TX: Highland Loch Press, 2012.

Aertsen, Jan A. "Aquinas's Philosophy in Its Historical Setting." In *The Cambridge Companion to Aquinas*, edited by Norman Kretzmann and Eleonore Stump, 12–37. Cambridge: Cambridge University Press, 1993.

Albright, William F. *From the Stone Age to Christianity: Monotheism and the Historical Process*. New York: Doubleday Anchor, 1957.

Alston, William P. *Divine Nature and Human Language*. Ithaca, NY: Cornell University Press, 1989.

———. *Perceiving God: The Epistemology of Religious Experience*. Ithaca, NY: Cornell University Press, 1991.

Alter, Robert. *The Art of Biblical Narrative*. London: George Allen and Unwin, 1981.

Aquinas, Thomas. *Summa Theologiae: Questions on God*. Cambridge Texts in the History of Philosophy. Edited by Brian Davies and Brian Lewftow. Cambridge: Cambridge University Press, 2006.

———. *The Summa Theologica: Complete Edition*. London: Catholic Way Publishing, 2014.

Aristotle. *Metaphysics*. Translated by Hugh Lawson-Tancred. London: Penguin, 1998, 2004.

Assmann, Jan. *Moses the Egyptian: The Memory of Egypt in Western Monotheism*. Cambridge, MA: Harvard University Press, 1997.

———. *Of God and Gods: Egypt, Israel, and the Rise of Monotheism*. Madison: University of Wisconsin Press, 2008.

———. *The Search for God in Ancient Egypt*. Translated by David Lorton. Ithaca, NY: Cornell University Press, 2001.

Augustine. "The Literal Meaning of Genesis." In *On Genesis*. Translated by Edmund O. Hill. New York: New City Press, 2002.

———. *On Genesis*. Translated by Edmund O. Hill. New York: New City Press, 2002.

Austin, J. L. *How to Do Things with Words*. 2nd ed. Oxford: Oxford University Press, 1962, 1975.

Avishur, Yitzhak. "The Narrative of the Revelation at Sinai (Ex. 19–24)." In *Studies in Historical Geography and Biblical Historiography*, edited by Gershon Galil and Moshe Weinfeld, 197–214. Leiden: Brill, 2000.

Barr, James. *History and Ideology in the Old Testament: Biblical Studies at the End of a Millennium*. Oxford: Oxford University Press, 2000.

Barth, Karl. *Church Dogmatics*. Edited by G. W. Bromiley and T. F. Torrance, translated by G. W. Bromiley et al. Four volumes in fourteen. Edinburgh: T&T Clark, 2004.

———. *Dogmatics in Outline*. Translated by G. T. Thomson. London: SCM, 1966.

———. *Protestant Theology in the Nineteenth Century*. Translated by Brian Cozens and John Bowden. Grand Rapids: Eerdmans, 2002.

Bartholomew, Craig G. *Contours of the Kuyperian Tradition: A Systematic Introduction*. Downers Grove, IL: IVP Academic, 2017.

———. "Old Testament Origins and the Question of God." *Bulletin for Biblical Research* 27/2 (2017): 169–84.

———. "Philosophy, Theology and the Crisis in Biblical Interpretation." In *Renewing Biblical Interpretation*. SAHS 1. Edited by Craig G. Bartholomew, Colin Greene, and Karl Möller, 1–39. Grand Rapids: Zondervan, 2000.

———. "Three Horizons: Hermeneutics from the Other End—An Evaluation of Anthony Thiselton's Hermeneutic Proposals." *EJT* 5 (1996): 121–35.

———. *Where Mortals Dwell: A Christian View of Place for Today*. Grand Rapids: Baker Academic, 2011.

Bartholomew, Craig G., and Bruce R. Ashford. *The Doctrine of Creation*. Downers Grove, IL: IVP Academic, 2020.

Bartholomew, Craig G., and Michael W. Goheen. *Christian Philosophy: A Systematic and Narrative Introduction*. Grand Rapids: Baker Academic, 2013.

Bartholomew, Craig G., and Heath A. Thomas. *The Minor Prophets: A Theological Introduction*. To be published in IVP Academic.

Barton, John. *The Nature of Biblical Criticism*. Louisville: Westminster John Knox, 2007.

Bavinck, Herman. *Reformed Dogmatics*. Volume 2. Translated by John Vriend. Grand Rapids: Baker Academic, 2004.

Bayer, Oswald. *A Contemporary in Dissent: Johann Georg Hamann as a Radical*

Enlightener. Translated by Roy A. Harrisville and Mark C. Mattes. Grand Rapids: Eerdmans, 2012.

Beebee, Helen, Christopher Hitchcock, and Peter Menzies, eds. *The Oxford Handbook of Causality*. Oxford: Oxford University Press, 2009.

Beiser, Frederick. *The Fate of Reason: German Philosophy from Kant to Fichte*. Cambridge, MA: Harvard University Press, 1987.

———. *Hegel*. London: Routledge, 2005.

Berkhof, Hendrikus. *Christian Faith: An Introduction to the Study of the Faith*. Grand Rapids: Eerdmans, 1979.

Berkouwer, Gerrit C. *The Providence of God*. Studies in Dogmatics. Grand Rapids: Eerdmans, 1952.

Berkovits, Eliezer. *God, Man and History*. Edited by David Hazony. Jerusalem: Shalem, 2004.

———. *Major Themes in Modern Philosophies of Judaism*. New York: Ktav, 1974.

Berlinerblau, Jacques. "'Poor Bird, Not Knowing Which Way to Fly': Biblical Scholarship's Marginality, Secular Humanism, and the Laudable Occident." *Biblical Interpretation* 10 (2002): 267–304.

Berman, Joshua A. *Inconsistency in the Torah: Ancient Literary Convention and the Limits of Source Criticism*. Oxford: Oxford University Press, 2017.

Betz, John. *After Enlightenment: Hamann as Post-Secular Visionary*. Oxford: Wiley-Blackwell, 2009.

Boff, Leonardo. *Passion of Christ, Passion of the World: The Facts, Their Interpretation, and Their Meaning Yesterday and Today*. Translated by R. R. Barr. 2nd ed. Maryknoll, NY: Orbis, 2001.

Bohatec, Josef. *Die Religionsphilosophie Kants in der "Religion innerhalb der Grenzen der blossen Vernunft": mit besonderer Berücksichtigung ihrer theologisch-dogmatischen Quellen*. Hildesheim: Georg Olms, 1966.

Bonk, Thomas. *Underdetermination: An Essay on Evidence and the Limits of Natural Knowledge*. Boston Studies in the Philosophy of Science 261. Dordrecht: Springer, 2008.

Brichto, Herbert C. *Toward a Grammar of Biblical Poetics: Tales of the Prophets*. Oxford: Oxford University Press, 1993.

Bright, John. *A History of Israel*. 3rd ed. Louisville: Westminster John Knox, 1959, 1972, 1980.

Brunner, Emil. *Dogmatics*. Volume 1: *The Christian Doctrine of God*. Translated by Olive Wyon. Philadelphia: Westminster, 1949.

———. *Dogmatics*. Volume 2: *The Christian Doctrine of Creation and Redemption*. Translated by Olive Wyon. Philadelphia: Westminster, 1952.

Buber, Martin. *I and Thou*. Translated by Walter Kaufmann. Edinburgh: T&T Clark, 1970.

Buckley, Michael J. *At the Origins of Modern Atheism*. New Haven: Yale University Press, 1990.

Burnside, Jonathan. *God, Justice and Society: Aspects of Law and Legality in the Bible*. Oxford: Oxford University Press, 2011.

Burrell, David B. "Aquinas and Islamic and Jewish Thinkers." In *The Cambridge Companion to Aquinas*, edited by Norman Kretzmann and Eleonore Stump, 60–84. Cambridge: Cambridge University Press, 1993.

———. *Freedom and Creation in Three Traditions*. Notre Dame: University of Notre Dame Press, 1993.

Cavadini, John C. "Can We Separate Scripture and Tradition? John C. Cavadini Responds to Benjamin Sommer's *Revelation and Authority*." https://marginalia.lareviewofbooks.org/can-separate-scripture-tradition/.

Cheyne, Thomas Kelly. *Founders of Old Testament Criticism: Biographical, Descriptive and Critical Studies*. London: Methuen and Co., 1893.

Childs, Brevard S. *Exodus*. The OT Library. Louisville: Westminster John Knox, 1974.

———. *Isaiah: A Commentary*. Louisville: Westminster John Knox, 2001.

———. *Old Testament Theology in a Canonical Context*. London: SCM, 1985.

Chirichigno, Gregory. "The Narrative Structure of Exodus 19–24." *Biblica* 68 (1987): 457–79.

Clayton, Philip. *God and Contemporary Science*. Edinburgh: Edinburgh University Press, 1997.

Coady, C. A. J. *Testimony: A Philosophical Study*. Oxford: Clarendon, 1992.

Craig, William Lane. *The Only Wise God: The Compatibility of Divine Foreknowledge and Human Freedom*. Eugene, OR: Wipf and Stock, 2000.

Cremer, Hermann. *The Christian Doctrine of the Divine Attributes*. Translated by Robert B. Price. Eugene, OR: Pickwick, 2016.

Cross, Frank Moore. *Canaanite Myth and Hebrew Epic*. Cambridge, MA: Harvard University Press, 1973.

Davidson, Herbert A. *Moses Maimonides: The Man and His Works*. Oxford: Oxford University Press, 2005.

Davies, Brian. *Thomas Aquinas's* Summa Theologiae*: A Guide and Commentary*. Oxford: Oxford University Press, 2014.

Davies, G. I. Review of Joe M. Sprinkle, *"The Book of the Covenant": A Literary Approach*. *VT* 48/2 (1998): 285.

Davies, Oliver. *The Creativity of God: World, Eucharist, Reason*. Cambridge: Cambridge University Press, 2004.

Day, Mark. *The Philosophy of History*. London: Continuum, 2008.

Dozeman, Thomas B. *Exodus*. Eerdmans Critical Commentary. Grand Rapids: Eerdmans, 2009.

Durham, John I. *Exodus*. WBC 3. Grand Rapids: Zondervan, 1987.

Edgar, A. "Kant's Two Interpretations of Genesis." *Literature and Theology* 6/3 (1992): 280–90.

Eichler, Barry L. "Law and Morality in Ancient Near Eastern Thought." In *Ethics, Politics, and Democracy: From Primordial Principles to Prospective Practices*, edited by J. V. Ciprut, 33–58. Cambridge, MA: MIT Press, 2008.

Eichrodt, Walther. "Offenbarung und Geschichte im Alten Testament." *Theologische Zeitschrift* 4/5 (1948): 321–31.

———. *Theology of the Old Testament*. Volume 1. Translated by J. A. Baker. Philadelphia: Westminster, 1961.

Emery, Giles, and Matthew Levering, eds. *Aristotle in Aquinas's Theology*. Oxford: Oxford University Press, 2015.

Feldman, Seymour. "Maimonides—A Guide for Posterity." In *The Cambridge Companion to Maimonides*, edited by Kenneth Seeskin, 324–59. Cambridge: Cambridge University Press, 2005.

Firestone, Chris L., and Nathan Jacobs. *In Defense of Kant's Religion*. Bloomington: Indiana University Press, 2008.

———. *Kant and the Question of Theology*. Cambridge: Cambridge University Press, 2017.

Firestone, Chris L., and Stephen R. Palmquist, eds. *Kant and the New Philosophy of Religion*. Bloomington: Indiana University Press, 2006.

Fishbane, Michael. *Sacred Attunement: A Jewish Theology*. Chicago: University of Chicago Press, 2008.

Flint, Thomas. *Divine Providence: The Molinist Account*. Ithaca, NY: Cornell University Press, 1998.

Frampton, Travis. *Spinoza and the Rise of Historical Criticism of the Bible*. London: T&T Clark, 2006.

Frankfort, Henri. *Kingship and the Gods: A Study of Ancient Near Eastern Religion as the Integration of Society and Nature*. Chicago: University of Chicago Press, 1948, 1978.

Gadamer, Hans-Georg. *Truth and Method*. Revised 2nd ed. London: Bloomsbury, 2004.

Gaybba, Brian P. *Aspects of the Medieval History of Theology: 12th to 14th Centuries*. Pretoria: UNISA, 1988.

Girard, René. *I See Satan Fall Like Lightning*. Maryknoll, NY: Orbis, 2001.

Goetschel, Willi. *Spinoza's Modernity: Mendelssohn, Lessing, and Hume.* Madison: University of Wisconsin Press, 2004.

Goheen, Michael W., and Craig G. Bartholomew. *Living at the Crossroads: An Introduction to Christian Worldview.* Grand Rapids: Baker Academic, 2008.

Goodman, Lenn E. "What Does Spinoza's Ethics Contribute to Jewish Philosophy?" In *Jewish Themes in Spinoza's Philosophy*, edited by Heidi M. Ravven and Lenn E. Goodman, 17–89. Albany: State University of New York Press, 2002.

Gorman, M. M. *The Unknown Augustine: A Study of the Literal Interpretation of Genesis (De Genesi ad litteram).* Dissertation, University of Toronto, 1975.

Grant, Edward. *God and Reason in the Middle Ages.* Cambridge: Cambridge University Press, 2001.

Grant, R. M., with D. Tracy. *A Short History of the Interpretation of the Bible.* 2nd ed. Philadelphia: Fortress, 1984.

Green, Arthur. *These Are the Words: A Vocabulary of Jewish Spiritual Life.* 2nd ed. Woodstock, VT: Jewish Lights, 2012.

Greenberg, Moshe. "The Book of Exodus." In *EncJud* 6:1056.

Greene, Theodore M. "The Historical Context and Religious Significance of Kant's Religion." In Immanuel Kant, *Religion within the Bounds of Reason Alone.* Translated by Theodore M. Greene and Hoyt H. Hudson. New York: Harper and Row, 1960.

Grene, Marjorie. *A Portrait of Aristotle.* London: Faber and Faber, 1963.

Gruenler, R. G. *Meaning and Understanding: The Philosophical Framework for Biblical Interpretation.* Foundations of Contemporary Interpretation 2. Grand Rapids: Zondervan, 1991.

Gunton, Colin E. *Act and Being: Towards a Theology of the Divine Attributes.* London: SCM, 2002.

———. *Actuality of the Atonement: A Study of Metaphor, Rationality and the Christian Tradition.* London: T&T Clark, 1988.

———. *Becoming and Being: The Doctrine of God in Charles Hartshorne and Karl Barth.* Oxford: Oxford University Press, 1978.

———. *The Promise of Trinitarian Theology.* 2nd ed. London: T&T Clark, 1997.

Gwynne, Paul. *Special Divine Action: Key Issues in the Contemporary Debate (1965–1995).* Rome: Editrice Pontificia Universitatà Gregoriana, 1996.

Hahn, Scott W., and Benjamin Wiker. *Politicizing the Bible: The Roots of Historical Criticism and the Secularization of Scripture, 1300–1700.* New York: Herder and Herder, 2013.

Halbertal, Moshe. *Maimonides: Life and Thought*. Princeton: Princeton University Press, 2014.

Halevi, Judah. *The Kuzari: An Argument for the Faith of Israel*. Translated by Hartwig Hirschfeld. New York: Schocken, 1964.

Halpern, Baruch. *The First Historians: The Hebrew Bible and History*. New York: Harper and Row, 1988.

Harkins, Franklin T. "*Primus Doctor Iudaeorum*: Moses as Theological Master in the *Summa Theologiae* of Thomas Aquinas." In *Illuminating Moses*. Commentaria 4. Edited by Jane Beale, 237–62. Leiden: Brill, 2014.

Harrisville, Roy A., and Walter Sundberg. *The Bible in Modern Culture: Theology and Historical-Critical Method from Spinoza to Käsemann*. Grand Rapids: Eerdmans, 1995.

Harvey, Lincoln., ed. *The Theology of Colin Gunton*. London: T&T Clark, 2010.

Hauge, Martin R. *The Descent from the Mountain: Narrative Patterns in Exodus 19–40*. JSOTSup 323. Sheffield: Sheffield Academic Press, 2001.

Herberg, Will. *Faith Enacted as History: Essays in Biblical Theology*. Philadelphia: Westminster, 1976.

Herms, Eilert. *Offenbarung und Glaube: Zur Bildung des christlichen Lebens*. Tübingen: Mohr, 1992.

Hertz, J. H., ed. *The Soncino Edition of the Pentateuch and Haftorahs with Hebrew Text, English Translation, and Commentary*. 2nd ed. London: Soncino, 1960.

Heschel, Abraham Joshua. "The Moment at Sinai." In *Moral Grandeur and Spiritual Audacity*. New York: Farrar, Straus and Giroux, 1996.

Hoch, Liron, and Menachem Kellner. "'The Voice Is the Voice of Jacob, but the Hands Are the Hands of Esau': Isaac Abravanel between Judah Halevi and Moses Maimonides." *Jewish History* 26 (2012): 61–83.

Höffe, Otfried. "Holy Scripture within the Boundaries of Mere Reason: Kant's Reflections." In *Kant's Religion within the Boundaries of Mere Reason*, edited by Gordon Michalson, 10–30. Cambridge: Cambridge University Press, 2014.

Hoffmeier, James K. *Ancient Israel in Sinai: The Evidence for the Authenticity of the Wilderness Tradition*. Oxford: Oxford University Press, 2005.

———. *Israel in Egypt: The Evidence for the Authenticity of the Exodus Tradition*. Oxford: Oxford University Press, 1996.

Holmes, Stephen R. "Divine Attributes." In *Mapping Modern Theology: A Thematic and Historical Introduction*, edited by Kelly M. Kapic and Bruce L. McCormack, 47–65. Grand Rapids: Baker Academic, 2012.

Howard, Thomas A. *Religion and the Rise of Historicism: W. M. L. de Wette, Ja-*

cob Burkhardt, and the Theological Origins of Nineteenth-Century Historical Consciousness. Cambridge: Cambridge University Press, 2000

Howell, Brian C. *In the Eyes of God: A Metaphorical Approach to Biblical Anthropomorphic Language.* Cambridge: James Clarke, 2014.

Illari, Phyllis, and Federica Russo. *Causality: Philosophical Theory Meets Scientific Practice.* Oxford: Oxford University Press, 2014.

Insole, Christopher J. *Kant and the Creation of Freedom: A Theological Problem.* Grand Rapids: Eerdmans, 2016.

Israel, Jonathan. *Radical Enlightenment: Philosophy and the Making of Modernity 1650–1750.* Oxford: Oxford University Press, 2001.

Ivry, Alfred L. *Maimonides' "Guide of the Perplexed": A Philosophical Guide.* Chicago: University of Chicago Press, 2016.

Jacob, Benno. *The Second Book of the Bible: Exodus.* Translated by Walter Jacob. Hoboken, NJ: Ktav, 1992.

Jenson, Robert. "A Decision Tree of Colin Gunton's Thinking." In *The Theology of Colin Gunton*, edited by Lincoln Harvey, 8–16. London: T&T Clark, 2010.

———. *The Knowledge of Things Hoped For.* Oxford: Oxford University Press, 1969.

———. *Systematic Theology.* Volume 1: *The Triune God.* Oxford: Oxford University Press, 1997.

Kant, Immanuel. *An Answer to the Question: "What Is Enlightenment?"* Translated by H. B. Nisbet. London: Penguin, 1970, 1991.

———. *Religion and Rational Theology.* Translated and edited by Allen W. Wood and George di Giovanni. Cambridge: Cambridge University Press, 1996.

———. *Religion within the Boundaries of Mere Reason and Other Writings.* Edited by Allen Wood and George di Giovanni. Cambridge Texts in the History of Philosophy. Cambridge: Cambridge University Press, 1998.

Kaufman, Gordon D. *In the Beginning . . . Creativity.* Minneapolis: Fortress, 2004.

Kaufmann, Yehezkel. *The Religion of Israel: From Its Beginnings to the Babylonian Exile.* Translated and abridged by Moshe Greenberg. Chicago: University of Chicago Press, 1960.

Kellner, Menachem M. *Maimonides on Judaism and the Jewish People.* Albany: State University of New York Press, 1991.

———. "Spiritual Life." In *The Cambridge Companion to Maimonides*, edited by Kenneth Seeskin, 273–99. Cambridge: Cambridge University Press, 2005.

Kelsey, David. *The Uses of Scripture in Recent Theology.* London: SCM, 1976.

Kenny, Anthony. *The Rise of Modern Philosophy.* A New History of Western Philosophy 3. Oxford: Clarendon, 2006.

Koerbagh, Adriaan. *A Light Shining in Dark Places, to Illuminate the Main Ques-*

tions of Theology and Religion. Translated and edited by Michiel Wielema. Brill's Texts and Sources in Intellectual History 12. Leiden: Brill, 2011.

Kraemer, Joel L. *Maimonides: The Life and World of One of Civilization's Greatest Minds.* New York: Doubleday, 2008.

Kreisel, Howard. *Prophecy: The History of an Idea in Medieval Jewish Philosophy.* Dordrecht: Springer, 2001.

Kroner, Richard. *Kant's Weltanschauung.* Chicago: University of Chicago Press, 1956.

Kuhn, Thomas S. *The Structure of Scientific Revolutions.* 50th anniversary edition. Chicago: University of Chicago Press, 2012.

LaCocque, André. "The Revelation of Revelations." In André LaCocque and Paul Ricoeur, *Thinking Biblically: Exegetical and Hermeneutical Studies,* 307–30. Translated by David Pellauer. Chicago: University of Chicago Press, 1998.

Lacoste, Jean-Yves. *Experience and the Absolute: Disputed Questions on the Humanity of Man.* Translated by Mark Raftery-Skehan. New York: Fordham University Press, 2004.

Lamm, Julia A. *The Living God: Schleiermacher's Theological Appropriation of Spinoza.* University Park: Pennsylvania State University Press, 1996.

La Montaigne, D. Paul. *Barth and Rationality: Critical Realism in Theology.* Eugene, OR: Cascade, 2012.

Lane, Tony. *The Lion Concise Book of Christian Thought.* Herts, UK: Lion, 1984.

Lazier, Benjamin. *God Interrupted: Heresy and the Imagination between the World Wars.* Princeton: Princeton University Press, 2008.

Lee, Sukjae. "Occasionalism." In *The Stanford Encyclopedia of Philosophy* (Winter 2016 edition), edited by Edward N. Zalta, https://plato.stanford.edu/archives/win2016/entries/occasionalism/.

Leftow, Brian. "Anselm's Perfect-Being Theology." In *The Cambridge Companion to Anselm,* edited by Brian Davies and Leftow, 132–56. Cambridge: Cambridge University Press, 2004.

———. "Classical Theism." Section within the article "God, Concepts of." *Routledge Encyclopedia of Philosophy.* Abingdon: Taylor and Francis, 1998. https://www.rep.routledge.com/articles/thematic/god-concepts-of/v-1/sections/classical-theism.

Lesslie, John. *Universes.* London: Routledge, 1989.

Levenson, Jon D. "Do Bible Scholars Need Theology? Jon D. Levenson on Sommer's *Revelation and Authority: Sinai in Jewish Scripture and Tradition*" (2018), https://marginalia.lareviewofbooks.org/can-separate-scripture-tradition/.

————. *The Hebrew Bible, the Old Testament, and Historical Criticism: Jews and Christians in Biblical Studies.* Louisville: Westminster John Knox, 1993.

————. *Sinai and Zion.* New York: Harper and Row, 1985.

Levering, Matthew. "Ordering Wisdom: Aquinas, the Old Testament, and *Sacra Doctrina.*" In *Ressourcement Thomism: Sacred Doctrine, the Sacraments, and the Moral Life,* edited by Reinhard Hütter and Matthew Levering, 80–91. Washington, DC: Catholic University of America Press, 2010.

Levinson, Bernard M. *"The Right Chorale": Studies in Biblical Law and Interpretation.* Winona Lake, IN: Eisenbrauns, 2011.

Licht, J. "The Sinai Theophany" [Hebrew]. *Studies in Bible and the Ancient Near East,* edited by Y. Avishur and J. Blau, 251–68. Jerusalem: Rubinstein, 1978.

————. *Storytelling in the Bible.* Jerusalem: Magnes, 1978.

Lilla, Mark. *The Stillborn God: Religion, Politics, and the Modern West.* New York: Vintage, 2007, 2008.

Loewenstamm, Samuel E. *The Evolution of the Exodus Tradition.* Translated by Baruch J. Schwartz. Jerusalem: Magnes, 1992.

Long, Burke O. *Planting and Reaping Albright: Politics, Ideology, and Interpreting the Bible.* University Park: Pennsylvania State University Press, 1997.

Lyon, David. *Postmodernity.* Concepts in the Social Sciences. Buckingham: Open University Press, 1994.

Macquarrie, John. *God-Talk: An Examination of the Language and Logic of Theology.* London: SCM, 1967.

Maimonides, Moses. *The Guide for the Perplexed.* 2nd ed. New York: Dover, 1904.

McCormack, Bruce L. *Karl Barth's Critically Realistic Dialectical Theology: Its Genesis and Development, 1909–1936.* Oxford: Clarendon, 1996.

Mendenhall, George E. "Law and Covenant in Israel and in the Ancient Near East." *BA* 17 (1954): 26–46, 49–76.

Michalson, Gordon E., Jr. *The Historical Dimension of a Rational Faith: The Role of History in Kant's Religious Thought.* Washington, DC: University Press of America, 1977.

————. *Kant and the Problem of God.* Oxford: Blackwell, 1999.

————, ed. *Kant's Religion within the Boundaries of Mere Reason: A Critical Guide.* Cambridge: Cambridge University Press, 2014.

Milbank, John. "The Theological Critique of Philosophy in Hamann and Jacobi." In *Radical Orthodoxy,* edited by John Milbank, Catherine Pickstock, and Graham Ward, 21–37. London: Routledge, 1999.

Miller, Patrick D. *The Way of the Lord: Essays in Old Testament Theology.* Grand Rapids: Eerdmans, 2004.

Miskotte, Kornelis H. *When the Gods Are Silent*. New York: Harper and Row, 1967.

Moberly, R. W. L. *At the Mountain of God: Story and Theology in Exodus 32–34*. JSOTSup 22. Sheffield: JSOT Press, 1983.

Molnar, Paul. *Divine Freedom and the Doctrine of the Immanent Trinity*. London: T&T Clark, 2002.

Moore, Megan Bishop, and Brad E. Kelle. *Biblical History and Israel's Past: The Changing Study of the Bible and History*. Grand Rapids: Eerdmans, 2011.

Morales, Michael, ed. *Cult and Cosmos: Tilting toward a Temple-Centered Theology*. Leuven: Peeters, 2014.

Nadler, Steven. *A Book Forged in Hell: Spinoza's Scandalous Treatise and the Birth of the Secular Age*. Princeton: Princeton University Press, 2011.

———. *Occasionalism: Causation among the Cartesians*. Oxford: Oxford University Press, 2011.

Nicholson, Ernest. *The Pentateuch in the Twentieth Century: The Legacy of Julius Wellhausen*. Oxford: Oxford University Press, 1998.

Niehaus, Jeffrey J. *God at Sinai: Covenant and Theophany in the Bible and Ancient Near East*. SOTBT. Grand Rapids: Zondervan, 1995.

Norris, Christopher. "Criticism." In *Encyclopaedia of Literature and Criticism*, edited by M. Coyle, P. Garside, M. Kelsall, and J. Peck, 27–65. London: Routledge, 1990.

———. *Spinoza and the Origins of Modern Critical Theory*. The Bucknell Lectures in Literary Theory. Oxford: Basil Blackwell, 1991.

Novak, David. "Can We Be Maimonideans Today?" In *Maimonides and His Heritage*, edited by Idit Dobbs-Weinstein, Lenn E. Goodman, and James A. Grady, 192–209. Albany: State University of New York Press, 2009.

———. *The Election of Israel: The Idea of the Chosen People*. Cambridge: Cambridge University Press, 1995.

Oakes, Kenneth. *Karl Barth on Theology and Philosophy*. Oxford: Oxford University Press, 2012.

O'Donovan, Oliver. *The Desire of the Nations: Rediscovering the Roots of Political Theology*. Cambridge: Cambridge University Press, 1996.

O'Neill, J. C. *The Bible's Authority: A Portrait Gallery of Thinkers from Lessing to Bultmann*. Edinburgh: T&T Clark, 1991.

O'Neill, Onora. "Vindicating Reason." In *The Cambridge Companion to Kant*, edited by Paul Guyer, 289–90. Cambridge: Cambridge University Press, 1992.

Owens, Joseph. "Aristotle and Aquinas." In *The Cambridge Companion to Aquinas*, edited by Norman Kretzmann and Eleonore Stump, 38–59. Cambridge: Cambridge University Press, 1993.

Parens, Joshua. *Maimonides and Spinoza: Their Conflicting Views of Human Nature*. Chicago: University of Chicago Press, 2012.

Penelhum, Terence. *David Hume: An Introduction to His Philosophical System*. West Lafayette, IN: Purdue University Press, 1992.

Plantinga, Alvin. "Christian Philosophy at the End of the 20th Century." In *Christian Philosophy at the Close of the Twentieth Century*, edited by Sander Griffioen and B. M. Balk, 29–53. Kampen: Kok, 1995.

———. *Does God Have a Nature?* The Aquinas Lecture, 1980. Milwaukee: Marquette University Press, 1980.

———. "Law, Cause, and Occasionalism." In *Reason and Faith: Themes from Richard Swinburne*, edited by Michael Bergmann and Jeffrey E. Brower, 126–44. Oxford: Oxford University Press, 2016.

———. *Warranted Christian Belief*. Oxford: Oxford University Press, 2000.

———. *Where the Conflict Really Lies: Science, Religion and Naturalism*. Oxford: Oxford University Press, 2011.

Plantinga, Alvin, and Nicholas Wolterstorff, eds. *Faith and Rationality: Reason and Belief in God*. Notre Dame: University of Notre Dame Press, 1983.

Popkin, Richard. "Spinoza and La Peyrère." In *Spinoza: New Perspectives*, edited by Robert Shahan and J. I. Biro, 177–95. Norman: University of Oklahoma Press, 1978.

Preus, J. S. "A Hidden Opponent in Spinoza's Tractatus." *HTR* 88/3 (1995): 361–88.

Provan, Iain, V. Philips Long, and Tremper Longman III. *A Biblical History of Israel*. Louisville: Westminster John Knox, 2003.

Radner, Ephraim. *Time and Word: Figural Readings of the Christian Scriptures*. Grand Rapids: Eerdmans, 2016.

Rae, Murray A. "Creation and Promise: Towards a Theology of History." In *"Behind the Text": History and Biblical Interpretation*, edited by Craig Bartholomew et al., 276–77. Grand Rapids: Zondervan, 2003.

Ramsay, Ian T. *Models for Divine Activity*. Eugene, OR: Wipf and Stock, 1973.

Reventlow, H. Graf. *The Authority of the Bible and the Rise of the Modern World*. London: SCM, 1984.

Ricoeur, Paul. "Religion, Atheism, and Faith." In Paul Ricoeur, *The Conflict of Interpretations: Essays in Hermeneutics*. Edited by Don Ihde. Evanston, IL: Northwestern University Press, 1974.

Rogers, Katherin A. *Perfect Being Theology*. Reason and Religion. Edinburgh: Edinburgh University Press, 2000.

Rogerson, John. *W. M. L. de Wette: Founder of Modern Biblical Criticism; An Intellectual Biography*. JSOTSup 126. Sheffield: Sheffield Academic Press, 1992.

Sarna, Nahum M. *Exodus*. JPS Torah Commentary. Jerusalem: Jewish Publication Society, 1991.

———. *Exploring Exodus: The Origins of Biblical Israel*. New York: Schocken, 1986, 1996.

Scheindlin, Raymond P. *The Song of the Distant Dove: Judah Halevi's Pilgrimage*. Oxford: Oxford University Press, 2008.

Schleiermacher, Friedrich. *On Religion: Speeches to Its Cultured Despisers*. Translated and edited by Richard Crouter. Cambridge Texts in the History of Philosophy. Cambridge: Cambridge University Press, 1988, 1996.

Schneidau, Herbert N. *Sacred Discontent: The Bible and the Western Tradition*. Baton Rouge: University of Louisiana Press, 1976.

Schniedewind, William M. *A Social History of Hebrew: Its Origins through the Rabbinic Period*. New Haven: Yale University Press, 2013.

Schumacher, Lydia. *Divine Illumination: The History and Future of Augustine's Theory of Knowledge*. Oxford: Wiley-Blackwell, 2011.

Schwöbel, Christoph. *God: Action and Revelation*. Kampen: Kok Pharos, 1992.

Scruton, Roger. *Kant*. Past Masters. Oxford: Oxford University Press, 1982.

———. *Spinoza*. Past Masters. Oxford: Oxford University Press, 1986.

Seeskin, Kenneth, ed. *The Cambridge Companion to Maimonides*. Cambridge: Cambridge University Press, 2005.

———. "Metaphysics and Its Transcendence." In *The Cambridge Companion to Maimonides*, edited by Kenneth Seeskin, 82–104. Cambridge: Cambridge University Press, 2005.

Silman, Yochanan. *Philosopher and Prophet: Judah Halevi, the Kuzari, and the Evolution of His Thought*. Translated by Lenn J. Schramm. Albany: State University of New York Press, 1995.

Ska, Jean-Louis. *Introduction to Reading the Pentateuch*. Translated by Sr. Pascale Dominique. Winona Lake, IN: Eisenbrauns, 2006.

Slonimsky, Henry. "Judah Halevi: An Introduction." In Judah Halevi, *The Kuzari: An Argument for the Faith of Israel*. Translated by Hartwig Hirschfeld. New York: Schocken, 1964.

Smith, Mark S. *God in Translation: Deities in Cross-Cultural Discourse in the Biblical World*. Grand Rapids: Eerdmans, 2008.

———. *The Pilgrimage Pattern in Exodus*. Sheffield: Sheffield Academic Press, 1997.

Sommer, Benjamin D. *Revelation and Authority: Sinai in Jewish Scripture and Tradition*. New Haven: Yale University Press, 2015.

Spinoza, Benedict de. *The Collected Works of Spinoza*. Volume 1. Translated and edited by Edwin Curley. Princeton: Princeton University Press, 1985.

————. *The Collected Works of Spinoza*. Volume 2. Translated and edited by Edwin Curley. Princeton: Princeton University Press, 2016.

Sprinkle, Joe M. *"The Book of the Covenant": A Literary Approach*. JSOTSup 174. Sheffield: Sheffield Academic Press, 1994.

————. "Law and Narrative in Exodus 19–24." *JETS* 47/2 (2004): 235–52.

Steiner, George. *Real Presences: Is There Anything in What We Say?* Chicago: University of Chicago Press, 1989.

Stern, Josef. "Maimonides' Epistemology." In *The Cambridge Companion to Maimonides*, edited by Kenneth Seeskin, 105–33. Cambridge: Cambridge University Press, 2005.

Sternberg, Meir. *The Poetics of Biblical Narrative: Ideological Literature and the Drama of Reading*. Bloomington: Indiana University Press, 1985.

Strauss, David Friedrich. *The Life of Jesus Critically Examined*. Translated by George Eliot. 4th ed. London: Swann Sonnenschein, 1902.

Strauss, Leo. *The Early Writings (1921–1932)*. Albany: State University of New York Press, 2002.

————. *Jewish Philosophy and the Crisis of Modernity: Essays and Lectures in Modern Jewish Thought*. Edited by Kenneth H. Green. Albany: State University of New York Press, 1997.

————. "On the Bible Science of Spinoza and His Precursors." In Leo Strauss, *The Early Writings (1921–1932)*, 173–200. Albany: State University of New York Press, 2002.

Stump, Eleonore. *Aquinas*. Arguments of the Philosophers. London: Routledge, 2003.

————. *The God of the Bible and the God of the Philosophers*. The Aquinas Lecture, 2016. Milwaukee: Marquette University Press, 2016.

Thielicke, Helmut. *Modern Faith and Thought*. Translated by Geoffrey W. Bromiley. Grand Rapids: Eerdmans, 1990.

Thijssen, J. M. M. H. *Censure and Heresy at the University of Paris, 1200–1400*. Philadelphia: University of Pennsylvania Press, 1998.

Thiselton, Anthony C. "Communicative Action and Promise in Hermeneutics." In Roger Lundin, Clarence Walhout, and Anthony C. Thiselton, *The Promise of Hermeneutics*. Grand Rapids: Eerdmans, 1999.

————. *New Horizons in Hermeneutics*. Grand Rapids: Zondervan, 1992.

Todorov, Tzvetan. *Introduction to Poetics*. Theory and History of Literature 1. Translated by Richard Howard. Minneapolis: University of Minnesota Press, 1981.

Tolland, John. *Christianity Not Mysterious: Or, a Treatise Showing That There*

Is Nothing in the Gospel Contrary to Reason nor Above it: And No Christian Doctrine Can Properly Be Called a Mystery. London, 1702.

Uffenheimer, Benjamin. *Early Prophecy in Israel*. Translated by David Louvish. Jerusalem: Magnes, 1999.

Unterman, Jeremiah. *Justice for All: How the Jewish Bible Revolutionized Ethics*. Philadelphia: Jewish Publication Society, 2017.

Vriezen, Th. C. *An Outline of Old Testament Theology*. 2nd ed. Oxford: Basil Blackwell, 1970.

Walzer, Michael. *Exodus and Revolution*. New York: Basic Books, 1985.

———. *In God's Shadow: Politics in the Hebrew Bible*. New Haven: Yale University Press, 2012.

Webster, John. "Gunton and Barth." In *The Theology of Colin Gunton*, edited by Lincoln Harvey, 17–31. London: T&T Clark, 2010.

Wellhausen, Julius. *Prolegomena to the History of Israel*. Cambridge Library Collection. Cambridge: Cambridge University Press, 2013.

Westphal, Merold. "Christian Philosophers and the Copernican Revolution." In *Christian Perspectives on Religious Knowledge*, edited by C. S. Evans and M. Westphal, 161–79. Grand Rapids: Eerdmans, 1993.

Wielema, Michiel. "Adriaan Koerbagh: Biblical Criticism and Enlightenment." In *The Early Enlightenment in the Dutch Republic, 1650–1750*, edited by Wiep Van Bunge, 61–80. Leiden: Brill, 2003.

Williams, Rowan. "What Does Love Know? St. Thomas on the Trinity." The Aquinas Lecture. Oxford, January 24, 2001, http://people.bu.edu/joeld/love-know.pdf.

Wolfson, Harry A. *The Philosophy of Spinoza*. Two volumes in one. New York: Meridian, 1934.

Wolterstorff, Nicholas. *Divine Discourse: Philosophical Reflections on the Claim That God Speaks*. Cambridge: Cambridge University Press, 1995.

———. *The God We Worship: An Exploration of Liturgical Theology*. Grand Rapids: Eerdmans, 2015.

———. *Reason within the Bounds of Religion*. Grand Rapids: Eerdmans, 1984.

———. *Selected Essays*. Volume 1: *Inquiring After God*. Edited by Terrence Cuneo. Cambridge: Cambridge University Press, 2010.

Wood, Allen W. "Rational Theology, Moral Faith, and Religion." In *The Cambridge Companion to Kant*, edited by Paul Guyer, 394–416. Cambridge: Cambridge University Press, 1992.

Wright, Christopher J. H. *God's People in God's Land: Family, Land and Property in the Old Testament*. Grand Rapids: Eerdmans, 1990.

Wright, G. Ernest. *God Who Acts: Biblical Theology as Recital*. SBT 8. London: SCM, 1952.

Wright, N. T. *The Lord and His Prayer*. Grand Rapids: Eerdmans, 1996.

Wyschogrod, Michael. *The Body of Faith: God in the People Israel*. Northvale, NJ: Jason Aronson, 1996, 1983.

Zakovitch, Yair. *"And You Shall Tell Your Son . . .": The Concept of the Exodus in the Bible*. Jerusalem: Magnes, 1991.

Zevit, Ziony. "The Priestly Redaction and Interpretation of the Plague Narrative in Exodus." *JQR* 66 (1976): 194–205.

Zimmerli, Walther. *I Am Yahweh*. Edited by Walter Brueggemann. Translated by Douglas W. Stott. Atlanta: John Knox, 1982.

INDEX OF MODERN AUTHORS

Holmes, Stephen R., 146
Howard, Thomas A., 134
Howell, Brian C., 213–14, 219
Hume, David, 119, 120–21, 144

Ibn Ezra, Moses, 46, 99, 102, 108
Illari, Phyllis I., 169
Insole, Christopher J., 116, 176–77
Israel, Jonathan, 89, 91
Ivry, Alfred L., 37, 39–40, 42, 45–46

Jachmann, R. B., 132
Jacob, Benno, 218, 220
Jacobs, Louis, 18
Jacobs, Nathan, 124
Jenson, Robert, 86, 143–45, 148–49, 151–52, 155–57

Kant, Immanuel, x, xvi, xviii, 10, 30–33, 82, 87, 89, 94, 143–44, 153, 176–77, 179, 190, 221, 228, 231–32
Kaufmann, Yehezkel, 196
Kelle, Brad E., 198, 212, 222
Kellner, Menachem M., 43
Kelsey, David, 86
Kenny, Anthony, 91
Koerbagh, Adriaan, 94
Köstenberger, Andreas, 192
Kraemer, Joel L., 36, 39–40
Kreisel, Howard, 40
Kretzmann, Norman, 75
Kroner, Richard, 125–26
Kuhn, Thomas S., 82, 190
Kuyper, Abraham, 170–71, 173

LaCocque, André, 200–201, 218, 229
Lacoste, Jean-Yves, 228–29
Lamm, Julia A., 111
La Montaigne, D. Paul, 116

Lane, Tony, 63
La Peyrère, Isaac de, 99, 106, 108
Laplace, Pierre-Simon, 181–82
Lee, Sukjae, 174–75
Leftow, Brian, 57, 61
Leibniz, G. W., 92, 120–21, 124, 175
Lessing, G. E., 10, 179
Lesslie, John, 181
Levenson, Jon D., 3–5, 8, 17, 19, 26, 28, 197
Levering, Matthew, 64, 83
Levinson, Bernard M., 19, 28, 88, 101, 107, 223
Licht, J., 212
Lilla, Mark, 90–91
Loewenstamm, Samuel E., 189
Long, Burke O., 221
Long, V. Philips, 222
Longman, Tremper, III, 222
Lyon, David, 125

Macquarrie, John, 178–79, 181
Malebranche, Nicholas, 174–75
McCormack, Bruce L., 116
Mendel, Menaḥem, 25
Mendenhall, George E., 196
Meyer, Lodewijk, 94
Michalson, Gordon E., Jr., 115, 139–40
Milbank, John, 116
Miller, Patrick D., 213
Miskotte, Kornelis H., 2
Moberly, R. W. L., 189
Molnar, Paul, 155
Moore, Megan Bishop, 198, 212, 222

Nadler, Steven, 89–90, 94, 96, 105, 175
Newton, Sir Isaac, 181

INDEX OF SUBJECTS

any and, 196–98, 215; universal,
97–98, 100
law codes, treaties, ancient Near
Eastern, 216–18, 224–25
liberation theology, 140
literary criticism, 196–98; readings,
22, 136; repetition, resumptive,
204–9; synchronic analysis, 204–12
liturgy, 22, 228–29; Sinai narrative,
216, 220, 227
Lutheran theology, 142, 169

Maimonides, 36, 57, 101, 109–10,
230–31; Aquinas and, 65–66,
84–86; Aristotelian philosophy, 10,
53, 59; biblical language, 59–60;
exegesis, 38–39, 52–53; God, view
of, 37–38, 40, 52–55, 153; *Guide for
the Perplexed*, 37–45, 52–53, 65;
inability of God to speak, 24–25,
29, 32, 35, 39, 42–43, 53, 59, 102–3;
perfect-being theology, xv–xvi, 32,
231; prophecy, 38, 40–43, 45; rationalizing Judaism, 38–40, 44, 45
Marcion, 171
medieval theology, theologians, 12,
174–75, 231; Christian, 63–65, 144,
176, 178; Jewish, 10, 18–19, 35, 47;
philosophy and, 41–42, 59, 81, 230
Mesopotamian law, 216–18
metaphors, 82, 152, 213–14
metaphysics, 10, 45, 89–90, 106, 121,
149–50; Greek, 145–46; hierarchical, 150–51
miracles, 98–99, 110, 129, 131, 136,
173–74; science and, 178–79, 181–83
monism, 112–13
monistic pantheism, 91–92, 106–7,
153, 159, 190, 231
monotheism, 112, 214–15, 222–23;

Jewish, Israelite, 10, 117, 195,
222–23, 225
morals, morality, ethics, 58, 97, 110;
in Bible, 19, 99–100, 216–17; community, 116–18; Decalogue, 220–21;
law, 30, 44, 100, 117, 125–27; true
religion, 124–27, 129–32
Mosaic distinction, 193–95, 224
Moses, 14, 210, 226, 229; burning
bush, 14n32, 85, 199–200; faith
of Israel, 221–22; God at Sinai,
24–25, 42–45, 72–73, 83–84, 102–3;
God, view of, 103–4; as imposter,
179–80; as prophet, 1n4, 9, 40–41,
43, 45, 85, 95; Torah and, 18, 22–23,
25–26, 97, 99, 104–5
Moses ben Ezra, 46
Muslim scholars, 35, 37, 62, 80, 175;
Alfarabi, 37, 42; Avicenna, 37, 42,
65
myth, mythology, 105, 135–36, 151;
neutrality, xvii, 31–33, 80, 108–9,
139, 141, 189–91; science and,
178–80

names of God, 49–50, 67–68, 83–84,
149, 220; Elohim, 49–50, 84,
197–98, 213, 215, 218, 220; YHWH,
16, 49, 56–58, 67, 78, 83–84, 86,
149, 199–205
naturalism, 68, 81, 106, 134, 179–80
negative theology, 70, 73, 143, 145,
148–51, 153
Neoplatonism, 37, 53, 68–69, 80, 151,
175
neutrality, myth of, xvii, 32, 80; historical criticism, 31, 33, 105, 108–9,
189–91; philosophy, 139, 141

obedience, 25, 49, 58, 98, 100–102, 117

INDEX OF SCRIPTURE REFERENCES